ULSTER 1641

Aspects of the Rising

English Protestantes striped naked & turned into the mountaines in the frost, & snowe, wheroef many hundreds are peryshed to death. & many lyinge dead in diches & Sauages upbraided them sayinge now are ye wilde Irish as well as wee.

ULSTER 1641

Aspects of the Rising

Brian Mac Cuarta S J
Editor

We had fed the heart on fantasies,
The heart's grown brutal from the fare;
More substance in our enmities
Than in our love

W.B. Yeats, 'Meditations in time of civil war', (1923)

THE INSTITUTE OF IRISH STUDIES
THE QUEEN'S UNIVERSITY OF BELFAST

First published 1993
This revised edition 1997
The Institute of Irish Studies
The Queen's University of Belfast

This book has received support from the Cultural Traditions Programme of the Community Relations Council, which aims to encourage acceptance and understanding of cultural diversity.

British Library Cataloguing-in-Publication Data. A catalogue record for this book is available from the British Library.

ISBN 0 85389 591 0

Printed by W & G Baird Ltd, Antrim
Cover design by Rodney Miller Associates

Cover illustrations

Front: Woodcut, harp with head, pamphlet,
*Mercurius Hibernicus: or, A discourse
of the late Insurrection in Ireland*
(Bristol 1644) [National Library of Ireland]

Back: Woodcut, two soldiers, pamphlet, *Two famous
battels fought in Ireland* (1642) [National
Library of Ireland]

Contents

Illustrations

Notes on Contributors

Toby Barnard, of Hertford College, Oxford, is the author of *Cromwellian Ireland* (1975) and is an authority on Protestant Ireland in the 17th century.

Aidan Clarke, professor of modern history, Trinity College Dublin, and president, Royal Irish Academy (1990–93), has written widely on early 17th century Ireland, including *The Old English in Ireland, 1625–42* (1966), and contributions to *A New History of Ireland, Vol III*.

Raymond Gillespie, St Patrick's College, Maynooth, has written a number of books and articles on 17th century Ireland, including *Colonial Ulster* (1985) and *The Transformation of the Irish Economy 1550–1700* (1991). He has also co-edited several collections of essays on Irish regional history.

Gráinne Henry, a history graduate of St Patrick's College, Maynooth, has written *The Irish Military Community in Spanish Flanders, 1586–1621* (1992).

Jacqueline Hill, St Patrick's College, Maynooth, has written articles on Irish political life in the 18th and 19th centuries and is on the editorial board of *A New History of Ireland* (published under the auspices of the Royal Irish Academy).

Phil Kilroy is the author of *Protestant dissent and controversy in Ireland, 1660–1714* (1994). She is currently writing a scholarly biography of the French educationalist Madeleine Sophie Barat (1779–1865).

John McCavitt is the author of *Lord Deputy Chichester 1605–16* (forthcoming), and has written articles on early 17th century Ireland. He has lectured at the Institute of Continuing Education, QUB.

Brian Mac Cuarta SJ studied history at University College Galway and theology at Sankt Georgen – Frankfurt/Main. He was co-chair of PACE Portadown (1991–2), and contributed articles to Irish historical journals.

Michelle O Riordan is the author of *The Gaelic mind and the collapse of the Gaelic world* (1990), and is publications officer with the School of Celtic Studies, Dublin Institute for Advanced Studies.

Michael Perceval-Maxwell is professor of history at McGill University, Montreal, and author of *The Scottish Migration to Ulster in the Reign of James I* (1973), and *The Outbreak of the Irish Rebellion of 1641* (1994).

Hilary Simms is a history graduate of TCD. An information studies graduate of London University, she has lectured on Irish bibliography, and works as an information consultant in Dublin.

Acknowledgments

The co-operation of many groups and individuals has made this volume possible. The success of the 1641 Conference organised by Protestant and Catholic Encounter (PACE) Portadown, in November 1991, indicated the extent of public interest in this area of our troubled history. Two of the essays here, those of Raymond Gillespie and John McCavitt, originated as papers at that Conference; an earlier version of Aidan Clarke's paper was given to the Columbanus Community of Reconciliation, Belfast. The generous financial assistance of Bord na Gaeilge [Irish language board], the Cultural Traditions Group of the Community Relations Council, and the Esme Mitchell Trust, has made publication possible. Raymond Gillespie provided inspiration and shared his infectious enthusiasm for seventeenth century Ireland. Kate Newmann and Brian Walker, of the Institute of Irish Studies, and Barbara FitzGerald, Irish Association, offered continual support. Thanks are due to the contributors themselves, and to Nicholas Canny, Alan Ford, Micheline Kerney Walsh, Joseph Liechty, Micheál Mac Craith OFM, Fr Raymond Murray, Mary O'Dowd, Diarmuid Ó Laoghaire SJ, and A.T.Q. Stewart, who, in regard to different contributions, have enriched the text by generously sharing their expertise. Anraí Mac Giolla Chomhaill and Ray Lawler SJ kindly read the proofs; Cyril Barrett SJ helped locate contemporary woodcuts. The staffs of the Irish Library, Southern Education and Library Board Headquarters, Armagh, and of the Special Collections Department, The Library, QUB were unfailingly helpful. *Rath agus bláth orthu, oíche agus lá!* [May they prosper at all times!]

For permission to reproduce illustrative material, the editor is grateful to the following: to the British Library, for the use of material from *Barbarous and inhumane proceedings against the professors of the reformed religion* (London, 1655); to Gill and Macmillan, for the use of the map 'English and Scottish settlement in Ulster, c. 1630' which appears in Philip Robinson, *The Plantation of Ulster*, (Dublin, 1984); to Loyal Orange Lodge No 273, for the reproduction of the banner; to the National Library of Ireland, for the illustrations on pp 62, 158, 172, and on the cover; the map, 'The Ulster Plantation', by T.W. Moody and R.J. Hunter, in T.W. Moody, F.X. Martin, F.J. Byrne (eds) *A New History of Ireland : Vol III Early Modern Ireland*, (Oxford, 1976) is used by permission of Oxford University Press; to the Royal Society of Antiquaries of Ireland, for the use of the illustration from John Hennig, 'Irish Soldiers in the Thirty Years War', *R.S.A.I Jn.*, lxxxii (1952). Thanks are due to Gill Alexander who drew the map on p 122.

FOREWORD

by

R.H.A. Eames
Archbishop of Armagh
The See House, Armagh

It has been said that any concept of history is of necessity selective and subjective. To examine any period of history is to accept the inevitable risk of interpretation which itself can be a commentary on personal opinion or outlook. Yet it is essential that every opportunity is taken to examine periods of history in the hope that contemporary society will come to understand more clearly where it has come from. Mythology and traditional outlooks have interacted in Irish history too often in a negative fashion. We are frequently told that the Irish spend too much time dwelling on their history and too little time looking ahead. But if we are reluctant to review the past we will never understand our relative identities or why we have to experience the differences of the present.

As one dedicated to reconciliation in Ireland I welcome any attempt to examine what has contributed to the history of our community. These essays examine a period of Ulster history which was to have a profound effect on later developments. They have been written from particular points of view but together present the reader with a most readable account. I gladly commend this book and hope it will help to enlighten all who still ask 'where have we come from and why?' I hope it is read objectively and will be a useful addition to the growing library of honest attempts to unravel our past.

+ Robert Armagh

Abbreviations

Anal. Hib.	*Analecta Hibernica.*
Archiv. Hib.	*Archivium Hibernicum.*
Bodl.	Bodleian Library, Oxford.
B.L.	British Library, London.
Cal. S.P. Ire.	*Calendar of the state papers relating to Ireland,* (24 vols, London, 1860–1911).
Commons' jn. Ire.	*Journals of the house of commons of the kingdom of Ireland* (1613–1791, 28 vols, Dublin, 1753–91).
E.H.R.	*English Historical Review.*
Gilbert, *Ir. confed.*	J.T. Gilbert (ed.), *History of the Irish confederation and the war in Ireland, 1641–3* (7 vols, Dublin, 1882–91).
H.M.C.	*Historical Manuscripts Commission* (London, 1870 –).
I.E.R.	*Irish Ecclesiastical Record.*
Ir. Econ. & Soc. Hist.	*Irish Economic and Social History.*
I.H.S.	*Irish Historical Studies.*
Ir. Sword	*Irish Sword*
N.H.I.	*A New History of Ireland* T.W. Moody, F.X. Martin, F.J. Byrne (eds), (Oxford, 1976 –).
O.F.M.	Order of Friars Minor [Franciscans]
P.R.O.	Public Record Office, London
P.R.O.N.I.	Public Record Office of Northern Ireland, Belfast.
R.I.A. Proc.	*Proceedings of the Royal Irish Academy.*
Strafford, *Letters*	*The earl of Strafforde's letters and despatches,* W. Knowler (ed), (2 vols, London, 1739).
SJ	Society of Jesus
T.C.D.	Trinity College Dublin.

INTRODUCTION

It would be hard to overestimate the significance of the breakdown in Ulster society in 1641 for future relations between the communities on this island. The memory of Irish attacks on English and Scottish settlers in 1641, often submerged but coming to consciousness at times of crisis, contributed to that sense of insecurity characteristic of the protestant community in Ulster. The aim of the present volume is to explore the 1641 uprising in Ulster, a central, highly complex event of Irish history, by making the fruits of modern scholarship available to a wider public. A vast array of pamphlets, books and articles has been generated by this subject over the course of 350 years. The first pamphlets on the alleged 'massacre' started circulating in England in November 1641, some illustrated with woodcuts designed to excite pity and revenge. Thus a word of apologia for the present volume is in order. The last sustained treatment of the topic in book form was Lord Ernest Hamilton's *The Irish Rebellion of 1641* (1920). In the past two decades, however, historians, including many of the contributors to this volume, have offered fresh perspectives – socio-economic, constitutional and political – on this many-sided subject. Special mention must be made of Michael Perceval-Maxwell's magisterial work, *The Outbreak of the Irish Rebellion of 1641* (1994). By making the perspectives gleaned by modern scholarship more widely available, it is hoped that this book will contribute solid historical insights to an area often characterised by denial, exaggeration and myth.

The fear of betrayal, the sense of being under siege, and the dread of massacre – the legacy of their seventeenth century experience – are etched deeply in the historical consciousness of the Ulster protestant community. The drowning of settlers at Portadown in November 1641 exemplified the reality of massacre, while siege and betrayal were crystalised in the events of 1689–90. While William on his horse, together with the half-closed gates of Derry, have provided the staple of loyalist iconography, it is striking that very few Orange banners depict an episode from 1641.[1] Out of sight, in this case, is not out of mind. Sir John Temple's *The Irish Rebellion* (the standard protestant version of 1641, first published in 1646) was reprinted again and again at times of crisis faced by Irish Protestants down to 1912. This is indicative of the enduring significance of 1641 for that community. Reflecting on some of the earliest protestant efforts to come to terms with the revolt, Aidan Clarke suggests that these have to be seen in the context of the evolution of settler

attitudes to Irish catholicism over the previous century. In this evolution
the religion of the majority was increasingly viewed as depraved. Thus
the myth of an Irish massacre of Protestants predated 1641, and in this
way conditioned interpretations of the attacks on settlers in 1641-2. As
Clarke has noted, 'the myth preceded the events, but it was sustained by
them as they happened'.[2]

'I procured a genuine account of the great Irish massacre in 1641.
Surely never was there such a transaction before, from the beginning of
the world! More than two hundred thousand men, women and children
butchered within a few months, in cool blood, and with such circumstance of cruelty as make one's blood run cold! It is well if God has not
a controversy with the nation, on this very account, to this day.' John
Wesley's reaction to a standard exaggerated account catches the flavour
of eighteenth century protestant perceptions of 1641. Edmund Burke,
writing in 1771, took a more critical view of the historiography of 1641,
in his opinion ' "That the Irish Rebellion of 1641 was not only (as our
silly things called Historys call it), not utterly *unprovoked* but that no
History, that I have ever read furnishes an Instance of any that was so
provoked". And that "in almost all parts of it, it has been extremely and
most absurdly misrepresented" '.[3] The enduring role of the memory of
1641 in shaping responses to each succeeding crisis is noted here by
Toby Barnard, a process in which annual 1641 sermons played a part
down to the end of the eighteenth century. Thus the way in which 1641
was commemorated, and drawn into contemporary debates, became
part of the legacy of that event. The nature and extent of native attacks
on settlers in 1641 provided the terms of reference of much writing on
Irish history. This was the case in the seventeenth and eighteenth centuries, and indeed, as Home Rule loomed, in the nineteenth century as
well. 'The massacre of 1641 was really an Irish St Bartholomew, only
more terrible and inhuman, and it is no wonder that, though more than
200 years have passed ... [the] memory has left behind in Ulster a dread,
amounting almost to terror, of being ever again placed in the power of
Rome'. Writing in 1887, the popular Presbyterian historian Thomas
Hamilton thus alluded to the place of 1641 in northern protestant
antipathy to Home Rule.[4] In one study of how 1641 influenced later
issues, offered here, Jacqueline Hill focuses on the part played by eighteenth century perceptions of 1641 in the debate on granting Roman
Catholics full political rights. This particular debate concluded only
with Catholic Emancipation in 1829.

Yet the studies presented here are limited largely to the area of high
politics: 1641 as a motif in popular culture remains to be explored.
Perceptions of past suffering are an enduring element in the Ulster psy-
che. Such memories have been transmitted through various forms of
popular culture, which have played a part in the continuing significance
of that troubled era. Bonfires and carnival marked the anniversary of

the rising as commemorated by Protestants in Irish towns in the later seventeenth and early eighteenth centuries. The anniversary of the rising, in the localities, became an occasion where current protestant concerns were aired.[5] Such celebrations would appear to have died out by the mid-eighteenth century. Yet the events of 1641 featured in popular storytelling in the first half of the nineteenth century.

According to the Tyrone writer William Carleton, describing a wake of his youth (1810s, 1820s), old men were 'talking over ould times – ghost stories, fairy tales, or the great rebellion of 41, . . .' The enduring place of 1641 in popular memory was reflected in the many references scattered throughout the Ordnance Survey Memoirs for counties Antrim and Londonderry, taken in the 1830s. Brief references occur also in the Memoirs for the other northern counties. Traditions from the 1640s touching battles, Irish attacks on castles and churches, massacres of Protestants, and miraculous escapes were noted. 'The wars of Cromwell' or 'Phelimy Roe', 'the persecution of 1641', 'the troubles of 1641' – in these ways the rising was designated in the folk memory of County Londonderry.[6] However the single incident which received the most extensive coverage in the oral tradition, as set down in the Memoirs, was the Islandmagee massacre of about thirty Irish by Scots in January 1642, in retaliation for earlier attacks on the settlers. The tradition that a mother with a child in her arms was killed by one of the Scots was recounted in the Memoirs, a detail later used by the poet John Hewitt. The notoriety of Islandmagee became embedded in the Irish folk memory, for according to the Memoirs people in Westport and Galway 'within memory' knew of its terrible reputation.[7]

Several Orange ballads of the mid-nineteenth century had verses, warning of romish perfidy, and drawing on the atrocities associated with the revolt, as in the following excerpt:

'Think, oh! think in time upon
The dreadful days of 'Forty-One',
When Rome's intrigues the mob set on,
To act their cruel part

Behold the Bann's polluted flood,
Purpled o'er with British blood;
There the persecutor stood
With unrelenting heart'.

One Orange ballad has the Bann drownings of 1641 as its theme. However such references would appear to have been few in the ballad repertoire. These hints suggest that 1641 was a persistent thread in popular loyalist culture, if perhaps a minor one, long after official commemorations had ceased.[8] A Gaelic Irish perspective, largely absent from the historiography, is afforded by Art Bennett's history of Ireland, composed in south Armagh and finished in 1858, entitled *Comhrac na nGael agus na nGall le Chéile* [The conflict of the Irish and the foreigners]. In this work the author interestingly follows an earlier catholic author and ignores protestant sufferings and concentrates on atrocities or alleged atrocities against Catholics. Pride of place was given to the Islandmagee massacre, a perspective perhaps indicative of how 1641 was remembered among the Irish-speaking poorer people of Ulster.[9] Thus more work needs to be done on elucidating how 1641 was commemorated at the local level, the place of 1641 in folk memory in different places and among the different communities, and how it impinged on successive political debates.

The literary treatment of the breakdown would repay further investigation. The Islandmagee massacre was the background to Samuel Ferguson's poem 'Una Phelimy', first published in 1831-2, Ethna Carbery's poem 'Brian Boy Magee', and John Hewitt's dramatic poem 'The Bloody Brae', composed in 1936. The Irish-language novel *Eoghan ruadh Ó Néill*, by the Donegal writer Seosamh Mac Grianna, and Breandán Ó Doibhlin's play, *Iníon Mhaor an Uachta* [The legacy steward's daughter], have mid-seventeenth century Ulster as their background. Ó Doibhlin's play, set in south-east Derry, explores religious and ethnic tensions on the eve of the rising, from the perspective of the dispossessed Gaelic gentry.[10] The rising did not feature highly in the platform rhetoric of unionist politicians in the decades before World War I. Nevertheless it was a theme in popular unionist literature from the 1870s onwards, in the works of William Johnston and Lord Ernest Hamilton.[11]

At each stage of heightened sectarian tension in Irish life, there have been commentators who have looked back wistfully to a golden age of peace and harmony which, allegedly, preceded present animosity. This vision of a harmonious past renders present strife all the more shocking, because unexpected. The beginnings of this process can be discerned in some of the contemporary responses to 1641, as indicated here by Raymond Gillespie. The early decades of the seventeenth century had been a time of severe dislocation for the Irish in Ulster. This happened through formal dispossession under the plantation, and through inability to adapt to the new political, economic and social order. At the upper social levels, the lands of the Gaelic lords were confiscated as part of the plantation. Perhaps of greater relevance to what happened in 1641, at the lower social levels native tenants were having to move onto the higher, poorer lands; on the more fertile plains, British tenants were replacing Irish. Whatever the nature of the processes involved, the Ulster Irish saw themselves within two generations become impoverished in the new society that had emerged by 1641. The nature and extent of native indebtedness to settlers in the 1630s, whereby, for example, the remaining Irish landowners were losing their lands through mortgage, could throw light on one source of Irish grievance. Harvest failures in the late 1630s, together with rising impositions of central government and an economic downturn, affected all groups in Ulster. Thus the worsening economic situation contributed to the build-up of tension. The interaction of natives and settlers under the new order, established in the wake of the plantation, needs close examination. Such interaction needs to be studied in social, economic, political, religious and cultural terms.[12]

Michelle O Riordan points to evidence of openness to the newcomers to be found in Ulster Gaelic poetry. Such an insight supports the view from other parts of Gaelic Ireland that adaptation, and not antagonism, often characterised native responses to the new order. Studies of the original leaders of the rising in Ulster – Sir Phelim O'Neill, Lord Conor Maguire, Philip O'Reilly, Rory Maguire, Rory O'More – are needed. These Irish in fact benefited as a result of the plantation, and were members of the Irish parliament. They must be set in their social and political contexts, if the genesis and limited aims of the insurrection are to be better understood. To what extent are these figures examples of adaptation or antagonism to the new order?

Any consideration of 1641 has to take into account the introduction and spread of English and Scottish settlers in Ulster, west of Antrim and Down, consequent upon the plantation. Recent historiography has tended to emphasise that British settlement in seventeenth century Ireland was the result of social and economic conditions on the two islands – population pressure on the one, and a low population density on the other. Thus Ireland was an attractive destination for Scottish and English immigrants, irrespective of government-sponsored plantation schemes. Yet, as John McCavitt reminds us, the Ulster Plantation was a political response of the London government to the need to pacify an unruly province. The government wanted to seize the opportunities presented by the departure of the native ruling class, in the Flight of the Earls, a move not anticipated by the authorities. This political background involved different proposals for the plantation and the threat of a successful return by O'Neill, with Spanish help. These considerations illustrate the precariousness of the plantation project in its first two decades.

Whatever about evidence of accommodation in other spheres, religious attitudes in early seventeenth century Ulster betray no hints of consensus. Indeed Irish antipathy to the religion of the newcomers was a marked feature of attacks on the settler community in 1641. By the beginning of the seventeenth century proponents of the Reformation in Ireland were becoming increasingly pessimistic about the chances of the reformed religion taking root on a broad scale. As Alan Ford has indicated elsewhere, such pessimism was underpinned theologically by an increasing acceptance of exclusivist Calvinist thought in Irish protestant circles. In such thinking the catholic majority were considered predestined not to enjoy divine favour.[13] Within Ulster such religious exclusivism was mightily strengthened by the emerging presbyterianism which the Scots brought with them from their homeland. Phil Kilroy traces the tensions within Ulster protestantism in this initial formative period. Reforming bishops, land-grabbing bishops, the growing influence of Scots presbyterianism, and Wentworth's efforts to impose doctrinal uniformity and to lessen lay control, were the diverging tendencies. A full study of Ulster catholicism for this period is still lacking. However the Counter-reformation in the Spanish Netherlands exercised an influence through the sizeable Ulster community there. The role of the Irish Franciscans would repay examination. They worked as preachers in Ulster itself and provided catechetical material, in the Irish language, which was based on the norms of the Council of Trent. As counsellors of the Ulster leaders in exile, they exercised influence in the political sphere. St Anthony's College in Louvain, an Ulster Franciscan foundation, thus played a pivotal role in the religious culture of the Ulster Irish at home and abroad. Grainne Henry refers to the ties between the religious and military groupings within the Ulster community in the Netherlands. Michelle O Riordan notes that antagonism towards protestantism characterised the catechetical writings of the Louvain Franciscans. Both authors point to the impact of the Counter-reformation. Yet more research on the speeches and remarks of the insurgents, as reported in the 1641 depositions, is needed before the sectarian rituals of bible-burning and desecration of places of worship can be understood.[14] Popular religiosity in that time of crisis reveals yet another level of response to the breakdown of order and consensus: Raymond Gillespie notes the prevalence of ghosts, prophecies and other manifestations of the supernatural in the efforts of the popular mind to make sense of what was happening. He shows that recourse to the supernatural as an interpretative framework was characteristic of all communities in the conflict.

Much ink has been spilt on the nature and extent of the sufferings endured by protestant settlers in the winter of 1641-2. It is tantalisingly difficult to give accurate figures of English and Scots killed, not to mention those who died from exposure and disease while fleeing their homesteads in the trek to the ports. From a detailed study by Hilary Simms of the relatively well-documented county of Armagh, given here, it is probable that between one-quarter and one-third of the protestant population of that area were killed in 1641-2. Evidence available for Armagh and other south Ulster counties – depositions taken in the mid-1640s – is not available for Donegal and east Ulster. Thus the sources need to be handled with great care. Already in August 1642, a clergyman from Tyrone who had been a prisoner among the Irish reported that 154,000 Protestants had been killed. This was a figure over four times greater than the number of settlers living in Ulster at that time.[15] The fact of exaggeration cannot blind us to the reality of widespread atrocities against the settler community in the winter of 1641-2. Within a few weeks of the start of the revolt in Ulster control had slipped from the leaders, who belonged to the lower echelons of the Old Irish aristocracy. These were men who to some degree had adapted to the new order of the early seventeenth century. A total collapse of law and order ensued, together with a breakdown in relations between the communities. Against this background spontaneous attacks on the settlers took place. In such a fearful atmosphere, rumour and a belief in the supernatural held sway in all communities. A study of the extant Ulster Gaelic literature, presented here, concludes by noting that there is no advocacy of the killing of the newcomers, in the native writings of the period. Although many English and Scots were killed, there is no evidence of a pre-arranged conspiracy to exterminate Protestants from Ulster, contrary to the myth which grew up almost immediately, and which was destined to endure. After the initial wave of attacks on settlers, groups of Irish were killed subsequently in the south Antrim – north Down area, in January 1642.[16] In the long-term history of Ulster, a comparison with killings in 1798 may be useful. It is possible to suggest that in east Antrim, proportionately more Protestants were killed by the forces of the crown in the 1798 Rebellion, than were killed in the same area by the Irish in 1641.[17] Further detailed studies of atrocities in areas other than Armagh are needed. The sectarian and economic dynamics of revolt in Ulster could be further elucidated by placing them in the context of popular revolt in early modern Europe generally.

Events in Ulster in 1641, however dramatic, cannot be understood in isolation. Among Irish Catholics, fear of invasion and of persecution by English and Scottish Puritans contributed to the crisis. A catholic correspondent noted at the end of December 1641, 'They [English parliament] are busily preparing to send 20,000 English and 10,000 Scots to Ireland to destroy and extirpate all that is there Irish and Catholic.' The insurgents saw themselves as latter-day Maccabees, prepared to defend their religion and their country against foreign oppression.[18] From Ulster the rising spread southwards, engulfing the whole of Ireland; popular attacks against Protestants occurred throughout the country, though these were less severe than in the north, while in December 1641 the gentry of the Pale joined in the revolt. Michael Perceval-Maxwell shows how the background of political crisis in the three kingdoms, Ireland, Scotland and England, interacted with the communities in Ulster in different yet ultimately explosive ways. Through the Scots' contacts with their homeland, political and religious developments in Scotland influenced attitudes in Ulster. The survey of Ulster Gaelic literature reminds us that the native community too enjoyed contacts with

Scotland, for Ireland and western Scotland enjoyed a common Gaelic literary culture at that time. The arrival of a Scots army under Robert
Monro in Ulster in April 1642, while outside the scope of this volume,
must be mentioned here.[19] Political and religious alignments on the continent, and the experience of both Irish and Scots in the European armies
of the Thirty Years War (1618-48), also clearly impinged on Ulster. In
July 1642 Owen Roe O'Neill landed in Donegal with 300 Irish troops,
who had served with the Spanish armies on the continent. These were
but a tiny fraction of the thousands of Ulster Irish, men and women,
who had migrated to the continent in the preceding forty years. To
resentment at displacement from Ulster was added the sharp sense of
confessional identity and antipathy to the religion of the planters, promoted by the Counter-reformation. Thus through the activities of Ulster
soldiers and Franciscans in the Low Countries we can speak of a
European dimension to the outlook of the native community in Ulster
by 1641. The continental experience of Scots from Ulster, a topic little
studied hitherto, must not be forgotten. Returned veterans of the Thirty
Years War made up much of the Scots military groupings which fought
effectively against the Irish in 1641-2, as in the Laggan corps in west
Ulster.[20]

Reliable and succinct accounts of several aspects of 1641 exist already,
as indicated in the modern section of the bibliographical essay in this
volume. The present work offers surveys of other dimensions of the
insurrection, and yet clearly there are regrettable omissions in the range
of topics addressed. Some of the unexplored topics have been already
mentioned – the stresses and strains of the 1630s, the backgrounds of the
Irish leaders, the whole range of relations between natives and newcomers, the sectarian dimension to the attacks, local case studies of individuals and events, the Catholic Church in early seventeenth century
Ulster, the European context of the conflict. It is worth noting here that
the 1641 depositions for Ulster are available on microfilm in the Public
Record Office of Northern Ireland, in Belfast. In this collection of essays,
an attempt has been made to cover some dimensions of a complex
event, without any claim to comprehensiveness. Yet by using a variety
of approaches, involving a short-term and a long-term focus, the aim is
to illustrate just how complex the event was, and how enduring its
legacy has been. Thus it is hoped that a variety of perspectives on the
cataclysm which was 1641 are offered here, and that the present contributions will serve to stimulate debate and further research.

THE POLITICAL BACKGROUND TO THE ULSTER PLANTATION, 1607–1620

John McCavitt

The Ulster plantation, as it eventually materialised, was a massive exercise in social engineering. Yet originally, the plans were much more small scale. Why did the English authorities undertake the project in the first place, increase it in scale so dramatically and consider abandoning it – all within the space of a short number of years? An analysis of the turbulent history of Ireland during the first two decades of the seventeenth century provides the answers to these questions.

The century began with the country embroiled in the Nine Years War, 1594-1603. It mainly involved Ulster lords and their followers and was led by Hugh O'Neill, earl of Tyrone. His base, in the heartland of Ulster, proved the launching pad for major successes against English forces. The most notable victory occurred at the Yellow Ford, 1598, when an English army suffered some 2000 casualties.[1] It was because of the magnitude of the threat which this rebellion posed, menacing 'the very survival of English rule in Ireland'[2], that its consequences proved so enduring.

Gaelic-style hit and run tactics often predominated in the war, but Tyrone was also capable of more sophisticated military strategy. This was manifested by his successful employment of trench warfare at the Yellow Ford in 1598 and later at the Moyry Pass in 1600.[3] A further testimony that Tyrone's forces were formidable adversaries was provided by the failure of a series of Elizabethan generals to quell the rebellion. Even the flamboyant earl of Essex, victor against the Spanish at Cadiz, made little or no progress, despite the fact that he commanded a large, well-equipped army. Lord Mountjoy, who finally brought Tyrone to terms, came close to personal disaster on numerous occasions. Fynes Moryson, one of his secretaries, described how

'My lorde himselfe had his horse shot under him, his Galloglasse carrying his helmet, had the same brused with the grasing of a bullet upon it, yea his Lordships very Grayhound, likewise using to waite at his stirrop, was shot through the body. Among

7

N.E. LIBERTIES OF COLERAINE

N.W. LIBERTIES OF DERRY

D O W N

A N T R I M

Lough Neagh

Coleraine
COLERAINE

KEENAGHT

Limavady

TIRKEERAN

Derry

FINISHOWEN

L O N D O N D E R R Y

LOUGHINSHOLIN

A

MOUNTJOY

Charlemont
ONEILLAND
Armagh
ARMAGH
FEWS (50%)

TIRANNY

B

ORIOR

A R M A G H

Dungannon
DUNGANNON

T Y R O N E

CLOGHER
Augher

OMAGH

Strabane
STRABANE

Lifford
LIFFORD

D O N E G A L

BOYLAGH

FANAD
TCD (10%)

DOE

Donegal

TIRHUGH
TCD (25%)

Ballyshannon

TIRKENNEDY

MAGHERABOY

LURG

F E R M A N A G H

Enniskillen
MAGHERASTEPHANA

CLANAWLEY

CLANKELLY
TCD (25%)

TULLYHAW

KNOCKNINNY

M O N A G H A N

TULLYHUNCO

Belturbet
LOUGHTEE

TULLYGARVEY

CLANKEE

CAVAN

Cavan
CLANMAHON

CASTLERAHAN

Assigned to Scottish undertakers
Assigned to English undertakers
Assigned to servitors and natives
Exceptional areas

A Formerly part of Loughinsholin
B Granted to Sir Turlough McHenry O'Neill
C Granted to Sir Thomas Phillips
TCD Baronies where land was granted to Trinity College Dublin
(25%) % of total barony granted
● Parliamentary boroughs 1613
County boundaries
Barony boundaries
Minor boundaries

Miles   50
Kms   80
0   0

'The Ulster Plantation, 1609–13', by T. W. Moody and R. J. Hunter; N.H.I. III.

his Lordships Chaplains, Doctor Lattware was killed, and Master Ram had his horse shot under him. Among his Lordships Secretaries, Master Cranmer was killed and my selfe had my thigh brused with a shot I received in my saddle.'[4]

The climax of the Nine Years War occurred in 1601 at the battle of Kinsale. Four thousand Spanish troops had landed to bolster Tyrone's war effort. This seemed to be the decisive intervention which the earl had long been expecting. The Ulster lord marched south to link up with the Spaniards who had been besieged by the army of Lord Mountjoy. In the ensuing battle Tyrone suffered a sensational reverse. Failing to link up with the Spaniards as planned, his army was routed. With the defeat at Kinsale, Tyrone's chances of outright victory over the English evaporated. The Spanish at Kinsale sued for terms and returned home.[5] Yet, Kinsale was not the death-knell of Gaelic Ireland as has sometimes been suggested.

Lord Mountjoy could not bring his adversaries to terms by conventional military means, despite his major battlefield success. A scorched earth policy had to be employed which affected large parts of Ulster. Tyrone later claimed that 60,000 people perished as a result of this policy.[6] Certainly large numbers died through famine. But Tyrone was not forced to make an unconditional surrender even though his position was dire. Instead, as a result of the treaty of Mellifont in 1603, he received extraordinarily favourable terms from the English. His only 'major loss' was the allocation of 300 acres for each of the forts of Charlemont and Mountjoy, but even this was 'more than offset by the recognition, contrary to Gaelic law and English promises, that he was absolute owner of the remainder of the O'Neill lordship and of O'Cahan's country'.[7]

Tyrone's treatment at Mellifont owed much to the vagaries of British dynastic politics; Queen Elizabeth I's imminent death was decisive. She was to be succeeded by the Scottish king, James VI, who had long been suspected by the English of clandestinely aiding and abetting the Irish during the Nine Years War. Consequently it was feared in English government circles that without a treaty Tyrone would be in a position to obtain more propitious terms from the new monarch. Besides, there was also a pressing financial consideration. The Irish revolt had cost the English exchequer some £2 million, a very substantial amount at the time.[8] Therefore, Mellifont released the English government from what was proving to be a severe financial burden.

All in all, the treaty of Mellifont proved a most unsatisfactory conclusion to the war for the English. It was a classic case of defeat being snatched from the jaws of victory. Previous Irish rebel leaders, particularly as the sixteenth century wore on, were punished by execution and confiscation of family lands. Yet the 'Grand Traitor', Tyrone, escaped unpunished. It was to be a decision that the English authorities had cause to regret as it spawned enormous problems for the future.

In the aftermath of the treaty Tyrone's position was paradoxically powerful. The nightmare experience of the Nine Years War had petrified the London government, temporarily paralysing its resolution. For several years thereafter it pursued a policy of appeasement towards him which greatly angered its representatives in Dublin. That financial embarrassment inspired the London government's kid-glove policy was exemplified by the fact that within three years of the treaty the number of English infantry in Ireland had been reduced to a skeleton force of less than 900.[9] This was a remarkably small insurance against the risk of renewed revolt, particularly as the earl's ambitions had not been quenched.

Tyrone was neither defeatist nor disillusioned following Kinsale and the subjugation of his rebellion. His flight to the continent in 1607 was by no means a foregone conclusion.[10] Rather, from the very first, he endeavoured to rebuild his powerbase. His determination to do so was manifested by his successful negotiations, begun as early as 1604, to obtain a Spanish pension.[11] What is more, his readiness to rejoin the fight against the protestant English was demonstrated by the fact that as early as 1605 he was fomenting a new 'catholic' revolt in Ireland. This time he had grounds for believing that he could secure substantial support among the Roman Catholic Old English who had largely remained aloof from his previous rebellion. Tyrone's flight to the continent was not the product of defeatism. Quite the contrary, it was precipitated by the fact that he had re-engaged in conspiratorial machinations.[12]

The Old English Catholics were descendants of the Anglo-Norman settlers in Ireland. The native Irish had been their traditional enemies. This state of affairs persisted for some time even after the Reformation when the English crown passed into the protestant fold. Throughout much of the sixteenth, and particularly the seventeenth, centuries the Old English catholics engaged in a complex high wire act, seeking to balance their loyalty to the English crown in temporal matters with their spiritual allegiance to the pope. In James I (1603-25) they anticipated a sovereign who would stabilise their position and grant them religious toleration. Instead, much to their chagrin, his reign heralded an unprecedented degree of persecution.

On a philosophical level James I favoured toleration but realised that he had to placate the more militant protestant tendencies of his English subjects. Thus, when lord deputy Chichester began a strident anti-catholic policy in Ireland in 1605, James found his room for manoeuvre restricted. Chichester believed that the long-term security of English hegemony in Ireland depended upon the conversion of the population to protestantism. His religious policy, it is worth emphasising, was very much that – religious not confiscatory. He undertook his anti-catholic campaign with a genuine view to protestantising Ireland, not as a pretext to confiscate valuables and land. While he acknowledged that persuasive measures were required to complete this task, coercion was employed in the short term to force the Old English Catholics, who had been initially targeted, to become Protestants. Heavy fines were meted out and spells of imprisonment imposed on a number of leading citizens while thousands of others were subjected to the one shilling fine provisions of Statute 2 Elizabeth for failure to attend the service of the established church on the sabbath.[13]

The earl of Tyrone sought to tap resultant indignation among the catholic Old English in an endeavour to form a 'league' to eject the protestant English from Ireland. To this end, during the period 1605-7 he set about orchestrating a revolt which he hoped would be underpinned by Spanish military help.[14] Fearing that he had been compromised by an informer, however, Tyrone, the earl of Tyrconnell, Cuconnaught Maguire and many of their leading followers departed Ireland in September 1607 in what has come to be known as the Flight of the Earls.[15]

In popular conception, the departure of the earls in 1607 is considered as the key event paving the way for the plantation of Ulster. After all, it provided the opportunity for widespread confiscation of lands. There is, of course, some measure of justification for this assertion. To a large extent also it is misleading. If anything it was O'Doherty's rebellion in the spring of 1608 which had greater importance for the plantation of Ulster.

Following the flight of the earls in 1607 Chichester dominated planning for the settlement of Ulster. The king considered the lord deputy as his 'oracle' in this matter.[16] Chichester's plan was decidedly limited compared to the grander plantation scheme which finally materialised. As far as the lord deputy was concerned, substantial amounts of land were to be redistributed to leading individuals among the indigenous inhabitants.

> 'to every man of note or good desert so much as he can conveniently stock and manure by himself and his tenants and followers, and so much more as by conjecture he shall be able so to stock and manure for five years to come'.[17]

The rest was to be allocated to servitors, who were mostly serving or ex-soldiers, while some was to be made available for English and Scottish settlers.

It is more than likely that what has been described by one historian as Chichester's 'much more equitable' plan would have been implemented but for O'Doherty's rebellion in April 1608.[18] This event resulted from the vortex of insecurity and distrust which swept Ireland following the flight of the earls. It consumed, besides O'Doherty, two other major Ulster lords as well, Sir Niall Garbh O'Donnell from county Donegal and Sir Donal O'Cahan from county Coleraine. Rumours abounded that Tyrone was seeking to return to Ireland, as indeed he intended. The fact that he did not want to leave in the first place made his eagerness to return, and the destabilisation which resulted from such rumours, understandable. O'Doherty's revolt provides the first illustration of the enormous influence which the earl continued to exercise on Irish affairs even after the flight.

Sir Cahir O'Doherty, the lord of Inishowen, appears to have been the innocent victim of the situation which prevailed in the aftermath of the flight. The sinister nature of this event, combined with the plethora of reports that Tyrone's return was imminent, caused acute consternation among English government officials and commanders in Ireland. They were inclined to be very suspicious of groups of men being assembled, particularly in Ulster. It was in these circumstances that O'Doherty and some of his men embarked by boat in October 1607 to Canmoyre wood for the purpose of obtaining timber to renovate one of his castles. The governor of Derry, Sir George Paulet, however, interpreted his actions as treasonable.[19]

Paulet attempted to arrest the Inishowen chieftain but failed to do so. Eventually, O'Doherty made his way to Dublin to seek the lord deputy's intervention in the matter. It was to be his misfortune, however, that he arrived there in the immediate aftermath of the escape of Lord Delvin from Dublin Castle. Delvin had admitted complicity in the conspiracy which the earls had been engaged in prior to their flight.[20] Incensed by Delvin's escape and regardless of O'Doherty's personal circumstances, the deputy decided to make an example of him to others showing any disposition which might be construed as treasonable. A 'great recognizance' of £1000 with two sureties of 500 marks were imposed on the Inishowen lord and he was imprisoned for some days while these arrangements were finalised.[21] It was only after the outbreak of O'Doherty's rebellion in April 1608 that the viceroy obliquely admitted his poor handling of the Canmoyre incident by acknowledging that 'all men believed he (O'Doherty) had been wronged'.[22]

In Sir George Paulet, it is evident, O'Doherty encountered an unusually abrasive official. Paulet was widely condemned in government circles, both before and after the revolt, for his demeanour in the position which he had purchased from the previous incumbent, the complaisant Sir Henry Docwra.[23] In February 1607, for instance, shortly after he took up his appointment, Chichester remarked that he was 'not fit for that command. Many dissensions have arisen since he came thither'.[24] Furthermore, before long, the Church of Ireland bishop of Derry was complaining about the treatment which he had received at Paulet's hands.[25]

The spark for the rebellion was provided by another incident involving O'Doherty and Paulet. It resulted from a visit which O'Doherty paid to Derry to deal with proprietorial matters. A dispute arose during which Paulet apparently struck the Inishowen lord. The youthful O'Doherty, spurred on by his embittered chief adviser, Phelim Reagh Mac Daibheid, reacted by organising a revenge attack on Derry.[26] Clearly, in the light of previous experience, he despaired of receiving satisfaction by appealing to the vice-regal authorities in Dublin.

The rebellion proved an affair of short duration and little military consequence. It ended in July 1608 with O'Doherty's death at Kilmacrenan in county Donegal.[27] At its height, it attracted a concourse of no more than 800.[28] Perhaps the relatively small-scale nature of the revolt owed something to the fact that following the flight of the earls Chichester had promised generous treatment for the Ulster Irish who remained peaceful. Partly, too, it may be accounted for by the dearth of weapons in Ulster following the implementation of a proclamation prohibiting the bearing of arms, which was promulgated in February 1605.[29] Even after O'Doherty's seizure of the royal fort at Culmore, not all of his 100 men were armed when the attack on Derry was launched. Of the handful of casualties sustained by either side in the subsequent hostilities there, one Lieutenant Gordon was only eventually slain after being knocked unconscious by a stone.[30]

What O'Doherty lacked in arms was made up for to some extent by ingenuity. The native Irish were noted for their inability to employ artillery in order to breach castle walls. O'Doherty's men overcame this previously often insurmountable problem on two occasions in the early stages of the revolt with ingenious ease. They contrived to go through the opened front gates of the castles at Culmore and Doe. In the case of Culmore, the captured warden's wife was forced to fake a story that her husband had been injured close by while returning from a social engagement at O'Doherty's home. When the warders on duty rushed to his aid, the rebel forces promptly availed of the opportunity to enter the fort through the open gate. Doe castle was likewise seized as a result of a ruse. A cow-herd approached the unsuspecting warders warning them that their livestock was being attacked by wolves. Once more, while the concerned warders fell for the red herring, the rebels rushed through the open gates.[31]

Rebel successes were transitory. Lord Deputy Chichester, a very experienced soldier, reacted in a phlegmatic manner to news of the events. Rather than waiting for reinforcements from England, he promptly dispatched the marshal of the army, Sir Richard Wingfield, with 'all available forces' to confront the rebels. He also made plans to participate in the operations himself. His instructions to Wingfield were to conduct the war in a 'thick and short' fashion.[32]

Following O'Doherty's death at Kilmacrenan in July 1608, the lord deputy arrived to take charge of the pursuit of dispersed rebel elements. He employed characteristically ruthless methods. His tactic of inducing rebels to obtain pardon by killing their former colleagues resulted in instances of desperate internecine strife, the most gruesome of which occurred on the island of Tory.[33]

Although O'Doherty's rebellion did not constitute a major military threat, its ramifications were enormous. Such was the state of alarm in London about the prospect of a prolonged rebellion in Ireland, and its financial implications, that the king and privy council in England panicked on hearing news of the attack on Derry in April 1608. They were concerned that this was but the prelude to Tyrone's return. At first they contemplated effecting a rapprochement with the earl but did not pursue this idea.[34] Two other precipitate policies, however, were implemented. In the first instance, it was decided to introduce 'impositions' in England to pay for the projected huge expenditure that the new rebellion was expected to entail. These were extra customs duties imposed by the crown. Such was the controversy associated with this measure that it played an important role in dividing the first Stuart king and his parliaments over finance.[35]

Even when O'Doherty's revolt was subdued with relative ease, the mood of consternation persisted in London government circles. It was as a result of the acute palpitations caused by this revolt that the king and his advisers in England took control of planning policy for the Ulster plantation. They proved amenable to overtures from other government officials, such as Sir John Davies, that the plantation of Ulster should be greatly increased in scope, not only in the area that was to be confiscated, but also in the proportion of each county that was to be taken from the indigenous inhabitants. A project emerged which resulted in one quarter, or less, of the lands in Ulster being allocated to the native inhabitants. The rest was apportioned to English and Scottish planters, servitors, the Church of Ireland and Trinity College Dublin.[36]

In combination, therefore, the flight of the earls and O'Doherty's rebellion played key roles in paving the way for the plantation of Ulster. Paranoia motivated this radical attempt to solve the Ulster problem. Inspired by the memory of the Nine Years War, an acute apprehension had persisted for some time in London about the dangers of renewed revolt in Ulster and the expenses that this might entail. The flight of the earls and O'Doherty's rebellion fuelled these fears. As a result, the London government resorted to root and branch measures to extirpate the menace of a northern revolt.

The amount and quality of land that was allocated to the native Irish in the Ulster plantation has been a controversy that has exercised historians for generations and may well continue to do so. For the purposes of this essay, it is the attitude of the lord deputy to the issue of distribution of lands which will be considered in detail because of the important shifts in policy which he embraced. In nationalist historiography Chichester has been villified through a variety of uncomplimentary reputations. In particular, he has been most often portrayed as the viceroy with the sticky fingers, the virtual clepto-maniac who found it impossible to resist any opportunity to defraud the native Irish inhabitants of their lands.[37] Undoubtedly, Chichester gained enormously from his career in Ireland and the manner in which he did so may well reflect adversely on his character. It is surely all the more remarkable, therefore, that he fought a passionate campaign, largely unsuccessfully it must be acknowledged, to ensure that an adequate proportion of lands remained in native hands.

As much for his desire for an equitable settlement for the deserving natives, as for its impracticality, Chichester rejected the idea of large-scale protestant settlement. He remarked of the proposals to inflate the scope of the plantation:

'I despair to see it effectually performed upon private men's undertaking; for such an act must be the work of a commonwealth, and upon the common charge, towards which a subsidy or two were well given; and that (if I be not deceived) will save many a subsidy in 40 years'.[38]

He realised, of course, that the London authorities would be unwilling to levy taxes to underpin a thorough-going plantation process. Without adequate capital, he considered that attempting to saturate the planta-tion lands with protestant settlers would prove to be not only unsuc-cessful but dangerous. Chichester warned that the natives would 'kindle a new fire in those parts at one time or other, if they be not well looked to or provided for in some reasonable measure'.[39]

The lord deputy's admonition was ignored and it was an immensely disappointed Chichester who reported that his plan to allocate at least half of each county to natives and servitors was rejected. Instead, according to the deputy, the natives were confined to a barony in each county and in some cases less.[40] One can only wonder what would have happened if he had been successful in allocating them a more substan-tial stake in the settlement scheme. Certainly, there would have been a much greater chance that attachment to the traditional lords living in exile would have been considerably weakened.

As it was, the knowledgeable Sir Toby Caulfield, who had resided in the heart of Ulster since the end of the Nine Years War, remarked of the response of the Ulster Irish to the plantation in 1610, 'there is not a more discontented people in Christendom'.[41] Overall, as Aidan Clarke remarked,

'Few of the favoured Irish received grants of the land which they actually occupied; none received as much as they believed

themselves entitled to. They had every reason to remain resentful
and unreconciled, and their discontent merged with that of the
majority, who had received nothing, to generate a hostility that
endangered the success of the project'.[42]

Chichester's fundamental disapproval of the fate of the Ulster Irish in the
plantation scheme was to be matched by his anger at the way the servitors
were treated. While the amount of land allocated to the natives has loomed
large in the historical debate about the plantation of Ulster, the treatment
of the servitors in the scheme has largely been ignored. In many ways, as
the very people who had subdued Tyrone's dangerous revolt (1594-1603),
they were the most deserving of the protestant settlers to get substantial
proportions of land. Yet they too were to be greatly disappointed with
their share. The lord deputy was very bitter about this, having championed the servitor cause during the plantation debate.[43]

   Two significant policy departures resulted from Chichester's disap-
pointment with the way the servitors and natives were treated in the
Ulster plantation. Aiming, partially, to provide lands for disappointed
servitors, he embarked on a series of minor plantations in Wexford,
Longford, Leitrim and elsewhere. In undertaking the new settlements,
the deputy adhered to his earlier preferred option of taking a limited
proportion of land to allocate to settlers, about a quarter of the total
available land in these instances.[44]

   At least for the servitors Chichester was able to devise some measure
of compensation. For the disappointed natives in Ulster there was little
positive he could do. Instead, confronted with the problem of a substantial number of disaffected natives menacing the proposed settlement of
the province, he embarked on a scheme to transport large numbers of
redundant native soldiers abroad, most of them from Ulster. He claimed
that some 6000 were shipped to Sweden.[45]

   The transportation policy almost dramatically back-fired on the
authorities. During the summer of 1609, a number of representatives
from the London companies received a guided tour of county Coleraine
in an endeavour to persuade them to invest in its settlement. Every effort
was made to provide them with the most favourable impression of the
area. It was with considerable satisfaction, therefore, that Chichester
reported that the Londoners had safely boarded for home. By a twist of
fate, however, their ship skirted the shores of Carlingford Lough just as
some 300 native transportees had seized control of their vessel in an
attempt to escape. The Londoners' ship was used to help suppress the
mutiny.[46] The incident did not deter the Londoners from embarking on
the plantation. Nevertheless, it did provide a foretaste of the instability
and violence that was to haunt the early years of the plantation process.

   The Ulster plantation was considered by its sponsors to be a refined
version of the previous plantation strategies employed in Ireland.

Indeed there was a certain symmetry to the government's plans. Estates of 2000, 1500 and 1000 acres were made available while an almost equal proportion of land was allotted to English and Scots landlords who were officially described as 'undertakers'.[47] They were thus known because they undertook to fulfil certain conditions which the government stipulated. These included requirements to reside on their property for five years, introduce a quota of twenty-four able bodied males per thousand acres and to provide arms and at least a bawn (a fortified enclosure) for defence of their property. The undertakers were given a three-year period to fulfil their building and settlement conditions.[48]

Although the official scheme was known as the plantation of Ulster only six of its nine counties (Armagh, Cavan, Fermanagh, Tyrone, Donegal and Coleraine) were affected. County Coleraine became the focus of special attention. Anxious to secure substantial private funding to ensure that the settlement was a success, most of the county was allocated to various London companies such as the Haberdashers and Vintners. As a result of this unique connection, county Coleraine was renamed county Londonderry and the name of the city of Derry was also changed to Londonderry.[49] Of the three Ulster counties not included in the official plantation Monaghan had been the subject of a settlement in the 1590s which was reconstituted in the early seventeenth century.[50] As for counties Antrim and Down, substantial progress had already been made in attracting lowland Scots settlers in the early seventeenth century as a result of private enterprise. Two Scotsmen, James Hamilton and Hugh Montgomery, played leading roles in this respect.[51]

The official Ulster plantation, in its early stages, did not live up to government expectations. Too many undertakers failed to abide by their conditions. In particular, the building programme proceeded slowly while the native Irish often remained on the estates of the English and Scottish undertakers. Furthermore, there was a slow rate of migration by British settlers until 1614. Between 1614 and 1619 there was a more rapid increase, followed by stabilisation and to some extent decline until 1630.[52] Overall, before the 1630s there was not a large-scale British migration to Ulster.[53] From the mid-1630s, large numbers of Scots, escaping unfavourable economic conditions in their homeland, began to arrive.[54]

The government's timescale of three years for the undertakers to fulfil their building and settlement conditions proved to be pitifully inadequate. On the whole, as Philip Robinson has pointed out, the plantation did not develop 'in response to political decisions taken in the early seventeenth century'. Instead he has emphasised how 'environmental factors were to prove more important than governmental controls in shaping the new settlement pattern'.[55] Had political circumstances been different during the early years, the government's plans might have met with more success.

   Life for the British settlers who migrated to Ulster was particularly
perilous during the first decade of the plantation. Attacks, or the threat
of attack, by discontented Irish retarded the development of the settlement. This occurred in spite of the fact that the initial steps in the
plantation process in 1610 encountered a passive response from the
indigenous inhabitants. The manner in which O'Doherty's rebels
were so ruthlessly treated by the authorities and the success of the
government's transportation policy both played a part in creating this
response.[56] Before long, however, this tranquility gave way to sporadic
violence while the threat of all-out attack remained possible. Two main
reasons may be adduced to account for this: the general dissatisfaction
of the Ulster Irish with the way they had been treated, and the fact that
Tyrone wanted to return to Ulster.

   It has already been suggested that the Ulster Irish were generally
displeased with their allocation of lands. This was even the case in
county Cavan, where government officials first implemented the plantation because it was felt that the natives there had received most
satisfaction. A judge had to be sent to the county in 1612 to try to resolve
the 'controversies between the servitors, undertakers and natives'.[57]

   Tyrone's desire to return also undoubtedly fuelled the attacks by
'woodkerne', or native Irish outlaws, on the Ulster settlers. His ambition also held out the prospect that an all-out assault would be launched
against the plantation. This remained a possibility until the earl's death
in 1616. Spanish government records indicate quite clearly that he was
to be returned to Ireland during the post 1607 period in the event of a
renewal of hostilities with England. However the Spanish were not
prepared to precipitate a new war for Tyrone's sake.[58]

   By a succession of emissaries, often priests, Tyrone sustained the
aspirations of his supporters in Ulster with a constant diet of news of his
imminent return. He hoped that not only many among the Ulster Irish
would have welcomed his return, but perhaps a substantial number of
Old English Catholics as well. As in the pre-1607 era, he hoped to count
on Old English support as they had been suffering from renewed
persecution since Chichester re-embarked on a vigorous and sustained
anti-catholic policy in 1611. The Old English Catholics again bore the
brunt of a range of penalties that can have done little to accentuate their
loyalty to the protestant administration in Dublin.

   These penal measures ranged from heavy fines and imprisonment,
to being deprived of municipal offices, while catholic lawyers were
debarred from practice and catholic wards were granted to Protestants.[59] Catholic disabilities were not codified at this time – they were
not enshrined in a body of parliamentary statutes – yet they amounted
in a practical sense to a penal code. Such was the intensity of the conflict
concerning the exclusion of Catholics from municipal offices that one
historian has referred to this period as the 'wars of the mayors'.[60] It has

been remarked of the 'momentous union' of Irish Catholics following the outbreak of the 1641 rising that it been 'achieved less by common interests than by protestant pressure'.[61] Such an amalgamation might well have been formed much earlier in the century as a result of protestant pressure.

At the very least, the Old English Catholics were intensely aggrieved by the government's renewed protestantisation policy. This disaffection was manifested by a number of dramatic incidents. The first occurred in February 1612 with the executions in Dublin on charges of treason of the octogenarian bishop of Down and Connor, Cornelius O'Devanney and a priest called Patrick Loughran, both native Irishmen from Ulster. Loughran had been a chaplain to O'Neill.[62] In the normal course of affairs native Irishmen could have expected little sympathy from the catholic Old English. Yet their executions precipitated serious disorder in Dublin, the crowds tore at the body of the dead bishop in order not to leave 'a scrap for the hangman' and succeeded in recovering his head.[63] Many historians now believe, indeed, that O'Devanney's death was critical in ensuring the success of the Counter-Reformation in Ireland.[64]

By the time of O'Devanney's execution preparations were also well under way for the convening of the Irish parliament. Traditional representation would have resulted in Old English Catholics dominating the legislature. This was unacceptable to the royal authorities who were determined to protestantise Ireland. As a result, elaborate plans were implemented to procure a protestant majority in the legislature, the newly planted areas of Ulster proving crucial in this respect. Owing to the completion of the English conquest in 1603 it was not unnatural that parliamentary representation should be extended throughout the country for the first time. However, it was the sectarian nature of the government's plans which amplified Old English catholic discontent. In a deliberate exercise in religious headcounting the Dublin government decreed that some 40 new boroughs were to be created, mostly in Ulster, with in-built franchise mechanisms to return Protestants. These would provide the authorities with a protestant parliamentary majority.[65]

For the Old English Catholics this rigged parliament not only meant an end to their traditional domination of the Dublin legislature but heralded the threat of the introduction of severe anti-catholic laws. Thus a contemporary catholic observer summed up the mood when he remarked:

'What keeps everyone in a state of suspense is the fear of the approaching Parliament, which is to assemble after St.John's festival, in which the heretics intend to vomit out all their poison and infect with it the purity of our holy religion and it is

expected that things will take place in it such as have not been
seen since the schism of Henry VIII began'.[66]

It was a measure of the Old English catholic response to these developments that the London and Dublin authorities believed that they were
on the verge of making common cause with the native Irish at a time
when Tyrone was making strenuous efforts to return to Ireland. The
violent mood in the country at the beginning of the Irish parliament in
May 1613 was encapsulated by a remarkable incident days before the
parliament assembled. Two Old English noblemen, Lord Barry and
Viscount Gormanston, got involved in an altercation while escorting
the lord deputy from church. Then, 'two of their followers drew their
swords, close by the Lord Deputy, whereupon he himself called the
guard. At least five hundred swords were drawn, everyone fearing that
there had been a massacre intended by the Papists'.[67]

As a result of this extraordinary tension, the London authorities took
precautionary measures which indicate the degree to which they feared
the threat of a pan-catholic revolt. As many as four warships patrolled
the coasts of Ireland from early 1613, at a time when the London
government was encountering serious financial difficulties.[68] It was
a further testament of government fears that this resolute action
contrasted sharply with previous practice, where only one ship
patrolled the Irish coasts in spite of the fact that a fleet of pirate ships
had been taking refuge in ports in the south of Ireland.[69]

Owing to the tense atmosphere, the Irish parliament was convened
inside Dublin Castle as a security measure. Truly bizarre scenes
occurred as the catholics attempted to nullify the government plans by
placing their candidate for speaker, Sir John Everard, on the speaker's
chair. In response, the protestants first deposited their candidate for
speaker, the corpulent Sir John Davies, on Everard's lap, before physi-
cally removing Everard from his perch. Following this, the catholic
MPs, the vast majority of whom were Old English, attempted to leave
the chamber en masse only to find their passage obstructed by locked
doors. Eventually they were permitted to exit.[70]

Certainly, Old English Catholics dominated recusant parliamentary
tactics. That large numbers of native Irish in Ulster, however, contributed to collections for a recusant delegation sent to London, evidences
a striking degree of catholic solidarity.[71] While Tyrone lived, and
against the background of a renewed protestantisation campaign in
1611, many among the Old English were being coerced, albeit against
their natural inclinations, to consider seeking common cause with the
native Irish. From the crown's viewpoint, the gravity of this situation
was compounded by the fact that Anglo-Spanish relations had
deteriorated so sharply by early 1613, as a result of mercantile
disputes, that many in England feared a Spanish invasion. So worried

had the London government become that more than a fleeting consideration was given to effecting a rapprochement with Tyrone during the summer of 1613.[72] For a time the future of the Ulster plantation was in the balance.

When the furore associated with the turbulent opening to the Irish parliament subsided, the negotiations with the earl were abandoned. As a result the exiled lord redoubled his efforts to return to Ireland, if possible with Spanish military aid, or, without it, if need be. So by 1615, O'Neill determined to return to his homeland with a handful of followers deeming it 'better to meet death with sword in hand'.[73] As part of his plans, he plotted to free his son, Con, from captivity in Ulster.[74] In the end, his intentions were frustrated by the Spanish who, having refused all requests to support his return with military help, effectively prevented it taking place at all by threatening to withdraw his annuity.[75] The enormity of Tyrone's decision to take flight, giving up his independence and placing his fate in the hands of the Spanish, could not have been more apparent.

Tyrone's plans coincided with the 1615 Ulster conspiracy. From a military point of view it was an affair of little consequence.[76] It is not clear to what extent the plotters acted in accordance with the earl's wishes or whether they were motivated by informed rumours at the time. Equally, it is hard to conjecture what might have happened had Tyrone returned. Lack of arms and men would surely have greatly hampered his activities. His very presence, alternatively, might have been sufficient to bring to terms what had been an habitually timorous Jacobean administration in London.[77]

While the conspiracy proved to be an ignominious failure and the earl was unable to return, it remains true that the sporadic attacks which continued to occur were sufficient to generate great alarm among the Ulster settlers. The damage which this caused to the plantation process must have been considerable, if unquantifiable. During the years 1616-19, most strikingly, some 300 woodkerne were killed or executed for attacking protestant settlers in Ireland. Counties Londonderry, Tyrone and Wexford suffered most in this respect.[78] Therefore, the contemporary protestant depiction of the Ulster settlers working under the constant threat of attack had substantial basis in reality in the early stages of the plantation.[79] By 1624, however, this high level of violence had temporarily subsided. Lord Deputy Falkland remarked in that year, cautiously it must be admitted, 'since Ireland was Ireland, there never was such universal tranquillity as at this instant'.[80]

Despite its precarious existence in the early years, the plantation survived. How did it affect Ulster society? Most obviously the demographic complexion of the province was transformed by the arrival of English and Scottish settlers. In other respects too the difference was marked.

'The social norms of Gaelic Ireland, already changing slowly in
the sixteenth century, were rapidly dismantled and replaced
with English standards of social order. Terms such as
"leaseholder" and "freeholder" became the normal description
of a man's place in the social order rather than the older
vocabulary of Gaelic Ireland'.[81]

In the legal sphere, the extension of the English common law system,
already underway prior to the plantation, was also institutionalised
before long. Regular twice yearly visits by judges of assize played a key
role in underpinning this process.[82] Government surveys of the plantation's progress, such as those in 1611 and 1622, make it clear that at
least some undertakers fashioned their estates according to the official
plantation mould. To some extent too Ulster was transformed into a
market economy as an embryonic urban structure developed.[83]

In other respects, by contrast, native Irish culture pervaded Ulster
society for some time. The majority of tenants, whether Irish or British,
resided in modified versions of primitive thatched cottages. Of this
development Nicholas Canny has concluded that 'for the overwhelm-
ing majority of British settlers in Ireland during the first half of the
seventeenth century it was a question of accommodating themselves to
Irish-style residences rather than the reverse process that had been
intended'. In the economic sphere, also, change was slow. The traditional Gaelic emphasis on pastoralism, as opposed to British tillage,
prevailed for some time. Once more, British settlers initially became
more acculturated to native Irish practice than vice versa.[84]

Overall, while the plantation wrought considerable changes in
Ulster society, in the short term these were not as radical as intended.
This probably explains in part why a substantial section of the Ulster
Irish eventually reconciled themselves to the settlement, at least for a
time. Furthermore, evidence shows that some of the 'deserving Irish'
tried to assimilate themselves into a British way of life. The plantation
also opened up new opportunities for large numbers of Ulster Irish to
negotiate favourable terms as tenants on the plantation estates of British
landlords, owing to the initial shortfall in available settler manpower.[85]
A major native Irish rising, such as occurred in 1641, was not a foregone
conclusion.

The 1641 rising cannot, therefore, be explained in simplistic terms, as
the inevitable and sole product of the alleged iniquities of the Ulster
plantation. All recent historiography indicates it was much more than
an attempt to right such perceived wrongs. Instead, the manner in
which the 'deserving Irish' ran foul of their attempts to assimilate
themselves to a British way of life and the fact that native Irish tenants
were subsequently jettisoned to make way for new British arrivals are
emphasised. So, too, short term political considerations are accorded

prime importance. In this respect, the threat to catholic interests in Ireland of the prospect of a parliament victory in its power-struggle with Charles I has been shown to have played a central role in fashioning the nature of the rising.[86] That the Ulster plantation endured and survived the upheavals of the 1640s was an indication of the fact that it had become firmly established, despite its shaky beginnings.

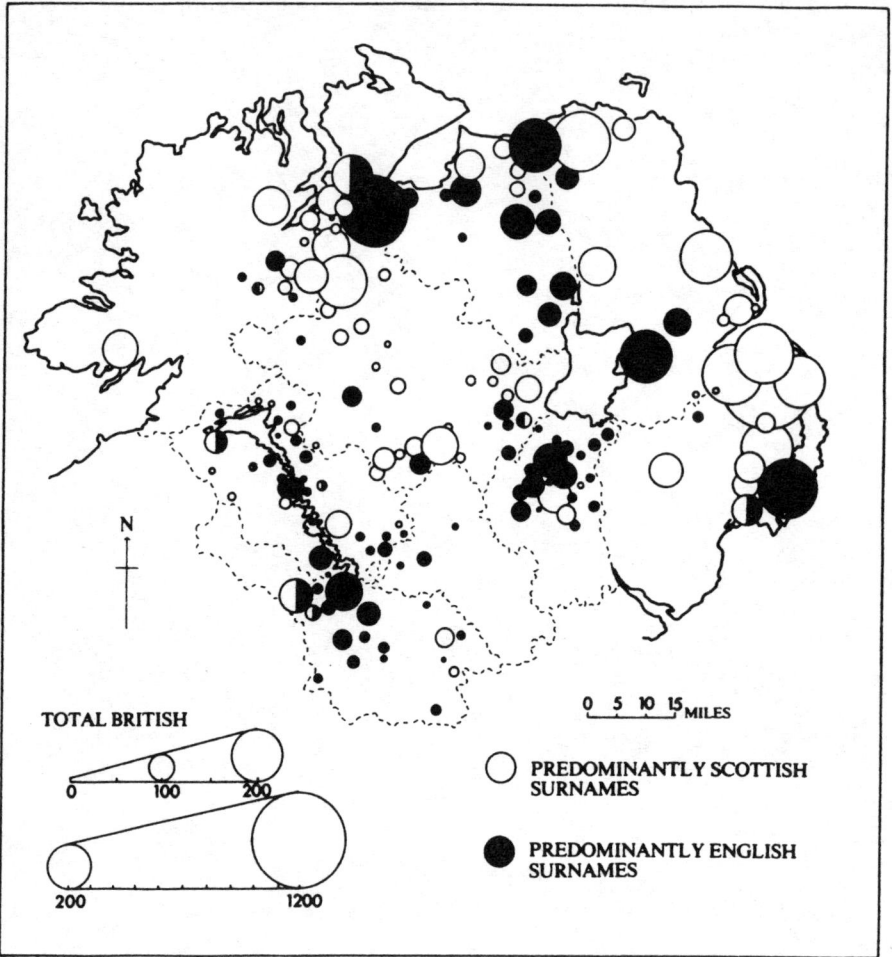

TOTAL BRITISH

0   100   200

200   1200

0 5 10 15 MILES

○ PREDOMINANTLY SCOTTISH
   SURNAMES

● PREDOMINANTLY ENGLISH
   SURNAMES

'English and Scottish settlement in Ulster based on numbers and surnames recorded in the muster rolls, c. 1630'; in Philip Robinson; *The Plantation of Ulster* (Dublin 1984).

PROTESTANTISM IN ULSTER, 1610–1641

Phil Kilroy

Within the first century of its existence the Church of Ireland was marked by several significant events: establishment by statute in 1560, articulation of its own creed as a national church in 1615, the challenging of that creed by Laud and Wentworth in the 1634 Convocation; the re-emergence of the Church after the Interregnum, symbolised by the Act of Uniformity in 1665. Although named the Church of Ireland in the 1536 Act of Uniformity, it was only established as a church by statute in 1560 and even at this stage had a different stamp and tenor from that of the Church of England. As early as 1567 the Church was provided with twelve articles of religion, significantly the broader set of Archbishop Parker, rather than the Thirty-Nine Articles of the Church of England. [1] Indeed, by the time of the Ulster Plantation the Church of Ireland had developed a theological stance which was quite distinctive and arose partly out of the situation peculiar to Ireland, and partly due to the theological background of its ministers. In itself this was quite an achievement, for initially legislation had attempted to change the existing sixteenth century Roman Catholic Church into one within the tradition of the Reformers. This proved an impossible task on several grounds and the Church of Ireland evolved into a new, small cohesive church, not the older church reformed, as intended.

This development occurred for several reasons. Firstly, the intentions of the secular legislators were not matched by their active and continuous support for the new church. For decades the church's internal administration was hampered by the rights of lay patronage and by lay control of its property. Whereas the legislation of 1560 intended that the new church would replace the older one, this was not possible since the structures and internal organisation of the older church were caught in a web of lay rights and control. For this reason and because it was not provided with adequate economic support, the Church of Ireland was unable to take root at any wide level in the country. This gradually led to a realistic assessment of the possible effectiveness of the Church of Ireland. It also contributed to the growth of a distinctive theology: the awareness of being a small, predestined community, elect among the damned, enduring opposition from the old church and suffering lack of real support from lay society and, with few exceptions, from the governments of the day.

Such articulation of theology arose out of practical experience and from the definite calvinistic influences which were prevalent in Ireland, particularly towards the end of the century. The foundation of Trinity College Dublin in 1591 contributed to the distinctive theology which developed in the Church of Ireland. For Trinity was modelled on Emmanuel College Cambridge and served by ministers from that college and by others who were distinctly puritan in theology and background. Such theology was particularly represented in the first provosts and fellows of the college.[2] In addition to English puritanism, the influence of the Scottish Reformation, itself in process of defining its own tradition, was also present in the college. This originated when James VI of Scotland sent agents to Dublin in 1597, hoping that they could gain the support of the Irish gentry in his bid for the throne of England. James Fullerton and James Hamilton set up a school in Dublin and James Ussher, future archbishop of Armagh, was one of their first pupils. They were also among the first fellows of Trinity College.

At the same time, the Church of Ireland was of necessity ambivalent in its attitude towards the conversion of the Irish nation. The new church was faced with a procedural problem: either to convert the Irish to the new church and exert all efforts towards this; or force conformity and the discipline of the church, with severity if necessary, and then introduce the deeper fruits of the reformation to a conforming people. This latter was seen as part of the introduction of civility and culture by the colonising power, going hand in hand with religious reformation. These two approaches to evangelisation certainly exercised the Church of Ireland throughout the seventeenth century, and the merits and drawbacks of each were debated, often within the context of the political crises of the day.[3]

While in its initial stages the Church of Ireland struggled to be the national church, it gradually faced into its inability to realise this purpose. Indeed by the time the Church of Ireland had gathered enough energy and insight to recognise this situation the counter reformation movement had begun to gain pace and momentum in the country. In a real sense it was an opportunity missed, for the reformation church had neither the support nor the impetus needed to root itself quickly in the land and so valuable time and opportunity were lost.[4] This situation further encouraged the Church of Ireland to develop into a church of the predestined and the saved, surrounded as it was by the Roman Church, by all the signs of Antichrist. In the Convocation of 1613–15, the Church of Ireland drew up its own quite distinctive articles, which were calvinistic in tone and content and which expressed their vision and experience of being the reformation church in Ireland.

Thus the plantation of Ulster took place within the religious context of a small reformation church, which though established as the national church was not effectively supported by the government or by the powerful lay landowners; nor did it hold the allegiance of most of the population. In the reign of James 1 there were great hopes that the plantation of Ulster could effectively enable the Church of Ireland expand into a true reformation church. Certainly the plantation had lasting effect on the Church, though not in the way originally intended. Indeed, several developments took place in protestantism in Ulster from 1610-1641 which both marked and defined the future path of the Church: increasing influence from Scottish protestantism; reforming activities of some bishops; and bishops acting as landowners, increasing their own power and prestige at the expense of the reformation they were appointed to serve.

At this time the reformation church in Scotland was in process of determining its own theology and practice. James 1 had imposed episcopacy on the church in Scotland after his accession to the throne of England, thus creating real potential for conflict in a church which had adopted a presbyterial form of government. However, since no minister had to be re-ordained, and bishops were described as permanent moderators of presbyteries and synods, this change did not lead immediately to dissent. When James made his only visit to Scotland in 1617, he imposed the Articles of Perth which provided for kneeling at the reception of the sacrament, private communion, private baptism, confirmation of children by bishops, and celebration of festival days of Christmas, Good Friday, Easter, Ascension Day and Pentecost. These Articles split the Church and provided the context for the Scottish Church to define further its own theology and practice.[5] Within this debate the Church of Ireland, with its own set of Articles which were distinctly calvinistic, was an attractive choice for disaffected Scottish ministers. In particular the Irish Church omitted any reference to the consecration of bishops[6] and this would have been most acceptable to the Scottish ministers. Moreover, despite initial hopes and designs that the Church of Ireland in Ulster would be served as far as possible by native clergy, bishops in Ireland were forced to look for clergy either in England or Scotland.

Indeed the plantation of Ulster was seen as a solution for many ills, not just those of the church:

> 'Now what an excellent diversion . . . is ministered by God's providence . . . in this plantation of Ireland . . . wherein so many families may receive sustentation and fortunes and the discharge of them out of England and Scotland may prevent the seeds of further perturbations. So shall ... this work have double commodity in the avoidance of people here and the making use of them there.'[7]

What seemed a simple solution to several problems in reality created
further complexities, particularly in the area of religion. These grew
slowly over the years and by 1641 the Church of Ireland had been caught
between the pressure of Laudian reforms, enforced by Wentworth and
Bramhall, and the growth of Scottish Presbyterianism in Ulster.[8] For
example, Robert Blair came to Ireland in 1623. He had been professor
of philosophy at Glasgow University, where he resigned his post on
account of his opposition to episcopacy. Lord Clandeboy invited him to
Bangor and there he was ordained. The bishop of Down and Connor at
that time was Robert Echlin, a Scot, educated at St. Andrews. He,
according to the presbyterian account, agreed to ordain Blair on these
terms:[9]

> "'I hear good of you, and will impose no conditions upon you
> . . . Only I must ordain you, else neither you nor I can answer
> the law, nor brook the land". I told him that that was contrary
> to my principles; to which he replied, both wittily and
> submissively, "Whatever you account of episcopacy, yet I know
> you account a presbyter to have divine warrant; will you not
> receive ordination from Mr. Cunningham and the adjacent
> brethren, and let me come in amongst them in no other relation
> than a presbyter ?"'

Similarly, Andrew Knox, bishop of Raphoe and a Scot, ordained John
Livingstone in 1630 with the same understanding that the bishop was
just one among presbyters.[10] Thus there was a degree of accommodation which these two bishops were willing to exercise, in order to enable
the Church of Ireland take root in Ulster. Neither bishop saw himself
going beyond his brief and later on Echlin was to defend his actions
in this regard and indeed proceed against the ministers in his own
diocese.[11] More than anything else it showed the state of change and
flux in church order that obtained at that time. Besides, both prelates
were from Scotland and were in need of well-educated ministers in
their dioceses.[12] While no other bishop was prepared to ordain Scottish
ministers simply as a presbyter among presbyters, neither were Scottish
ministers denied the right to be appointed as incumbents in the Church
of Ireland. Moreover, Primate Hampton and his successor, James Ussher,
both held distinctly calvinistic views on election and predestination.
They both hoped that some accommodation could be reached with the
Scottish ministers, and indeed with other members of the Church of
Ireland, on the questions of ceremonies.[13]

An insight into the religious vitality of the Scottish ministers and
settlers who came to Ulster in the early part of the seventeenth century
is given through the Six-Mile-Water Revival of 1625. The Revival itself
was begun by James Glendinning, a minister who preached powerfully

but lacked both sufficient content in his sermons and the capacity to answer the needs of his hearers.[14] In response to this crisis, several Scottish ministers grouped together and decided to hold a monthly lecture at Antrim. This meeting began with a sermon on Thursday evening, followed by sermons all day Friday, three in the winter months and four in the summer. In time these meetings became very popular in Ulster and hundreds came to them from far and wide. The ministers used the opportunity for holding conference among themselves, especially on matters concerning their congregations. It was at one level the forerunner of the Antrim meeting and at another the beginning in Ireland of large, open-air meetings for the renewal of piety, a practice which Presbyterians had already established through holding large communion services.[15]

Although Scottish ministers were officially appointed by the Church of Ireland, and their actual theology was in many respects not remarkably different from that held by many of the bishops, their way of leading worship and their attitude toward the office of bishop was a source of unease. In 1621 the archbishop of Armagh, Christopher Hampton, complained to the duke of Buckingham:[16]

> '... certain factious and irregular puritans which of late be settled in the lands of Hugh Montgomery entertaining the Scottish discipline and liturgy. They offer wrong to the church here established and the rites of the administration of the sacraments, with extraordinary contempt which I may not suffer to take place, or deepen root...'

These remarks reflect growing unrest and division in the Church of Ireland as a whole at this time. Throughout the early decades of the seventeenth century in Ireland the church struggled to maintain unity in the midst of growing Arminianism[17] and an increasingly articulate counter reformation movement.[18] Nevertheless, the growing polarisation between the Scottish ministers and the Church of Ireland was balanced by the actual need of the church for ministers to place in parishes. This practical concern overrode the latent theological conflict, at least until the arrival of Wentworth as lord deputy in 1633.

For its part there was no strong leader among the Church of Ireland bishops in Ulster who could command conformity to the ceremonies and discipline of the Church. Hampton died in 1625 and was succeeded as primate by the bishop of Meath, James Ussher. Ussher had enormous stature as a writer and scholar and he was both marked by and contributed to the independent stance of the Church of Ireland and its calvinistic thrust in theology. Indeed, the presbyterian form of church government attracted Ussher and in later years his tract *'The reduction of episcopacy'* was used several times in efforts to forge some agreements between episcopalians and dissenters.[19] Therefore during his term of office there was little risk that Scottish presbyterian ministers in Ulster would be challenged.

At the same time, bishops themselves differed greatly in approaching their task. Some were convinced that only by suppressing the entire structure and practice of the old church could the reformation have any hope of success in Ulster. When George Montgomery was appointed bishop of the three dioceses of Derry, Clogher and Raphoe in 1605 he set about trying to implement such a policy, without success.[20] His successor in Raphoe, Andrew Knox, pursued a threefold policy of coercion, persuasion of the native clergy and people, and secured some preachers from Scotland, and to the extent as indicated of ordaining ministers who were evidently presbyterian. For a short time he was successful but by 1634 the native ministers who had been won over to the new church had been replaced by either Scottish or English clerics.[21]

By contrast, Bishop Bedell of Kilmore and Ardagh saw it as his duty to persuade and win over the native population in his diocese to the church. To this purpose, he tried as far as possible to get preachers who could speak Irish, for the vast majority of people in the diocese were Gaelic speakers. Bedell himself set about his work of translating the Old Testament and he had a small catechism printed in Irish in 1631.[22] He also made a point of contacting Roman Catholics in the diocese and tried to accommodate some of their resistances to the liturgical practices of the Church of Ireland. He was prepared to get in touch with the Roman Catholic bishop of Kilmore 'lately chosen Primate', Hugh O'Reilly, causing resentment and suspicions among his own colleagues.[23] He also proceeded against his own clergy, against those who held several church livings at the same time and non-residents, and he clashed with Ussher on these issues several times.[24] Indeed, when Bedell set about trying to reform his own diocese and confronted the extortions of the clergy, particularly of his chancellor, Alan Cooke, he was accused of being 'a papist, an arminian, a politician, a neuter'.[25]

James Spottiswood, bishop of Clogher, was in a different mould from Bedell. His concerns were entirely taken up with court cases against Lord James Balfour of Clonawly, Fermanagh, Sir James Areskins and Sir John Wishard.[26] His predecessor, George Montgomery, had managed to get 100,000 acres for the church, instead of the original 75,000 acres laid down in the plantation. This land included most of Fermanagh, and parts of Tyrone and Monaghan. In the royal visitation of 1622 it was noted that half of the incumbents in Tyrone and Fermanagh were non-resident, that three quarters of the churches were in ruins or very inconveniently placed and that the surrounding undertakers were trying to deprive the church of its endowments. Spottiswood was appointed in 1621 and spent most of his term of office in litigation.

Clearly, throughout the early decades of the Ulster plantation bishops in the several dioceses had different emphases: Hampton and

Ussher avoided confrontation in order to maintain unity and provide actual ministers to parishes; others like Knox and Echlin were prepared to accept theological and disciplinary modifications from the Scottish ministers, at least for a time; others like George Montgomery of Clogher and his successor, James Spottiswood, were more concerned with building up their own power and position; a reforming bishop like Bedell encountered great opposition to his views and activities from his own colleagues in the ministry.

In addition to this complex development within the Church of Ireland in Ulster, its own particular theological position, articulated in 1615 at the convocation held in Dublin, continued to evolve. For the Church saw itself as an elect people, who were destined to live in a country where Antichrist reigned, and where they were called to serve the God who had saved them from damnation in this world and the next. Such a stance gave them purpose and justification in every sense. But it did not prevent inner tensions and divisions growing from within. Indeed the marked increase of discord within the Church of Ireland in the early seventeenth century was a source of concern, particularly in the north of Ireland. This dissension further defined protestantism in Ulster, and though there was division within the entire Church of Ireland, there were aspects of it which were peculiar to Ulster. Underlying such tensions was a fundamental difference in approach to the task of the reformation church in Ireland.

For example, the bishop of Derry, George Downame (or Downham) and the bishop of Kilmore, William Bedell, debated the issue of predestination. This controversy sharpened within the reformation churches once the Synod of Dort in 1619 had defined the teaching of the reformed churches on the question of election and reprobation: no one, on their own, could merit either election to life or damnation to hell. Any attempt to say that the human person could in any way accept or reject salvation was to concur with the errors of Arminius and his followers. Downname was bishop of Derry from 1617-34, a diocese where Roman Catholicism was strong. Prior to his appointment, Downame's views were well known and indeed published.[27] Three years after his arrival in Derry Downame published his 1603 work 'The Pope is Antichrist', this time in Latin possibly in the hope that some of the Roman Catholics would read it. Latin was suggested as 'the most suitable lingua franca between the native Irish and foreigners'.[28]

Then in 1631 the bishop published a work which dealt with the question of predestination. It was dedicated to the lords justice, Adam Loftus and Richard Boyle, and in this work he was very critical of those who denied strict predestination to life or to damnation:[29]

> 'The new creation is a motion from our not being of grace and spiritual goodness to a being thereof which serves notably to

confute the erroneous concepts of the patrons of free will, the Pelagians, the Papists, the Arminians and our new Anabaptists.'

In the appendix to the work, Downname appended a tract:'*A treatise on the certainty of perseverance, maintaining the truth of the 38th Article of the National Synod in Dublin in the year 1615*'. It was written at a time when many in the Church of Ireland felt that Roman Catholicism was being allowed too much freedom both in law and practice. It was feared that the Church of Ireland could not sustain such freedom granted to Roman Catholics and Downname had plenty of evidence of this in his own diocese.[30] However, he was particularly critical of William Bedell, whom many suspected of being Arminian and even half-papist, for Bedell accepted the Roman Church as a church, though in error.[31]

This attitude to Bedell was not new; for some time he had been held in suspicion by many in his church. While provost of Trinity College Dublin from 1627-29 Bedell was at the centre of controversy. Firstly there was 'a schism among the fellows arising from national antipathy; the society consisting partly of British and partly of Irish'.[32] The second source of friction was due to Bedell's positive attitude towards the Roman Church; he was accused of contracting the differences between the two churches, even to the extent of recognising that the Roman Church was a church. Prayer was made in public for ' a good head, no Arminian, no Italianated man'.[33] This tag of being an Arminian and half-papist followed Bedell into his episcopate. He maintained his views and told Ussher:[34]

> 'I have not changed one jot of my purpose or practice or course with papists from that which I held in England or in Trinity College, or found, I thank God, any ill success but the slanders only of some persons discontented against me for other occasions'.

John Richardson, who succeeded to the see of Ardagh when Bedell surrendered it in order to avoid holding a plurality, was urged by Ussher and others to find out exactly what views Bedell held on the question of predestination. In 1629 Richardson accused Bedell of holding the doctrine of free will. Bedell denied this and insisted all his teaching was based on the Synod of Dort.[35] The following year, Downame and Bedell exchanged views by letter.[36] Bedell indicated that both he and Dr. Ward of Cambridge disagreed with Downame's views expressed in the 'Covenant of grace' . And Bedell was careful to remind Downame that Ward and himself had already differed from such views when Downame taught them as professor of logic at Cambridge.[37] Certainly it was Bedell's insistence that a person could have an active trust in God, 'affiance in Christ', which caused controversy and suspicion regarding predestination orthodoxy. Nevertheless, he asked Downame to agree to differ and desist from further controversy. While Bedell may not have been an Arminian theologically, he certainly was pastorally, and this caused unease among his colleagues in the church. They felt themselves surrounded by Antichrist, and when Charles I held out the Graces to Catholics in 1629, they must have felt that religion was being sold in the market place. Thus any accommodation with the Roman Church was seen as capitulation.

However, accommodation within the reformation tradition was a different matter and in the early decades of the seventeenth century there were continuous efforts to maintain unity within the Church of Ireland. Yet by 1622 the strains were showing. In that year Henry Leslie preached before the king's commissioners for Ireland, at the beginning of the royal visitation and reflected:[38]

> 'contention extinguishes the very life of religion . . . and therefore they who make so much ado about ceremonies had need to take heed that in the meantime they lose not that which is more precious . . . Let us labour to reconcile ourselves, and at length to embrace unity.'

Christopher Hampton, archbishop of Armagh, had already raised the issue of disunity within the Church of Ireland in 1613 and sought to contain it:[39]

> 'It may be that some small debates come from our own brethren and comburgesses, moving unnecessary and unprofitable questions in ceremonies, things indifferent . . . If I believe and am persuaded in mind and conscience that the cross in baptism, the ring in marriage, kneeling at the Lord's Supper etc. work nothing with God, I enjoy the full benefit of my Christian liberty.'

This was a statement of moderation and comprehension quite impossible twenty years later. Even by 1621 Hampton had recognised that the situation in Ulster was beginning to polarise sections of the church.[40] The Church of Ireland was being threatened by Scottish presbyterian ministers who had been accommodated within the church. In 1636 Leslie, who succeeded Robert Echlin as bishop of Down and Connor in 1635, complained:[41]

> 'Would to God that you who came out of Scotland had followed this advice [authority of the bishop] and so conformed yourselves into the orders of this church and [not] sought facetiously to bring ..amongst us the customs of the place from whence you came . . .'

By this time the whole tenor and theology of the Church of Ireland had officially changed. For Wentworth had been appointed lord deputy in 1633 and immediately set about reforming the reformation church. He was a firm supporter of William Laud and wished to model the Church of Ireland as closely as possible on the Laudian model of the Church of England. To both Laud and Wentworth it was evident that the Church of Ireland had been the victim of governments which almost always could not offer support either of policy or finance, and which at the same time had granted progressive toleration to Catholics.

Both Wentworth and Laud found support in William Bedell. In 1634, drawing upon his experience in the diocese of Kilmore, Bedell preached:[42]

> 'We that seem to the forwardest in Reformation are not yet so come out of Babylon, as we have many shameful badges of her captivity; witness her impropriations [church property in lay hands], being indeed plain church robbery, devised to maintain her colonies of idle and regular irregulars, idle to church and state, zealous and pragmatical to support and defend her power, pomp and pride, by whom they subsisted; witness their dispensations, or dissipations rather, of all canonical orders, bearing down all with her non obstante, her simoniacal and sacrilegious venality of holy things, her manifold extortions, in the exercise of canonical jurisdictions, which we have not yet wholly banished. Let each of us therefore account it as spoken to himself: Come out of her my people.'

This was the diagnosis made by Wentworth and with the help of his chaplain, John Bramhall, he set about trying to lessen lay patronage in the church, especially the laity's hold on the lands intended for the support of clergy and the practice of laity presenting to livings. At the same time Wentworth attempted to impose doctrinal uniformity in every part of Ireland. When Bramhall visited the north he found 'the resident clergy absolute irregulars, the very ebullition [sudden outburst of civil commotion] of Scotland'.[43] Laud himself was named chancellor of Trinity College Dublin and began amending its statutes; in addition he recommended William Chappell, a known Arminian, to be provost of the college, which Ussher resisted but could not prevent. During the 1634 parliament in Dublin, convocation met and examined the state of the church. Bramhall represented Wentworth in the upper house, as did James Croxton in the lower house. Both were articulate supporters of the changes and reforms Laud wished to see in the church. The upper house petitioned the king for sound financial support for the church, without which the work of reformation in Ireland was impossible. A sub-committee in the lower house presented a commentary on the English Canons of 1604 and also proposed an article for confirming the

1615 Articles under pain of excommunication.[44] Furious at this independence Wentworth insisted that the Thirty-Nine Articles be accepted
'for he would not endure that the articles of the church of England be
disputed'.[45] Though he was forced to accept the Thirty-Nine Articles,
Ussher refused simply to adopt the existing canons of the Church of
England. Instead he adapted the English canons for the Irish Church. In
an effort to retain some comprehension within the church and indeed
maintain a token independence from the Church of England, Ussher
omitted some detailed references to outward conformity to the ceremonies and discipline of the church.[46]

Certainly some of the northern bishops responded to the changes
positively. Bedell showed enthusiastic support for reform of the church
by holding a synod in his diocese which drew criticism from his clergy
and even Bramhall. Ussher however supported Bedell seeing the
reform as the act of a free, national church, independent of the Church
of England.[47] In the diocese of Down and Connor, Henry Leslie used
his legal authority both to challenge and depose Scottish presbyterian
ministers, culminating in the Black Oath of 1639.[48] But there was not
sufficient time for Wentworth's plans to be implemented fully in
Ireland, for by 1641 he had been impeached and the country was in
rebellion. In such a short time no long-term change could have been
effected and by 1647 the Church of Ireland had been effectively suppressed. What survived was the spirit of the 1615 Articles, even though
they had been superseded legally by the Thirty-Nine Articles of the
Church of England. Moreover, the very deep sense of being a church
predestined to live among a reprobate people continued and indeed
was heightened by the 1641 rebellion. Most of all, the church's sense of
being a national church, the Church of Ireland, remained strong and
was in fact one of the arguments used by the clergy in Dublin, pleading
their right to exist.[49]

Protestantism in Ulster in the first part of the seventeenth century
was formed out of several diverse experiences. It had emerged from the
late sixteenth century with a theology which suited its experience as a
church of the élite, the saved. By the early seventeenth century it had
accepted that it was a church primarily of the settlers in Ireland and it
had an uneven policy towards the evangelisation of the native people.
In general the church hoped that when the native people had been
brought to civility and outward conformity, then the work of reformation in the entire country could begin. This must have seemed endlessly
postponed with the evident increasing strength of Roman Catholicism
in Ireland. The strength of that religion, tolerated by the government,
was a continual source of fear and dread which motivated the members
of the church to try and contain differences among themselves in face of
the common enemy. Lacking a native clergy of any substantial numbers
forced the church to rely on ministers from England and Scotland.

These in turn brought their own issues and theology, which in the early stages of the plantation were generally accommodated in the church. However, gradually the inherent tensions of such a modus vivendi emerged. By the time Wentworth began to implement his religious policy, to the extent of imposing the Thirty-Nine Articles on the Irish Church, the old way of trying to live with differing theological views and practices was over.

Such reforms as were thrust on the Church of Ireland must have convinced the Scottish ministers in particular that Arminianism had invaded the Irish Church. For its part, the Church of Ireland realised that it was no longer able to tolerate Scottish presbyterian ministers in Ulster and it set about expelling them from parishes. The sense of crisis within the Church of Ireland was compounded in 1641 when the rebellion seemed to prove that Antichrist had come, both as a scourge and a judgement. Twenty years later, the Church of Ireland, silenced during the Interregnum, re-emerged as the established church of the land. From the early years of the Restoration, its statements made it clear that the old days of comprehension were over. The spirit of accommodation, especially in Ulster, was consigned to the past. Instead, membership of the Church of Ireland was no longer a universal obligation and dissent within the church would not be tolerated.[50]

ULSTER EXILES IN EUROPE, 1605-1641

Gráinne Henry

In 1597 Sir Henry Harrington wrote to Mr Waad about the misery being then endured by the inhabitants of county Cavan. He noted that due to 'famine and extremity' they 'eat horses, a qua[r]ter of a bad garron is sold for five schillings, their stud mares, their best relief'. The context of their suffering was the Nine Years War (1594-1603) which in its final stages witnessed the confrontation between Hugh O'Neill, earl of Tyrone and the lord deputy, Charles Blount, lord Mountjoy. Harvests in Ulster could not be gathered during the war, while every available kerne as well as professional swordsman was called upon to fight, whether on the rebel Irish side or as part of the army of the lord deputy. The scorched earth policy adopted by Mountjoy against the forces of Hugh O'Neill further ensured that the population of Ulster was starving, and some years after the war finished, Fynes Moryson, Mountjoy's secretary, recounting its progress, noted that 'multitudes lay dead in the ditches of towns and other waste places, with their mouths all coloured green by eating nettles, docks and all things they could rend above ground'.[1] While this description may have been a deliberate exaggeration to discredit Hugh O'Neill as far as possible, there is no doubt that there was a good deal of truth in it. From as early as 1597 the 'wild Irish' began to leave Ulster in their hundreds reaching a high point between the years 1600-1 when the corn harvest failed drastically all over Ireland. This probably represented the first widespread dislocation of population in Ulster for over a hundred years. Although some of these particular migrants were shipped back again from England and continental Europe, their departure and the socio-political context of their migration was a pattern that was repeated again and again in the early Stuart era up to 1641. This essay aims to examine those who left Ulster in the early seventeenth century under three headings, firstly, who left Ulster for continental Europe and why, secondly, the formation of an Ulster military community in the Spanish Netherlands or Flanders as it was often called then, and thirdly, to examine that community's links with its new European world and the impact this had on the Ulster emigrés' perception of Ireland.

Plate VI, No. 124, facing p. 35, John Hennig, 'Irish Soldiers in the Thirty Years War', R.S.A.I. Jn., lxxxii (1952).

Those leaving Ulster from the poorer classes in the early seventeenth century probably fall into two categories. The first consisted of vagrants and beggars. We learn about these generally from the numerous complaints made against them by contemporaries. In November 1605, the lord deputy, Arthur Chichester, upon receiving complaints from England about the 'multitude of Irish beggars' there, defended his own position by reference to the restrictions he had lately introduced to curb this flow of people out of Ireland. Referring to the Nine Years War period, he maintained that

'The multitude now there [in England] are rather of the former remnant, increased by the resort of others from France and Spain, to which kingdoms they fled, in time of the rebellion upon the beginning of the famine, out of the provinces of Munster and Connaught and of Ulster.'[2]

Between 1628 and 1631 there was another mass movement of people from Ireland to England, Scotland and continental Europe. On 27 August 1628 the English privy council noted that 'of late great numbers of poore Irish people have been landed in divers parts of Wales'. They ordered that 'no such Irish' be permitted to land and in the ensuing months heavy penalties were imposed on all shipowners who transported them.

While beggars from all parts of Ireland landed in Wales and Bristol, making their way usually down the main routes leading to London, there was also a traffic of poor Irish to Scotland at this time, almost certainly coming exclusively from Ulster. In November 1629 for example the Scottish privy council noted the 'great nombers of strong and sturdie Yrish beggars' who

'goe in troupes throw the countrie, and not contenting themselffes with the benevolence and charitie of the people whilk is freelie offered unto thame they extort almous, and . . . they committ sindrie insolenceis upon his Majesteis good subjects who ar not able to withstand thame'.

In this case the beggars were given fourteen days to leave and landlords were ordered to apprehend these beggars and have them transported back to Ireland if found on their land.[3] The existence of this and similar decrees indicate that Irish migration to Scotland at this time was an urgent problem.

The English privy council noted in August 1628 that these Irish were leaving Ireland due to the 'great death of cattell and want in that kingdome' while in January 1629 a report from the mayor and aldermen of Bristol noted that 'the scarcitie of corne in his Majesties Realme of Ireland is such at this presente as the poore people of the said Realme are enforced for the avoyding of famine to come over into this kingdome'. The population of Ulster between the close of the Nine Years War and the outbreak of rebellion in 1641 increased by at least fifty percent so that it was hardly surprising that there was greater pressure on the food supply. Rapid urban growth during the same period, due mainly to the implementation of plantation policies, further increased the number of households dependent on the market for food. Thus, while famine and harvest failures weren't new, the population in Ulster as in Ireland as a whole was increasingly coming to rely on a good harvest and surplus agricultural output. Significantly the two most disastrous periods of harvest failure in Ulster – 1603-5 and 1628-31 – were also the very years when migration from Ulster, whether to Scotland, England or the continent, was at its highest.[4] The comparatively lenient terms of reference used particularly by the English privy council for these Irish refugees further strengthen the view that these Irish came to England out of economic necessity. It is particularly noteworthy that during the periods 1603-5 and 1628-31 the Irish were mostly referred to as 'the poore Irishe' or 'Irish Beggars' thus indicating a certain degree of sympathy towards their plight. Such terms did not preclude the local authorities from giving such beggars harsh treatment, usually a whipping followed by immediate transportation back to Ireland. They do, however, indicate that the authorities saw this group of Irish beggars as a separate entity from the 'ordinary vagrants'.[5]

The second category of poorer people leaving Ulster in the early seventeenth century were those who left as part of a voluntary levy or expedition to one of the foreign armies of Europe. In many parts of Europe it was not unusual to conscript men into foreign service. However the official emphasis in Ireland for all levies conducted between 1605 and 1641 was definitely on the voluntary nature of such recruitment. Men could join up as they wished by presenting themselves at the recruiting points and were then usually paid an 'impress' or advance of their wage. Recruitment took place either in the form of a military expedition where the commanders as well as the food, clothing and transportation of troops were fully organised by the Dublin and English administrations (this was the case in the Swedish expedition 1609-11 and the expedition to La Rochelle and the Isle of Ré in 1627) or under the contract system. Under this system, negotiations took place between England and a representative of a foreign country which agreed to take a certain number of troops out of Ireland. Contractors, usually captains, would then be employed by the foreign state to come to Ireland and recruit a given number of soldiers (usually 200-300) whom they fed, clothed, and transported out of the country at the foreign state's expense. Spanish territories were particularly favoured, in that companies recruited by contractors from there could be automatically reinforced by new recruits each year from Ireland.[6] Under this contract system troops were regularly transported out of Ulster in the first four decades of the seventeenth century. Levies for the Spanish army of Flanders in the Spanish Netherlands took place between 1605-6, 1621-2 and from 1629 right through to 1641 with the exception of two short bans – one for the years 1637-8 and the other for a short period in 1640. Under this system troops were also levied for Poland in 1621, Denmark in 1627, Sweden in 1629 and 1631 while France recruited companies in 1635 and continuously from 1638 to 1641. (See Table 1).

The voluntary nature of the recruitment was emphasized at official level whether the troops were taken as part of a military expedition or under a contractor. Significantly, the word 'voluntaries' was employed right throughout the 1620s and 1630s to refer to these recruits levied in Ireland for foreign service even though manpower for all the armies involved in the Thirty Years War (1618-48) was becoming extremely scarce by the second half of the 1630s.[7] Despite the emphasis on voluntary recruitment however, there is little doubt that the English administration in Ireland welcomed these levies for foreign service as a means of getting rid of undesirable elements in the country and in particular those of Ulster. Those professional soldiers or swordsmen who played such a vital role in maintaining the strength and autonomy of a rebel Anglo-Irish or Gaelic lord were the chief target-group for foreign service. After the Nine Years War, lord deputy Mountjoy wrote to the earl of Salisbury:

> 'there rests little now to settle this kingdom but some way to rid the idle swordsmen of both sides, and that the English owners would or were able to inhabit their own lands'.

The 'way' found was a request made by the Swedish king in 1608 for some recruits from Ireland, and the military expedition to Sweden organized in the years 1609-11 was undoubtedly an attempt to rid Ulster of swordsmen and of the Gaelic military class – the 'kerne' – a group who appear to have acted both as farmers and as light infantry for a Gaelic lord when the need arose.[8] In 1609 Chichester, commenting on the success of the initial levy of 240 troops for Sweden, noted that 'most of them (were) idle swordsmen that served on the one side or the other in the last rebellion of Tyrone, and some of them were with O'Dogherty'. It is noteworthy that the disbanded soldier from the English army was as feared as the rebel, a concern that was shared by most early modern European societies who saw the disbanded soldier as the worst type of 'masterless man' – a trained fighter who could easily organize himself into a group.[9]

However, large numbers of those incorporated into all the levies were men outside the military class who might also be thought to present a threat to the political stability or social order in Ulster. Sir John

TABLE 1   *Military levies from Ireland, 1605–41*

Year	Destination	Approx. number of companies [1]	Approx. number of men	Type of Recruitment
1605–6	Spanish Netherlands [2]		1,260	Voluntary Levy
1609–11	Sweden		1,000	Expedition
1611–13	*Moscow / Poland*	*No figures available*	*6,000* [3]	Expedition
1621–2	Spanish Netherlands	10	2,000	Voluntary Levy
1621	Poland	10	2,000	Voluntary Levy
1627	France	1 regiment	2,000	Expedition
1628	Denmark	1	200	Voluntary Levy
1629	Sweden	1 (Ulster) [4]	200	Voluntary Levy
1629	Spanish Netherlands	7	1,400	Voluntary Levy
1631	*Sweden*	*Not allowed to go ahead*	*3,500*	Voluntary Levy
1631	Spanish Netherlands	9	1,800	Voluntary Levy
1634	Spanish Netherlands	30	6,000	Voluntary Levy
1635	France	4	800	Voluntary Levy
1636	Spanish Netherlands	35	7,000	Voluntary Levy
1637–8	**BAN**	–	–	–
1638–9	France	1 regiment	1,100	Voluntary Levy
1639	France	3 regiments	3,000	Voluntary Levy
1639	Spanish Netherlands	2	400	Voluntary Levy
1639–40	France	1 regiment	1,000	Voluntary Levy
1640	**BAN**	–	–	–
1641	Spanish Netherlands	1 regiment	1,500	Voluntary Levy
1641	*Spain* } [5]	–	} *16,000*	Voluntary Levy
1641	*France* }	–		Voluntary Levy
TOTAL			**32,660** [6]	

Source: A.G.R.E.G. reg 22/399v. – reg. 41/12v; Jennings, *Wild Geese*, 81–345.

These figures only reflect the military records available from Brussels and miscellaneous English sources. Simanca military sources and particularly those of the Spanish military treasury – *Pagadores Generales, Datta a tropas irelandesas* – would need to be examined thoroughly to give an overall accurate picture of the number of recruits for imperial armies drawn from Ireland up to 1641.

1. Companies could contain between 200–300 men but since not all companies might be complete 200 has been taken as a basic estimate.
2. This levy was also meant to have been for the United Provinces (Holland) but none appear to have been taken for there.
3. Chichester claimed to have sent 6,000 'swordsmen' out of Ulster to Sweden, Moscow and Poland between 1609 and 1613. As I could find no evidence of the latter two levies I've excluded this 6,000 from my total.
4. This levy organized by Lord Reay in Scotland was later banned (see 1631) but at least one company under Patrick Barnwall was taken from Ulster and probably a lot more.
5. These two levies, eventually totalling 10,000 and 6,000 for Spain and France respectively, were forbidden by the English parliament, 30 July 1641.
6. Note that at least a quarter of these recruits were levied on more than one occasion so that this figure does *not* represent the total number of Irish who left Ireland during this period as part of foreign levies. The figure excludes those in italics.

Davies and Chichester were proud of the fact that the Swedish expedition included 'thieves', 'vagabonds', 'wild malefactors' and other 'unprofitable' people and in September 1609 Davies wrote to the earl of Salisbury that Chichester had

'. . . . left the province of Ulster in more complete peace and obedience than has ever been seen since the conquest. For the Lord Deputy has taken in all the woodkerne and loose people in every county, and has bound them with sureties to depart into Sweden'.

Sir Ralph Bingley who raised 400 recruits for France out of Ulster in 1627 noted that 'the exportation of idle men will be good for the country'.[10] The emphasis in these reports was significantly on 'loose' and 'idle' people, terms which were certainly not confined to a redundant Anglo-Irish or Gaelic military class. Rather such terms were the references used in Elizabethan and Stuart society to denote any person who was unemployed or on the road – in short, a person who departed from the realms of manor, lord and master.

In the face of such anxiety to be rid of these people one is tempted to ask just how 'voluntary' the levies for foreign service were. There can be little doubt that conscription did take place. In August 1609 Sir John Davies noted that no execution had taken place recently in Coleraine prison as the prisoners had been 'spared and reserved . . . .to fill up the companies that are to be sent into the wars of Swethen [Sweden]'. It is not likely that the prisoners would have argued with their fate in this case but the practice was undoubtedly more widespread.[11] Such practices could only have increased in the late 1630s when Sweden, France and Spain competed fiercely for recruits from Ireland. 'Voluntaries' were all very well when available but when in short supply as was certainly the case in Ireland between 1639 and 1641 conscripts were just as acceptable. Thus in Stuart policy foreign levies were used as a means of social control, and the authorities did not hesitate to employ dubious means in attaining this goal.

Despite this rather harsh official attitude towards levying for overseas service it is nevertheless true that people voluntarily left Ireland in large numbers to join foreign armies, outside of the official levies sanctioned. Between 1611 and 1620 inclusive at least twenty grants 'to serve' in the army of Flanders were issued to Irish soldiers at a period when no official recruiting took place, while in 1632 such were the numbers departing in secret from Ireland that the lords justice and council felt the need to consult on the matter with the English privy council. They noted that

'The unconformed natives here have lately departed in large numbers to foreign countries secretly in small parties without leave or licence, leaving from remote harbours. They leave their homes usually for England, whence they take passage to the territories of the archduchess of Flanders'.[12]

Their destination was the army of Flanders where a second Irish regiment under Colonel Hugh O'Donnell was just being set up. (See Table 2).

Of course it was not only the lower classes in society who went to the continent to make a living. Foreign service attracted many members of the upper classes from Ulster. Men whose families had traditionally fought in the English army were now finding themselves out of work in the widespread demobilization that occurred in the English army after the Nine Years War. Obviously the place to continue a military career was henceforth in the armies of Europe. Captain Neale Oge M'Art O'Neill, for example, fought on the side of the English army against Cahir O'Dogherty in 1608, before enlisting with Sir Robert Stewart in 1609 to go to Sweden. Chichester noted that Neale had 'ever been in opposition to the Earl [Hugh O'Neill] and his sept . . . . and is verily believed to be a loyal subject'. Those whose inheritance was severely encumbered also went to foreign wars often only for a short time simply to make some extra money. Hugh Boy O'Dogherty, son and heir to Sir John, served with Colonel William Stanley in Flanders until he came home in 1595 to assist the rebels in the Nine Years War. A later example was Phelim MacHenry O'Neill, heir to the title and lands of Henry MacShane, who had fought against Hugh O'Neill in the Nine Years War. He joined the Irish regiment of John O'Neill in the Spanish Netherlands for a short period in 1623. It was undoubtedly in this context that Hugh O'Neill advised Rory O'Donnell regarding his debts in 1607, to recruit a company of soldiers with England's permission and bring them into foreign service.[13]

However by far the largest two groups from the upper levels in Ulster society attracted to foreign service were the élite swordsmen or personal bodyguards of a Gaelic lord, and those Gaelic and Anglo-Irish rebels against the crown who had had their lands confiscated. In the plantation policies of early seventeenth century Ulster there was certainly no room for professional retainers – usually relatives of a lord – who had maintained the lord's position by brute force. Such retainers could in fact become a financial as well as political burden to a lord who had successfully defended his title and lands within the English legal system and who now wished to advance his fortunes under crown patronage. Turlough MacHenry O'Neill was a case in point. Formerly one of the military retainers of Hugh O'Neill, he had three sons described by the English authorities as 'swordsmen'. These three were singled out by the Dublin administration in 1609 as men 'fitter to be employed elsewhere' and all three ended up in the service of Spain or the Archduke Albert. Similarly Sorley Boy MacDonnell, described by the English authorities as a 'pirate and rebel', spent a number of years as a pirate operating along the islands of Scotland before joining the Irish regiment in the army of Flanders in 1622 at the rank of captain. With their old position in society now redundant these professional fighters felt they had little choice but to make their living in foreign armies.

Those branded as traitors and rebels to the crown particularly after the parliament of 1613–15 were likewise obliged to leave Ireland. Oghy O'Hanlon, John Maguire and Cormac O'Neill testified in memorials to Philip III that the 'heretics' of England had deprived them of their estates forcing them to come to the Spanish Netherlands. The three received captaincies in the Irish regiment of John O'Neill, son of Hugh. In fact many grants to Irish arriving in Spanish territories followed the pattern of that given to Roderick O'Dogherty in 1619. He received a grant of ten escudos a month from Spain 'in consideration of his birth and good parts, and of the services of his father in defence of the Catholic cause'.[14]

Given official hostility to soldiers returning from foreign armies,[15] it was extremely difficult for a soldier to return to Ireland. Official leave for an ordinary rank and file soldier was almost impossible. In the army of Flanders, for example, it was granted only on three conditions: an incurable illness or wound, the taking up of an inheritance or the fulfilment of a religious vow. Between 1610 and 1621 for example, only 101 licences to come to Ireland were granted to Irish soldiers despite the fact that most companies were disbanded at this time due to the Twelve Year Truce with Holland (1609-21). Of course desertions were widespread (at least one percent a month) but in order to leave any part of the Spanish territories for Ireland, even officers had to have a passport and a letter of recommendation from an English 'person of quality' in residence in the Spanish domains. In 1624 the privy council in England gave specific directions to the five ports on the west coast as to the legal restraints to be imposed on any Irish passing through who had 'bene or are employed in the service of forreigne princes'. Of course soldiers or indeed vagrants probably evaded all the bureaucracy, landing at lonely creeks in the middle of the night as the Irish had done in Pembroke in 1630. However any movement between countries, particularly in the war-torn Europe of the 1620s and 1630s, was likely to be greeted with the utmost suspicion on the part of any authorities. Such legal restraints must have prevented any large groups of soldiers or vagrants returning to Ireland from the continent. In 1601 lord deputy Mountjoy noted that three out of four people who went into the service of a foreign army from Ireland never returned.[16] Of approximately 32,000 recruits (see Table 1) taken for the continent from Ireland, and particularly Ulster, during the period 1605-1641, a substantial proportion were never to return to Ireland. This is proven by the numbers who did in fact settle on the continent.

II

During the period of our study (1605-41) numerous little Irish communities appeared on the continent mainly in Spain, northern France and
around the headquarters of the Irish military group in the Spanish
Netherlands, where in 1605 scattered independent Irish companies
were consolidated into one regiment. Such communities can be identified by the existence of Irish names in certain parish records. Such
records exist in the French towns of Nantes, Rouen, St Malo and
Bordeaux while in Spain Bilbao, Seville, Cadiz and Madrid attracted
most Irish outside of Galicia in the north-west which became almost an
Irish province in this period. So many Irish at all levels crowded into
Corunna in Galicia that a member of Philip III's council of state, the
conde [count] de Punonrostro, was specifically appointed in April 1604
with the title 'Protector of the Irish' to look after the interests of the Irish
there. Within those towns clusters of Irish names in the parish records
of certain churches indicated the existence of closely knit Irish communities. The area of San Martin in Madrid, the parish of San Anton in
Bilbao and the large parishes of St Michel et St Gudule and St Catherine
in Brussels were all examples of parishes with records of Irish interest.[17]

The important role played by kin-groups in early seventeenth
century migration from Ireland contributed to the development of
these Irish communities. Given the fact that the vast majority who left
Ireland between 1605 and 1641 did so as part of a military expedition or
levy for foreign service, it is significant that these levies were very
localized indeed. It was common practice for captains to recruit their
own tenants and retainers and this was particularly true for Ulster. In
the 1609-11 Swedish levies from Ulster, eighty men were taken from the
'O'Cahane country' while the captains chosen for this expedition were
encouraged to take any of their followers with them. In later levies
recruitment in Ulster was always undertaken by captains who were
themselves of northern origin. In the levies of 1621-2 for the Spanish
Netherlands Carlos O'Neill, John Maguire, Patrick Daniel or O'Donnell
all carried out their recruiting in Ulster, Maguire in particular being
accused of employing his time in 'spying and prying, [and] riding into
the counties of Fermanagh, Monahan, Donegall'. Others of the wealthier
Old Irish from Ulster simply brought their followers with them to the
continent in the hope that they would find employment in some army
there. In 1610 for example Donogh O'Brien who had accompanied
O'Neill, O'Donnell and Maguire to Italy in 1608 requested Philip III that
he be appointed captain and 'be allowed to form a company from many
of his vassals who are in Spain and with whom he would go to Flanders
to serve in the regiment of Colonel Henry O'Neill'. Likewise in 1612
Charles O'Daly asked the Infanta Isabella that she recommend him for a
position as captain in the service of the king of France. He wrote that he

had fled Ireland 'with two hundred of his relations, kinsmen, and friends to France' and that they were all now waiting in Paris in the hope of employment.[18]

Not surprisingly army records also indicate the existence of family or kin-groups within the ranks of the Irish. Close family ties are easy to identify among the upper ranks of those serving in foreign armies. Captains, for example, were often related to their officers. James Bellewe of Louth acted as ensign to Captain James Gernon to whom he was related through marriage, while Arthur and Terence O'Hagan served in the company of their father Henry in 1626. In a memorial to the Spanish ambassador at Brussels in 1635, John Barry, later to have an Irish regiment of his own in 1636, noted that he had two brothers and 'two other relatives' captains in the service of the archduke and the king of France.

In 1596 the Spanish authorities completely restructured their armies by organising their companies and regiments into 'national' groupings, and while no Irish regiment was then set up, independent wholly Irish companies under Irish captains such as Edward Fitzgerald and Alexander Eustace were established. These were finally merged together in 1605 into the Irish regiment under Henry O'Neill, son of Hugh, and the arrival of Hugh O'Neill with O'Donnell and Maguire on the continent (the Flight of the Earls, 1607) had a huge impact on the structure of this regiment. Not only were many in this 'company . . . disposed into the regiment' in 1608 but in the following years Hugh O'Neill consistently used his influence to recommend his allies for positions in the Irish regiment. In 1612 O'Neill made a special request to the Archduke Albert that Cornelius O'Reilly receive the *entretenimento* (permanent monthly salary or grant) O'Reilly had previously enjoyed in the army of Flanders. O'Neill's suit was successful and in 1613 he went as far as to ask Philip III that seven Irish companies which had been dismissed by the king of Poland be incorporated into the Irish regiment. These men had been part of the expedition to Sweden organised in Ulster by Chichester to serve 'against the King of Poland' but they seemingly had passed over to the catholic army. The circumstances of this plea made by Hugh O'Neill on their behalf were interesting. The Spanish ambassador at Rome, conde de Castro, noted:

> '. . . the poor men go begging from door to door and many of them have come to the Earl for they feel he has an obligation towards them; this is true for, in his cause, they were exiled.'

These soldiers had obviously been dependants of either Hugh O'Neill or Rory O'Donnell in Ulster. It was a measure of O'Neill's determination that these men be established 'as soldiers among those of their nation' in Flanders, that he turned to Philip III after a flat refusal from the archduke. He achieved partial success in that Philip promised to arrange some 'manner of admitting them'.[19]

There is no doubt that Hugh O'Neill's ambition was to make the Irish regiment as strong as possible for his own political uses. In expressing concern to Philip III in 1608 on the numbers of Irish either sick or leaving the regiment, he wrote 'It is of great importance to the service of Your Majesty and to the benefit of our country that the Irish regiment should be preserved', and further begged his majesty to 'ensure that the soldiers remain in their regiment'. Already by July 1608 there were several references in discussions in the Spanish council of state to 'The Regiment of Tirone', in place of the Irish regiment, and in October 1610, the conde de Castro wrote to Philip III on the occasion of Henry O'Neill's death:

> '. . . at the end of his days, Colonel Don Enrique Onel begged Your Majesty not to allow his appointment as Colonel to be filled by any other than a person nominated by the Earl of Tirone his father.'

Hugh O'Neill was in fact so successful in identifying his interests with the Irish regiment that this request made by Henry O'Neill was granted. Against the wishes both of the English ambassador at Brussels and such an influential person as the Franciscan Fr Florence Conry (adviser on Irish affairs to the Spanish council of state), who favoured Owen Roe O'Neill, it was Hugh O'Neill's own son John who was appointed as Henry O'Neill's successor as colonel of the Irish regiment in 1610.[20]

In fact it became customary for the king of Spain to appoint each successive earl of Tyrone in Spain as colonel of this regiment. With Hugh's son John as colonel of the Irish regiment on the continent for twenty eight years (see Table 2) it is not surprising that the influence of this northern Irish group continued to be felt even after Hugh O'Neill's death in 1616. Significantly when Oghy O'Hanlon, John Maguire and Cormac O'Neill petitioned the Spanish authorities for a position in the Irish regiment in 1617, they emphasized their own relationship to Hugh O'Neill. The first two were nephews of Hugh O'Neill while Cormac was his grandson. Later levies taken up for this regiment in Ireland by those connected to Hugh O'Neill incurred considerable wrath on the part of the English administration. A letter to the lords justice in Ireland from the English privy council in July 1622 recommended that captains John Maguire and Carlos O'Neill be forbidden

> 'to leavie or raise any men at all either for that [Spanish] or any other service (for they were) . . . descended from the late traitor Tyrone and . . . might breed some trouble in the thoughts of the subjects and undertakers of those parts [Ulster]'.[21]

In fact all the Irish regiments right from 1605 to 1634 were either under an O'Neill or an O'Donnell (see Table 2) and this had obvious effects on the structure of the military group in Flanders. For example in Owen Roe O'Neill's regiment, six of the forty-six commissions for companies were granted to an O'Neill while at least ten captains of Henry O'Neill's and thirteen of John O'Neill's were captains from Ulster who had either taken part in the Nine Years War or were relatives of those who had.

Table 2

Irish Regiments in Spanish Flanders, 1605-42

The 'Old Irish regiment' (El tercio viejo irlandes)	
Under Colonel Henry O'Neill	1605-10
Under Colonel John O'Neill [*1]	1610-38
The Regiment of Hugh Alberto O'Donnell [*2]	1632-8
The Regiment of Owen Roe O'Neill	1633-42
The Regiment of Thomas Preston	1634-41
The Regiment of John Barry [*3]	1636

The Ulster group was certainly perceived by other groups in the Irish regiment to be favoured by the Spanish army administration especially with regard to posts and promotions in the companies. In June 1609 Thomas Edmondes noted that within the Irish regiment it was felt that Henry O'Neill favoured 'the standing of the captains which are Northern men and employs himself to procure the cashiering of those which be Palesmen'. These same sentiments were echoed some thirty years later by Colonel Maurice MacSweeney who wrote bitterly in 1640 that 'men of his own nation of the province of Ulster . . . will not permit any others, especially men of the province of Munster, to obtain any promotion in the army of our King [of Spain]'. MacSweeney not surprisingly was from Munster! However, the amount of influence exerted by the 'northern group' was exaggerated. During the years 1609 to 1622, in the Irish regiment eleven of the thirty captains were Old English, three were of Munster Old Irish extraction while significantly five of the ten captains who levied troops for the army of Flanders in 1621-2 were from areas outside Ulster. It is important to note also that Thomas Wentworth (lord deputy 1633 – 1640) did all in his power to increase the influence

---

* 1 This regiment was transferred to Spain in 1638 where it continued under the command of John O'Neill, until his death in 1641.
* 2 Also transferred to Spain in 1638.
* 3 Due to difficulties in recruiting, only two companies of John Barry's regiment ever came into existence.

of the Old English group in this military community. He exerted the strongest pressure possible on the Spanish government to increase the number of senior posts granted to Old English while at the same time severely curtailing recruiting in Ireland for the regiments of Hugh O'Donnell and Owen Roe O'Neill. This strategy achieved a good deal of success with the formation of two new Irish regiments under the leadership of Old English – the regiment of Colonel Thomas Preston established in 1634 and that of Colonel John Barry in 1636.[22]

Ultimately real power over the structure of the Irish military was in the hands of the governors of the Spanish Netherlands. The priority of these rulers was to maintain a strong military presence in what they saw as a vulnerable Spanish Netherlands between their enemies France, England and the United Provinces. These Spanish governors might be favourable to a northern Irish group who had thrown in their lot with Spain against England but essentially they pursued whatever diplomatic strategies were currently in the interests of Spain. The important point was not the amount of power that the Ulster group had over the Irish military group in Flanders but the power they were perceived by others to have. Ulstermen from all over Europe looked to the banner of O'Neill and O'Donnell in these regiments. This resulted in an Irish military group in Flanders that was not only dominated by a northern élite but whose rank and file largely consisted of their dependants and retainers.

The second factor that influenced the development of Irish communities was that early seventeenth century migration from Ireland included a substantial number of women and children. While studies done in England have shown that couples and their children were relatively small elements in any vagrant population, this does not appear to have been the case with Irish migrants. Ulster women certainly accompanied their menfolk to the foreign wars. In 1607 there were fifteen women, including Catherine Magennis, Nuala O'Donnell and Rosa O'Dogherty, who formed part of the train of O'Neill, O'Donnell and Maguire to the continent, though this obviously was a small proportion of the ninety nine claimed by O'Cianain to be on board the ship leaving Lough Swilly, in what came to be known as 'The Flight of the Earls'. In 1629, when Hugo O'Shaughnessy of the Irish regiment was killed, his wife Mariana MacMahon applied for a licence and passport for 'her and another honest widow . . . to go through the country asking for alms', while in the army of Flanders' list of widows and orphans in 1635 at least eight of the widows appear to have been of Ulster origin.[23]

The proportion of Ulster women who went to the continent is hard to determine. There must have been many like the wives of Murtagh O'Quinn, Henry O'Hagan and Henry Hovenden who remained in Ireland when their husbands left with the earls in 1607. These wives

actually received some of their husbands' goods to maintain themselves and their children in Ulster. Yet women, whether as wives or
companions, formed a customary part of the Ulster military group on
the continent.[24] The combination of family migration and kingrouping
outlined here pointed to the existence of very close, almost introverted
Irish communities on the continent.

III

The final section of this essay is concerned with the links forged
between this Ulster community and their new environment, that of
counter-reformation Europe. The southern provinces of the Netherlands [present-day Belgium], where most of the Ulster contingent
congregated, were dominated by Catholic Spain. Not only did these
provinces owe political allegiance to Spain but they were characterized
by an emerging catholic identity and the flowering of a counter-reformation movement that was directed largely by the Habsburg government. From the patronising of traditional shrines and new religious
orders to the implementation of regulations regarding discipline and
education for the laity and the clergy, Philip III and Philip IV and the
papal nunciature at Brussels as well as the archducal couple Albert and
Isabella (1598-1633) consciously reshaped the Catholic church of the
Spanish Netherlands in the Tridentine [referring to the Council of Trent
1545-63] fashion. From the early 1600s the Spanish Netherlands became
a home to hundreds of refugees fleeing from protestant governments
among the Germanic states, the United Provinces, Scotland, England
and Ireland. These people not only received political asylum in Flanders but became part of a movement of revived catholic spirituality and
learning where the history and culture of catholic peoples were becoming important. The Ulster group was one of many such groups who
had left their homeland. The army of Flanders in which they served
remained at an average of 65,000 men throughout the Eighty Years War
between Spain and the United Provinces (1565-1645) and consisted of
soldiers from different 'nations' – Spain, Italy, Burgundy, Germany and
James I's three kingdoms (England, Scotland and Ireland) serving alongside the local troops of the Spanish Netherlands – the Walloons. Thus
the small military group of Ulster men and women in Flanders lived in
an environment where a multiplicity of nationalities, languages and
cultures was the norm but which had as a unifying feature counter-
reformation catholicism.[25]

   This Ulster military group integrated remarkably well into their new
environment, despite the dynamics of family migration and kingrouping
outlined already. From both marriage and baptismal certificates it is
clear that at least some members of this group intermarried with the

local Walloon (French-speaking) and Flemish populations while a majority had at least one foreign godparent for their children.[26] Secondly, unlike the English or Scottish subjects, the Irish living in Spanish territories were accorded the same legal rights as a Spaniard so that they were able 'to live, trade and acquire property' there without any legal hindrance. This meant in effect that there were no bars to Ulster people becoming established socially in the Spanish Netherlands. Some Ulster merchants in particular not only traded but bought lands in Spanish territories while Ulstermen like Owen O'Sheil and Nial O'Glacan forged out particularly successful medical careers for themselves on the continent.[27]

It was however in the military arena that such legal privilege was most to benefit the Irish and particularly the Ulster Irish. A decree of Charles II of England in May 1680 noted that 'no obstacle has ever been placed in the way of [the Irish] obtaining political or military appointments' in Spanish dominions and in two areas this was particularly true. The first was the particular status accorded to all Irish regiments whereby they were put on an equal footing with the Spanish regiments. Although there was some dispute between Owen Roe O'Neill and the archduchess Isabella regarding the flexibility of promotion within the Irish regiment in 1631, this status meant that in general all Irish regiments, together only with the Italian regiments, enjoyed the same 'honours, favours, pay and precedence' as their Spanish counterparts. Secondly, several of those Irish with suitable backgrounds were admitted into the Spanish military orders of Santiago, Alcantara and Calatrava. Among the Ulster contingent, Hugh Albert O'Donnell, son of Rory, was made a knight of Alcantara while John O'Neill and Dermot O'Mallun became knights of the prestigious order of Calatrava before 1633.[28] This was an extraordinary achievement. Entry into one of these orders combined with a commandery carried with it an income equal to a large country estate and was very difficult for a non-Spaniard to achieve.

Perhaps the most important links established by the Ulster military group in the Spanish Netherlands were with the Irish religious community there. This religious community, consisting of Irish students and clergy at the counter-reformation colleges and convents in the Spanish Netherlands, was effectively started by Christopher Cusack when he founded the Irish college at Douai in 1594. The training of Irish priests and nuns for the Irish mission grew to such an extent that during the 1620s Douai had appendages at Lille, Tournai and Antwerp while other Irish colleges and institutions were founded at Dunkirk, Nieuport and particularly Louvain before 1630. These colleges were to form the Irish centres of post-tridentine catholic learning.

Not surprisingly, close family ties existed between the Irish religious and military groups. For example, of the twenty-eight Irish names listed as clerical students in the archdiocese of Malines (including

Louvain) between 1600 and 1610, there were only five who did not have either brothers or near kin serving during the same period in the Irish regiment. In 1625, six of the seven founders of the Irish Poor Clare Order of nuns appear to have had brothers or relatives serving in the army of Flanders.

A formal channel of communication between the religious and military groups was initiated by the Spanish army officials. It was the usual practice in the army of Flanders to appoint a chaplain to each company of soldiers. For example, Nicholas Brae, William Barry, Edmund O'Donoghue, John White, Dermot O'Hullacayn and John Delahide were appointed by the Spanish authorities as chaplains to six of the fifteen companies established by 1608 in the Irish regiment under Henry O'Neill. Another category called 'sacerdotes' [priests] appear to have been employed in the specific capacity of preachers or confessors to the soldiers and between 1605 and 1621 at least twenty-five chaplains and sacerdotes had been officially appointed to Irish companies.

Religious instruction and ministration among soldiers were not confined to the chaplains or priests appointed by the army authorities. In the Jesuits' annual letters of Tournai in 1606 a report related the activities of 'two Jesuits from the novice house of Tournay' who went to the Irish soldiers in winter quarters in Mildeburg. There, it claims, 'they converted thirty-eight heretics, taught soldiers to say the angelus on their knees', and encouraged soldiers to give up swearing, observe fast days and do penances. Such a report indicated the close relations established between the soldiers and the religious houses in their proximity. Likewise in Louvain, Hugh MacCaughwell's [Aodh Mac Aingil] dual appointment as chief chaplain of the Irish regiment in 1606 and guardian (superior) of the Irish Franciscan convent at St. Anthony's, Louvain in 1607 ensured that there was frequent contact between the Franciscan friars and the soldiers. In fact the friars were granted special leave by the archbishop of Malines to carry out religious duties within the Irish regiment and it was no coincidence that Bonaventure O'Hussey's Irish-language catechism was produced at Louvain, to cater 'for the instruction of Irish soldiers in the doctrine of Trent'. Based on the Jesuit Bellarmine's *Copiosa Explicatio*, and the teachings of Trent, the essential articles of faith in verse form and the simple presentation of the catechism were ideal for the instruction of the predominantly Irish-speaking soldiers.[29]

The chaplain's role however was by no means restricted to religious instruction and devotional work. Chaplains in the army of Flanders were until 1596 wholly responsible for the wills and testaments of soldiers and even after this date continued to assist in this area. It was customary to leave orphaned children under the care of Irish chaplains, and priests often gave loans to soldiers. In the will of Captain Patrick Fleming in 1637 one of his first requests was that the sixty pounds lent to him by 'Father Geillis' be returned. In return for such services and the duties carried out by the religious, regular collections were made amongst the soldiers for the religious houses. The building of the Irish college at Paris in 1623 for example was greatly assisted by generous endowments from the Irish officers serving the king of France while in the Spanish Netherlands Henry O'Neill organized a collection within the regiment towards the building of St. Anthony's College and chapel at Louvain (1615-16). In a similar collection organized by Captain James Gernon in his company in 1616 most of the soldiers gave four to eight escudos, the equivalent of a month's salary.

In fact a measure of the extent to which the Spanish authorities acknowledged a close relation between the Irish religious and military groups can be seen in the number of contributions made frequently to religious institutions from army funds. In 1596 the money allotted to the Irish infantry included a grant 'to the fifty-three students at Douai', while in 1614 nine Irish and English institutions, including the college of Douai, lost all or part of their annual allowance due to the last *'reformacion'* or rationalization of the army. The official appointment of chaplains and priests to cater for the soldiers' spiritual needs, the family ties between the two groups and the close association between clerical students and the army camp represented a deep bond between the army and religious personnel. It was a bond that was probably strengthened by the growth in the number of Irish colleges and the number of Irish students going to study in the Low Countries.

The clergy also had much influence on the promotion and recruitment of Irish soldiers in the army of Flanders. From the time of his appointment as one of the chief advisers to the Spanish council on Irish affairs, the Franciscan Florence Conry [Flaithrí Ó Maolchonaire] (archbishop of Tuam in exile) vouched for several of the Irish then entering Spain, recommending them for service or *'entretenimiento'* in the Spanish armies. Charles Wilmot, joint commissioner for Munster, noted in 1606 that 'all Irish' had pensions or military positions allotted to them by 'religious men of the Irish nation'. This however was an exaggeration and the authority of the Irish priests lay in their literacy and their intimate knowledge of genealogies and social divisions in Ireland. Within a military context the priests' role was almost certainly to advise Spanish authorities on the backgrounds of people claiming *entretenimiento*, promotions or honorary titles.[30]

In the area of recruitment in Ireland for foreign service, the priests seem however to have exerted considerable influence, even by 1605. Captain William Nuse wrote in January 1606 that 'it was almost impossible to recruit a company in Ireland for the United Provinces [Calvinist Holland] because the Irish under the influence of the priests would not serve against the King of Spain'. By the late 1620s it was taken for granted that levies in Ireland for countries other than catholic ones would meet with opposition. In 1627 George Hamilton, recruiting a company of soldiers for Denmark from Ulster, complained to the lord deputy that the 'Papists in the North objected to their idle swordsmen leaving the country or entering the king of Denmark's service'. This levy went ahead but since there isn't any evidence of similar complaints about those going into Spanish service, one can conclude that it was the service of the protestant Danish king that was particularly objectionable. In 1634, according to English sources, the French only enticed Irish troops into their army with assurances that they would not be put into service against any of their own religion, while in 1631 Gustavus Adolphus, the protestant king of Sweden, objected to the raising of 3,500 'footmen' from Ireland on the grounds that he did 'not trust the Irish papists'.[31]

The links between the clergy and the Old Irish Ulster nobility both in family ties and social co-operation had traditionally been very close. This tradition was continued by Hugh O'Neill and Rory O'Donnell particularly in relation to the friars in the Spanish Netherlands. Henry O'Neill (son of Hugh O'Neill) was a typical example of the close relations that existed between the Old Irish and the Franciscan friars. As a boy he was tutored by Hugh MacCaughwell [Aodh MacAingil] (author of *Scathán Shacramuinte na nAithridhe* – a treatise on the sacrament of confession) and was sent by his father to Philip III in 1600 'to be reared and instructed in the Catholic faith'. Henry and MacCaughwell stayed at the convent of the friars in Salamanca where he made several friends amongst those Irish studying for the priesthood and Henry in fact actually 'adopted the Franciscan habit'. The contacts, particularly those with Florence Conry, appear to have been ones which he maintained over the period of his colonelship of the Irish regiment. In July 1607 a report by an English agent claimed that Henry O'Neill was being advised by several key clerical figures in the Low Countries, particularly Dr Robert Chamberlain, Dr Eugene MacMahon and Hugh MacCaughwell, while in October 1607 information by one James Bathe, brother to Captain John Bathe of O'Neill's regiment, noted that 'Henry O'Neill' was 'conversant and very great with . . . Father Florence'. Apart from Conry who was a native of Roscommon, three of these men had northern origins and all had close associations both with the O'Neill family and the problems confronting Gaelic society. They had all supported the Nine Years War as a catholic crusade and, with the possible exception of MacCaughwell, continued actively to support counter-reformation militancy on the continent.[32]

With Hugh MacCaughwell's appointment as chief-chaplain of the regiment of Henry O'Neill, the priests and chaplains appointed after 1605 included for the first time Old Irish and Franciscans. Of the eight religious appointments made between 1605 and 1610 to Irish companies, four were of Old Irish stock, and the strong presence of such a militant group within the Irish religious community of the Spanish Netherlands was clearly indicated by the reception given the northern earls in 1607 by the Irish colleges. Tadhg O Cianain in his account of the earls' (O'Neill and O'Donnell) arrival at Douai noted that they were met there by Florence Conry and Robert Chamberlain while 'assemblies of the colleges received them kindly and with respect, delivering in their honour verses and speeches in Latin, Greek and English'. Similarly at the Irish college at Antwerp they received a great welcome while at St. Anthony's, Louvain, where the earls left their children, they were, according to James Roche 'often entertained . . . very sumptuously'. The conclusion of one of the Latin orations recited at Douai in their honour makes clear the role envisaged for Hugh O'Neill by at least some members of the college of Douai.

> '. . . for it sufficeth not to have once subdued the enemy and chased him out of the borders of that kingdom, but you must wrest this afflicted country (which at length by reason of the sins thereof is come into the power of cruel tyrants) out of their jaws and impious dominion. For this cause doth Ireland lift up to you humbly suing hands, hoping that you will speedily succour her, and beseecheth you, by Him who hath suffered death for all of us, that you will not leave her any longer under the unworthy oppression and bondage of faithless enemies'.[33]

This oration was an obvious statement not only of a determination to withstand the spread of protestantism, but a determination to overthrow English authority in Ireland. Its significance with regard to our study however was the assumption that the earl's flight signalled not the end, but the beginning of a glorious era. Within this context, the Irish regiment, under O'Neill's son Henry, and incorporating by this time so many of those who had fought in the Nine Years War, was inevitably seen by this militant clerical group to have a specific role in the establishment of the Catholic counter-reformation in Ireland.

Some of the clergy who returned to Ireland, particularly the friars, appear to have equated the interests of the Catholic Church in Ireland with an invasion spearheaded by the Irish regiment. Complaints to the Dublin administration, particularly from Ulster between 1609 and 1610, were numerous, concerning 'priests' who were 'inciting' the people with stories of Henry O'Neill's imminent arrival in Ireland with his regiment.[34]

In the military expedition planned for Ireland by Hugh O'Neill in 1615, Franciscan friars such as Florence Conry and Durley O'Conor played a crucial role in carrying messages between the courts of Madrid, Brussels and Rome where O'Neill was based. In a letter to the duke of Lerma in September 1615, Conry pleaded that the Spanish council reconsider its decision to abandon this expedition 'before the English forestall all possible moves and complete the ruin of what little remains in the country'. Interestingly he suggested that Hugh O'Neill with the Irish regiment should join forces with Red Hugh O'Donnell's uncle, James MacDonnell, lord of Islay and Cantyre, who was then in revolt against the English crown with 1,500 men in Scotland.

Conry retained his position as adviser to the Spanish council on Irish affairs until his death in 1629 and he continued to keep in close contact with Owen Roe O'Neill during this period. He was largely instrumental in getting the position of major in the regiment of John O'Neill for Owen in 1611 while Conry, Owen Roe O'Neill and Dr Robert Chamberlain met regularly in Brussels and Louvain with a view to keeping the Irish regiment intact and its members in accord with each other. In their turn John O'Neill (after 1616, earl of Tyrone) and Hugh O'Donnell, earl of Tyrconnell (grandson to Red Hugh) played an important part in maintaining the influence of this militant clerical group by having Ulster clerics sympathetic to their cause appointed to key ecclesiastical positions. In petition after petition to both the Spanish authorities and the papacy these earls were largely responsible in the 1620s and 1630s for the appointment to bishoprics of Hugh O'Reilly, bishop of Kilmore (1625-28) and later archbishop of Armagh (1628-53), Edmund Dungan, bishop of Down and Connor (1625-29), Hugh MacCaughwell, archbishop of Armagh (1626) and Bonaventure Magennis, bishop of Down and Connor (1630-40). All were from Ulster and, with the exception of Hugh O'Reilly, all were Franciscans. Neither O'Neill nor O'Donnell on the continent lost sight of their ambition to be restored to their lost titles and lands in Ireland and in these ecclesiastics they found allies in their aim to launch an invasion of Ireland in the name of the Catholic Church.[35]

It was in this context of an ongoing close alliance between the militant clerical and political groups on the continent that the Franciscans Hugh Burke, commissionary general of the Order of St Francis, and Luke Wadding, adviser to the Spanish ambassador in Rome, assisted Owen Roe O'Neill in 1642 when he wanted to join the catholic uprising in Ireland. Wadding and Burke as Old English loyalists were not necessarily opposed to the authority of the English crown in Ireland but were certainly anxious to assist in defending the religious and political rights of the Roman Catholics there. Luke Wadding sent 10,000 crowns from Rome for 'artillery and munitions' for Owen Roe O'Neill and Preston, the catholic military commanders, while Hugh Burke raised a loan from amongst the religious communities of the Spanish Netherlands towards the buying and equipping of a frigate for O'Neill. Nor was it just the Irish religious group who were involved in these preparations for military assistance to Ireland. The archbishop of Malines personally contributed £500 sterling towards the purchase of the frigate for Owen Roe O'Neill. The papal nuncio in Brussels, Stravio, did all in his power to persuade the governor of Flanders – Francisco de Melo – to let Owen O'Neill and Thomas Preston set out legally for Ireland with the Irish regiments in the army of Flanders. When his requests fell on deaf ears Stravio wrote to Cardinal Barberini, a friend of Luke Wadding and another sympathizer to the Irish cause:

> 'Preston and O'Neill deserve support but the authorities in Flanders are hesitant, as England has threatened to break off relations with Spain if help is given to Ireland'.

Nevertheless Stravio promised to do all he could 'to get help for the Irish' and managed to procure 12,000 muskets for Ireland.[36]

The ambitions of Owen Roe O'Neill (c.1590 – 1649) do not seem to have been dissimilar to those of Hugh O'Neill.[37] Although Owen was a nephew to Hugh with no direct claim to any of the titles previously held by the O'Neills as earls of Tyrone before 1607, he seems to have wanted to acquire some land in Ulster even if it meant doing so under an English administration. The papal nuncio Rinuccini claimed that Sir Phelim O'Neill and Owen were locked in a bitter feud over their respective claims to the earldom following the death of Hugh O'Neill's son John in 1641. In 1649, just before he died, Owen in a letter to the marquis of Ormond seemed to identify his interests with the Old English loyalist group. He wrote to Ormond that his ambition had been 'truly and sincerely to the preservance of my religion, the advancement of his Majesty's (Charles I) service, and just liberties of this nation'.[38] Owen's immediate reason for this declaration was that he wanted his son Colonel Henry O'Neill to be treated favourably under any terms of agreement reached with Charles I. It is however, a significant document in two other ways.

Firstly it is clear that even in a letter which hoped effectively for a reconciliation with Charles I, Owen was not going to compromise his loyalty to the Catholic church. Hugh Burke verified Owen's commitment to catholicism in a letter to Luke Wadding in 1642, noting that Owen's reason for taking part in the rebellion in Ireland was not to claim the earldom of Tyrone but rather for the 'common cause of religion and realm'. His constant assertions of loyalty to the Catholic faith in both *English* as well as Spanish correspondence, his very close friendship with the papal nuncio Stravio at Brussels and the Franciscan Hugh Burke at Louvain, and the extraordinary level of assistance given him by the religious group in Flanders and Luke Wadding in Rome when embarking for Ireland, leads one to believe that his commitment to catholicism was sincere.

Secondly, Owen's reference to the liberties of a nation in this letter is significant. In 1646, in a letter to Charles I, Owen similarly referred to the war that 'this nation of Ireland' was engaged in against 'the parliament rebels of England' and there are two important points here. Firstly it shows that Owen's sympathies were with the monarchy as opposed to the parliament and this was hardly surprising coming from a man who had fought for thirty-three years in the service of the imperial armies of Spain. Secondly the reference to Ireland as a 'nation' or 'our nation' was one that frequently occurred, particularly in his correspondence with Fr Hugh Burke or Fr Luke Wadding. Owen was always anxious to disassociate himself from his image, especially in England, as one of those 'traytor Tyrone's children' who wanted to set himself up as petty ruler in Ulster. Like Hugh O'Neill, Owen hoped to transcend provincialism and factionism in Ireland by an appeal to catholicism as a common cause amongst many of the different groupings in Irish society. Unlike Hugh's efforts however, the respect and trust with which Owen was regarded by such Old English as Burke and Wadding showed that to a large extent he had succeeded. In 1642 Burke wrote to Wadding that as general of the 'Catholic army' in Ireland he would favour Owen Roe O'Neill above Thomas Preston. He noted that whereas Preston was 'very brave' and 'more popular than the other', Owen was 'of great prudence and conduct, very adroit and crafty in the handling of great matters'. He concluded that there was 'absolutely no comparison between the two talents for our purpose'.[39]

Although Owen hoped to regain some of the former O'Neill territories in Ulster for himself, he was very much a product of the counter-reformation world in which he had grown up and his vision was broader than that of Hugh O'Neill. Owen hoped to see Ireland take its place alongside the other catholic 'nations' of Europe even if she still owed allegiance to a protestant king.

There is considerable evidence that the thousands of Ulstermen who served in the army of Flanders between 1605 and 1641 – and their womenfolk – were conscious of their Irish roots and hoped some day to return to Ulster. In a study of the register of the Santa Cruz hospital in Spain, Dorothy Molloy noticed among the personal details of the sick and wounded soldiers the tendency of Irish soldiers born on the continent to give their fathers' birthplace as their own, while from a number of wills found at Barcelona there is evidence of Irishmen who bequeathed their lands and estates 'at present confiscated' in Ireland to their families.[40]

In July 1642, few of these rank and file soldiers were able to accompany Owen Roe O'Neill to Ireland. However like Owen and the 300 soldiers who landed in Donegal with him, many had been on the continent for at least twenty years and this had changed their perception of Ireland. By 1641 most of the Ulster military group on the continent had come to identify themselves and therefore Ireland with counter-reformation Catholicism while at the same time becoming conscious amongst the different nationalities in catholic Europe of a separate Irish identity. These men and women continued of course to regard themselves first and foremost as 'Ulster people' and clashes between O'Neill, O'Donnell or Maguire factions frequently occurred. Nevertheless, Ulster men and women at all levels on the continent were becoming conscious of a homeland which most were not likely to see again. As such they have merited the title 'Ulster exiles' given to this essay.

Transcription of illustration on p 62: *Scathan Shacramuinte na hAithridhe, arna chuma don bhrathair bhocht dord San Froinsias Aodh Mac Aingil leaghthoir diadhachta a ccolaisdi na mbrathar nEirionnach a Lobhain. Emanuel Telaph. Iarna chur a cclo maille re hugdarrdhas. 1618*
[The mirror of the sacrament of penance, composed by the Franciscan Aodh Mac Aingil [Hugh MacCaughwell], lecturer in divinity in the Irish Franciscan College, Louvain. Emanuel Telaph. Printed with permission. 1618]

THE NATIVE ULSTER *MENTALITÉ* AS REVEALED IN GAELIC SOURCES 1600–1650

Michelle O Riordan

Leath Cuinn is the traditional Irish term for the northern half of Ireland. *Leath Mogha* is the corresponding southern half. The expressions serve as rough terms for Ulster and Munster respectively. They are terms extensively used by Gaelic poets referring to matters northerly or southerly, and used by the poets who took part in the 'Contention of the Bards' (*Iomarbhágh na bhFileadh*)[1] – a dispute between poets, conducted through the medium of their art, extolling the claims of each half to pride of place in antiquity and honour.

Leath Cuinn is the province which will be accounted for in this discussion. It is the Ulster addressed by the poets, in the poetry which they provided for members of the Gaelic élites in the period up to the outbreak of the 1641 Rebellion. The poets' account of notable events in *Leath Cuinn*, and their comments on the behaviour of different leaders, are different in emphasis and in intention to accounts of the same events and occasions documented by non-Gaelic sources. This can be accounted for partly by the fact that, as in the present discussion, the Gaelic sources are often the products of literary men, who were following a traditional set of rules in the manner in which they presented their material, and consciously sought to produce works of art. The poets were following the dictates of a traditional profession which excercised its own restrictions in content, style and subject.[2] Their traditional role in the Gaelic polity means that their work has a central part to play in our understanding of the mentality of the Gaelic élites of the period.

The disintegration of the Gaelic polity of individual lordships, with its characteristic struggles within septs and between neighbouring septs, meant death for the professional poets as a distinctive and important group in so far as their traditional duties and special relationship with the chief were concerned. However, the nature of the profession was such that the undermining of the poets' traditional source of patronage and focus of attention did not mean that the poets ceased abruptly to articulate the traditional perceptions of the society they were trained to

61

scathan
SHACRA
ṁuinte na haiṫ
ridhe,
a r
Na ċuma ḋon bṙáṫḟ boḟ
ṫoṙḋ San ḟṙoinsias
aoḋh ṁac aingil
léġṫóir ḋiaḋaḟa a ccoléiṡḋi
na mbṙáṫḟ Néirioñać
a lúḃáin

emanuel
telaṡḣ.

Iḟ na ċur a cclo maille ṙé
húḟoḟnóḟ. 1618

address in their poetry. Poets writing for patrons who no longer appear to enjoy their traditional role in an integral Gaelic political culture often seem to ignore the changes in the status of the patron. Poems written in the first half of the seventeenth century for chiefs, ex-chiefs and their near kinsmen, seem to address the traditional chief, or aspiring candidate for chieftainship, in a way that appears to neglect the changed circumstances of the addressee and the poet himself. Sometimes this occurs in a poem of praise, where the individual addressed is hailed as the new saviour of Ireland's honour. In elegies, for example, the death of the poet's patron or chief is still lamented as the most unfortunate event, a devastation of the hopes of Ireland for any respite from her troubles.

It is possible to let the work of the poets and writers alone take us through the events of the period: the heart-breaking poems of loss and grief they wrote after the death of Aodh Rua/Red Hugh; the equally moving poems of despair on the disappearance of the Earls in 1607; in between, euphoric poems of welcome for James 1's accession to the throne in 1603; poems of support and advice for the unfortunate O'Donnell prisoners in the Tower and regular poems of praise for different individuals. The death of Owen Roe [Eoghan Rua O'Neill] in 1649 effectively ended the traditional base of political power of the native leaders of Ulster, though poets continued to eulogize members of those leading families who survived in the new order imposed by the victors of the Eleven Years War (1641–1652).

From the death of Red Hugh O'Donnell/Aodh Rua Ó Domhnaill in Spain in 1602, to the death of Owen Roe O'Neill in Ireland in 1649, the history of Ulster, as portrayed in the learned poetry dedicated to the most prominent members of the political élites, is one of great gain, and great loss. Great rejoicing and celebration greet success, great sorrow and grief are expressed at defeat or failure. Success, defeat and failure are measured according to the traditional expectations of the individual addressed – sometimes in apparent self-contradiction. A brief sketch of some of the poems composed for prominent members of the Gaelic polity and a look at some prose accounts of events which affected them are presented here to convey a sense of the outlook of the Gaelic literary and political élites of the period. We find that the behaviour of chiefs and leaders is measured according to a criterion which takes into account the status of the chief and the traditional aspirations of his sept. The yardstick of pro- or anti- English is not one which makes much sense in the poetry looked at here. We find that poets lament the loss of Red Hugh O'Donnell, and his rival kinsman Niall Garbh O'Donnell, with equal fervour. The poet's allegiance to his traditional patron and the patron's family means that criticism of the chiefs' activities may be muted. It may also be the case that poems of dispraise did not survive as long as eulogies and elegies. In the surviving body of poetry it appears that the chief's allegiance to the traditional values of the sept was a trait to be praised rather than condemned. This seems to be the case even where the pursuit of traditional goals meant that the chief became involved in expeditions which led to the destruction of the Gaelic world – as did Niall Garbh's defection from Red Hugh O'Donnell at a vital point in Hugh O'Neill's campaigns in Ulster. The poetry highlights the sense of independence of the Gaelic Irish at the beginning of the seventeenth century – when their own evaluation of the importance of unity or disunity in the face of English encroachments and plantations was made with a confidence in their own ability to defeat or absorb their enemies.

Along with the poetry, some contemporary prose accounts in Irish of the career of Red Hugh O'Donnell,[3] of the departure of the earls of Tyrone and Tyrconnell and their retinue to the continent (the Flight of the Earls)[4] and of the progress of the 1641 rebellion[5] will be looked at cursorily as sources which reinforce the impressions of the political outlook of the Gaelic leaders that we get from the poetry.

The discussion here is confined to the most well-known characters and incidents of the period in the interests of simplicity. The death of Red Hugh O'Donnell in Spain in 1602 was lamented in a poem by the poet Fearghal Óg Mac an Bhaird – 'Teasda Éire san Easbáinn' ('Ireland has perished in Spain').[6] The learned family of Mac an Bhaird of Tír Chonaill [Donegal] seemed to enjoy the status of *ollamh taoisigh* [principal poet of a chief][7] to the Ó Domhnaill. But Fearghal Óg's compositons are by no means confined to members of that family, and in this he can be regarded as typical of the poets of this period.[8] Red Hugh O'Donnell had gone to Spain in January 1602, after the defeat at Kinsale, to seek military aid from Philip III. He was around thirty years of age at the time.[9] He died the following September. An annalistic account of the life of O'Donnell gives a very vivid account of his career. The 'life' is attributed to Lughaidh Ó Cléirigh, and is thought to have been compiled sometime after 1616 and before 1630. It is full of detail concerning the emergence of Red Hugh as chief and detailed descriptions of battles in which he excelled, or directed; it provides scant analysis of his actions in a context which a modern reader would regard as significant politically. The account hardly concerns itself with revealing the political context of decisions outlined in the narrative beyond those of most immediate importance. In the context of the poem by Fearghal Óg Mac an Bhaird, it is interesting to have a contemporary prose composition on O'Donnell's career, and a description of his final days. In the 'life' of Red Hugh, the author puts O'Donnell to the fore in any undertaking that he shared, for instance with the more powerful Hugh O'Neill. The preoccupations of the prose narrative and the poem are identical in their focus on the person of the addressee, and in placing that individual in the centre of the events depicted. This does not mean that

the poet or the historian was in any way unaware of the wider implications of events they chronicled in their different ways. Nor does it
indicate that the decisions made by various chiefs were the result of
simplistic and naive incomprehension of contemporary politics. It
suggests, rather, that the poets and the chiefs shared a view of the world
and current events which was articulated in the writings of the poets.
The prose accounts, briefly looked at here, support the view from the
poetry of chiefs conducting their affairs with reference to their traditional criteria, without being unaware or uncomprehending of the alter-
natives. Many of those who produced prose works in Irish were also
poets and this is the case for Aodh Mac Cathmhaoil, archbishop of
Armagh [d. Rome 1626], Flaithrí Ó Maolchonaire, archbishop of Tuam
[d. Madrid 1629] and Seathrún Céitinn [d. 1649], who produced devotional literature in support of the reforms urged by the Council of Trent
(1545–63). In any event, those who produced literature in prose or
verse, in Irish, belonged to similar social and cultural backgrounds in
the Gaelic world or that of the Old English.

The poet speaks of Red Hugh's death in Spain as the death of Ireland.
Suggestions that he had been poisoned by a spy in the crown's service
are not supported by either the 'life' or the elegy by the poet.

In Lughaidh Ó Cléirigh's prose narrative, Red Hugh is represented
as being extremely disappointed and angry at the poor performance of
the troops at Kinsale:[10]

> 'His own people were greatly afraid that he would bring on his
> death, through the suffering which seized him, so that he did
> not sleep nor eat in comfort for three days and three nights
> after.'

He determined to go to Spain for help from Philip III. Ó Cléirigh reports
great scenes of grieving, people clapping their hands together in
anguish, and general lamentation in O'Donnell's camp on the eve of his
departure:

> 'When this plan was heard by all and sundry pitiful and sad
> were the great clappings of hands, and the violent lamenta-
> tions, and the loud wailing cries which arose throughout
> O'Donnell's camp the night before his departing.'[11]

Another poet of the Mac an Bhaird family, Eoghan Rua Mac an Bhaird,
marked the occasion of Red Hugh's departure with at least one poem. His
poem beginning 'Rob soruidh t'eachtra, a Aodh Ruaidh' (Happy be thy
journey, Aodh Ruadh!)[12] brings to our attention some of the sorrow and
anxiety indicated in the passage from Ó Cléirigh's prose above, in a moving
poem which is really a blessing for Red Hugh and a prayer for his safety:

Rob soruidh t'eachtra, a Aodh Ruaidh,
an Coimsidh do-chí ar n-anbhuain,
gabhaidh sé t'innfheitheamh air,
go mbé ag rinnfheitheamh romhaibh.[13]

(Happy be thy journey, Aodh Ruadh! The Lord who seeth our distress, He taketh upon Him thy care, may He prepare thy way before thee.)

People of every quality and condition, even as indicated by Ó Cléirigh above, are anxious for his success, and fear for his life:
'Warriors, by reason of their love, women, clerics, the children of our nobles, the sons of our serfs, they are all united in fear for thee, Aodh'.[14]
The poet declares that Ireland – referred to as 'Conn's Isle' – and pre-eminently *Leath Cuinn* will suffer the loss should any misfortune thwart O'Donnell:
'Conn's Isle that hath been practised in suffering, it is she, in short, that would feel the blow, if thou should'st be opposed in thy journey over the raging perilous sea.'[15]
The poet lists some heroes of tradition who undertook similar journeys for the sake of their honour, or for the good of Ireland. Red Hugh personifies the sovereignty of Ireland, and all that he means to Ireland is committed to a frail ship:[16]

Atá san luingsin tar lear
oireachas Insi Gaoidheal,
a síodh, a guaisbhearta, a glóir,
díon a huaisleachta, a honóir.[17]

(There are in that ship beyond the sea the soveranty of the Island of the Gaels, her peace, her perilous exploits, her glory, the defence of her nobility, her honour.)

Lughaidh Ó Cléirigh recounted the final days of Red Hugh in Spain, telling us that he died in Simancas in the palace of the king of Spain, and indicating how nobly Red Hugh was treated because of his nobility and reputation:

'When he came to the town called Simancas (two leagues from Valladolid, the King's palace) God granted, and the ill-luck and misfortune attending the island of Eremon and the Irish of fair Fodhla too, that O Domhnaill should catch his death disease and his mortal illness. He was for sixteen days on his bed of sickness ... It was in the palace of the King of Spain himself in the town of Simancas he died. His body was then taken to Valladolid, to the King's Court, in a four-wheeled ornamental chariot, with countless numbers of State officers, of the Council, and of the Royal Guard all round it, with lighted lanterns and bright torches of beautiful fair wax blazing all round on each side of it.'[18]

This magnificent ceremony was fitting for the great hero which Ó Cléirigh's account presented. The elegiac passage with which he concludes gives an indication of how such a chief was perceived traditionally by the literary élites:

'Alas! it brought sorrow to multitudes the early withering of him who died there for his thirtieth year was not yet full run when he died. He was the head of support and planning, of counsel and disputation of the greater number of the Gaels of Ireland whether in peace or war . . . a lion in strength and force, with threatening and admonishing so that it was not allowed to gainsay his word, for whatever he ordered had to be done on the spot, a dove of meekness and gentleness to privileged men of the church and the arts, and everyone who did not oppose him . . . A man who did not allow himself to be injured or afflicted, cheated or insulted without repaying and avenging it immediately; a determined, fierce, and bold invader of others' terrritories; a destroyer of any of the English and Irish that opposed him; . . . a prophesied chosen one whom the prophets foretold long before his birth.'

This powerful and strongwilled chief was a great loss to his territory, to his clients and to the whole polity which his traditional virtues supported. His death transformed Ireland for the worse:

'Pitiful, indeed, was the state of the Gaels of Ireland after the death of the true prince, for they changed their characteristics and dispositions. They gave up bravery for cowardice, courage for weakness, pride for servility. Their hatred, valour, prowess, heroism, triumph, and military glory vanished after his death.'[19]

It is no wonder to us then that a lament for Red Hugh should be characterized by expressions of excessive grief at his loss, at the loss of his potential, and of its effects on Ireland.

The *marbhna* [elegy] by Fearghal Óg Mac an Bhaird opens thus:

Teasda Éire san Easbáinn,
do deaghladh a dīleasdáil:
an sēn fuair tre theasdáil thoir
uainn san Easbāinn do fhāgaibh.[20]

(Ireland has perished in Spain; her faithful tryst has been broken; the prosperity she found, he through dying in the east has
left it in Spain, out of our reach.)

Not only the race of Conn (the men of the northern half, *Leath Cuinn*) are
affected by Red Hugh's death, but the Munstermen also, in whose
territory he fought at Kinsale, are equally affected. Ireland is a rudder-
less ship – *arthach gan sdiúir* – and as such she has been overwhelmed by
a mighty wave:

> .....
> tug tar tealaigh Dha-Thí thuinn
> deaghail dí ris Ó nDomhnaill.[21]
> (... Her parting with O'Donnell has brought a wave over
> Ireland.)

The poet goes on to compare Red Hugh's fate to that of Hercules who
took his weapons with him when he died: unlike Hercules, Red Hugh
has not carried his weapons of victory to his grave, but has taken
Ireland with him. Red Hugh is more like Caesar, who was killed before
he could enjoy the fruits of his efforts in many gory battles. After ten
years of hard battling, Red Hugh's death deprives him of the victory he
deserves. But there were other *Gaeil* before him who suffered that fate,
Brian Boru had suffered and died to save Ireland's honour, as did his
son Murchadh. Therefore, why should a hero as great as Red Hugh
expect a less heroic fate:

'O'Donnell is in their mould: he gave himself and his life in the
defence of royal Niall's seat. The misfortune that befell him was to be
expected.'[22]

The poet despairs of Ireland's future after the death of Red Hugh. In
a stanza at the end of the poem he mentions another patron of his, Mág
Aonghusa [McGuinness].[23] His death – in 1595 – also caused the overthrow of the Ulstermen and the regression of their honour. Since Mág
Aonghusa died the family of noble Ros is unfenced tillage-land; Ulstermen have been overthrown after him and their honour has taken a step
backwards.[24] This stanza at the end of Fearghal Óg's *marbhna* for Red
Hugh, dedicated to a former patron of the poet's, uses the same
language of desolation and devastation to articulate the loss of that
particular patron. The loss felt by the Mág Aonghusa sept is extended to
include a loss to all of Ulster. Within the genre of this poetry, the
generalization of such loss is commonplace and will be evident in many
of the poems examined in this study.

In the poetry, nature and the cosmos always mirror the status of the
chief. If he is well and victorious and a true chief, the land and the
cosmos thrive and are fruitful. If he dies, the heavens bewail his loss,

and the earth shrivels up in his absence. The death of the earth is also a sign of an unlawful king or a corrupt ruler. The motif is as old as the concept of kingship itself, and it is as a mere shadow of its power in the earliest times that the concept survives as a literary motif in the bardic poetry. However, the poets made very frequent use of it to indicate the health of the polity and the influence of the chief. In this instance, because of Red Hugh's death, the crops have failed, trees are bare, streams have dried up and are empty of life; the Boyne is a mere miserable stream.[25] The wind, waves, and the heavens reflect the horror of the loss:

> Tuar uathbháis treathan na dtonn;
> tuar uilc ruithneadh na rēltonn;
> ruar dībheirge niamh na néll;
> sgiamh fhírfheirge ar an aiér.[26]

> (The fury of the waves is a portent of horror; the shining of the stars is an omen of evil; the colour of the clouds is a presage of vengeance; the sky has a look of true anger.)

All of the motifs outlined above are to be found in bardic poetry from the thirteenth century onwards. The changed circumstances over the centuries did not leave the genre untouched. The relevance of the sentiments and beliefs expressed in the poetry at different times must have been at some odds with the contemporary reality. However, the poets continued into the latter half of the seventeenth century to address poems of this kind to different patrons. The fact that they did so, and that their work was preserved seems to indicate that the genre was understood to represent a facet of the world view of both the poets and the chiefs and leaders to whom they were addressed. It indicates further that the particular expressions of grief, elation, anxiety etc. in the poems were relevant for both the writers and the recipients at a time when the familiar world of both groups was disintegrating.

In that context it is worth looking at a eulogy by the same poet for James VI of Scotland – 'Trí coróna i gcairt Shéamais' ('The three crowns in James's charter')[27] – and at another poem by the northern poet Eochaidh Ó hEodhusa hailing his accession to the throne of England – 'Mór theasda dh'obair Óivid' ('Much is wanting from Ovid's work').[28] Ó hEodhusa's principal patrons were the Maguires of Fermanagh.

The poem beginning 'Trí coróna i gcairt Shéamais' is attributed to Fearghal Óg Mac an Bhaird, and it is suggested that he wrote it prior to James VI's accession to the English throne after Elizabeth I.[29] Both poems welcome unreservedly the prospect of James' accession to the throne of England. Fearghal Óg begins his poem with the prospect of

James VI assuming the sovereignty of the three kingdoms. The poet examines the legitimacy of his claims to the three kingdoms. In this examination the poet exercised his professional duty – in the Gaelic system – to scrutinize the chief and to find him suitable. The two poets in question had no difficulty in eagerly anticipating James VI's accession to the English throne, and at the same time, by implication, becoming king of Ireland too (Fearghal Óg), and rejoicing in his success (Eochaidh Ó hEodhasa). Before the middle of the 1620s two poets, one northern, Aodh Ó Domhnaill, and one southern, Tadhg Mac Dáire Mac Bruaideadha – both contributing poems to the Contention of the Bards – insisted respectively that James I sprang from the northern hero Iughoine, and the southern hero Corc.

The *Iomarbhágh* [Contention] in its published form consists of thirty poems by some twelve poets, each joining in support of the primacy of *Leath Cuinn* or *Leath Mogha*. The poems are dated[30] to between *c*.1604 and 1624. The poetic competition envigorated the poetry of the early part of the seventeenth century with its learned displays of the store of traditional material at the poets' disposal. It also articulated some of the enduring preoccupations of the poets' profession – with the participating poets rivalling each other in knowledge of the tradition and in their ingenuity in applying their knowledge to their craft for the enhancement of their patrons' sept. The original cause of the 'contention' itself was ostensibly a poem written by the southern poet Mac Bruaideadha, which disparaged the claims of the north to primacy among the divisions of Ireland. Whatever the origins of the dispute, and whatever its real nature, the poems which survive further illustrate matters which occupied the poets in the early seventeenth century – one of which was the necessity to come to terms with the expansion of the power of King James I, for the rule of English law had been declared throughout Ireland in 1605. The poets in the following extracts contended for the honour of claiming James I as descendant of the mythical heroes of each 'half' of Ireland, and thereby legitimating his claims over Ireland in that way.

Aodh Ó Domhnaill, of *Leath Cuinn* (possibly a great-uncle of Red Hugh O'Donnell)[31] found it possible to claim, in his poem beginning 'Measa do thagrais a Thaidhg' ('Worse have you argued, O Tadhg'), sometime before the death of King James I:

> Do Shíol Iughoine as bhuan bladh,
> ríoghradh uaisle na hAlban
> le Séamus aniú ma le
> Sacsa Alba agus Éire.[32]

(Of Iughoine's ever-glorious stock are the princes of the nobility of Alba. To James belong to-day England Alba Éire.)

Iughoine/Úghoine Mór was a mythical king of Ireland who divided the land between his twenty-five children on his death.[33] In response to this claiming of James I for *Leath Cuinn*, the poet championing *Leath Mogha*, Tadhg Mac Dáire Mac Bruaideadha (poet of the O'Briens of Thomond), in his poem 'Bhar rí Éireann aithne dhaoibh' ('Your king of Éire – you know it'), counter-claimed for the southern half:

'The king you mention, God preserve him! – far be it from me to yield him up to you! He is of the race of Maine Leamhna, Corc's son, Alba's famous Leamnach.

To us completely, and without any connection with you, belongs his stock on his father's side – unless you trace his line on the female side, and near to us was his mother too.'[34]

Maine Leamhna, the progenitor of the house of Lenox in Scotland,[35] was the son of a mythical king of Munster, Corc son of Lughaidh[36], who first sat as king at Cashel.[37]

The poets were well versed in the history and pseudo-history of their country. The great kings, heroes and villains of this history were referred to as familiar characters for comparisons and examples in the poets' works. They took it for granted that their peers and their patrons understood the significance of these historical and mythical figures.

Eochaidh Ó hEodhusa's poem welcoming James VI into his sovereignty over Ireland and England in 1603, ('Mór theasda dh'obair Óivid'), was written some years before those of Aodh Ó Domhnaill and Tadhg Mac Dáire Mac Bruaideadha above. He hailed the accession of James I to the English throne, and his sovereignty over Ireland, as a brilliance following the darkness of Elizabeth's death.[38] The success of James I's efforts to attain the throne after Elizabeth are seen by Ó hEodhusa as a source of joy to Ireland in particular. She forgets her many troubles in the glory of her king:

'Indeed, more remarkable than that are we, the troubled people of Ireland, in that each one of us forgot the tribulation of all anxieties.'[39]

Ó hEodhusa specifically refers to James I as 'ar ríogh' – our king – and insists that anxieties are banished by his accession:

Oirchios dúin, ge a-dēirim sin,
ceiliobhradh dār ccuing imnidh;
súil chobhartha ar ríogh do-róigh
tar bríogh ndomharbhtha ar ndobróin.[40]

(It is fitting for us, if I say that, to bid farewell to our yoke of anxiety; the helping eye of our king reaches beyond the lasting force of our sorrow.)

Could some of the anxieties thus dispelled have included the loss of
Red Hugh O'Donnell for whom the poet Fearghal Óg Mac an Bhaird, in
his 'Marbhna', lamented:

> Ní hionand is Éire iar nAodh;
> danair indte in gach éntaobh
> iar mbás gach duine dhīobh soin;
> nī bhīodh ruire a*cht don* rīoghr*oidh*.[41]

(After Hugh Ireland is no longer the same: there are foreigners
in her on every side following the death of all those; it used to
be that a chieftain came only from the royal line.)

The poets' insistence on emphasizing James I's links with the ancient
royal septs of Ireland does not contradict Fearghal Óg's assertion that
chieftains used only come 'from the royal line'. Fearghal Óg himself, in
his poem for James VI ('Trí coróna i gcairt Shéamais') – anticipating his
accession to the English throne – seems to have recovered his hopes for
Ireland, even after Red Hugh. Again, he points out the royalty of
James's blood, maybe with some exaggeration:
   'Myrrh or incense is not more fragrant than thy wine-blood; gold is
not equal to it; no exaggeration can describe it.'[42]
   Whatever the merits the poets saw in the new king, Red Hugh's
brother, Rury, had to contend with the king's men in Dublin after
his death. Rury O'Donnell surrendered under terms similar to those
obtained by O'Neill, but he was in no position to exploit his position in
the manner of Hugh O'Neill. In 1603 he was created earl of Tyrconnell.[43]
Eoghan Rua Mac an Bhaird, the poet to whom the poem above, wishing
Red Hugh safety and success on his fateful journey to Spain, is attributed, is also credited with a poem for Rury O'Donnell, who is embarking on a different kind of journey. His poem beginning 'Dána an turas
tríalltar sonn' ('Bold is the journey attempted here') refers to Rury's
journey to Dublin to make terms with the government.[44] The poem is
dated 1603 by Bergin. The poem emphasizes the danger to Rury of such
a journey, considering the vehemence of his opposition to the government in Dublin, and that his enemies will be aware of the injuries and
fatalities such a warrior as Rury has inflicted on their forces. The danger
to him is indeed lessened because of his enemies' desire to make peace
with such a valiant enemy.[45] They welcome his arrival because it means
the end of hard battling for them:

> Atáid re a ucht a n-Áth Clíath
> óig ar ar himreadh mídhíach,
> mór ngoimhfhéchsin ré a ghnúis ngloin,
> cúis roidhéistin a rochtoin.[46]

(There are ready for him in Dublin warriors on whom misfortune has been inflicted; many a painful glance at his bright face;
to reach them is an occasion for great loathing.)

Lughaidh Ó Cléirigh, in his *Beatha Aodha Ruaidh* [Life of Red Hugh],
lamenting the fact that Red Hugh's cousin and brother-in-law, Sir Niall
Garbh O'Donnell and his brothers, had defected from Red Hugh in 1600,
remarked on the embattled condition of the crown forces as follows:

> 'The English needed, too, that Niall and his brothers should
> come to them, for they were weary and fatigued in battle array
> and call to arms every night through fear of O Domhnaill, and
> they were distressed and distempered owing to the narrow
> quarters they were in and the old musty victuals and bitter salt
> meat and want of every condiment which they needed, and of
> tasty fresh meat especially. Niall O Domhnaill supplied them
> with everything they lacked, and released them from the nar-
> row prison in which they were'.[47]

The poet acknowledged the humiliating nature of Rury's journey – suing
for peace and pardon – but mitigates its effect by suggesting that the 'grim
warriors' in Dublin cannot but be relieved at his coming to terms with
them. They were indeed relieved to see the end of Tyrone's campaign and
the terms granted to both O'Neill and O'Donnell seemed to indicate that
they were willing to make generous terms for the time being.[48]

To the same poet is attributed another poem – 'Rob soruidh an
séadsa soir' ('Prosperous be thy journey eastward'). Eoghan Rua Mac
an Bhaird's poem for a different traveller – Toirdhealbhach Mac Airt
Óig, grandson of Turlough Luineach O'Neill – wishes him success in
his journey to England, to negotiate with the king.[49] The occasion of this
trip, some time later than that of Rury to Dublin, appears to have been
Toirdhealbhach's effort to release his father's land from Hugh O'Neill's
extended authority, following the terms Hugh secured at the treaty of
Mellifont. Sir Art Óg O'Neill [d. 1600] (father of Toirdhealbhach of the
poem), had joined Sir Henry Docwra – in Docwra's words:

> 'On the first of June, Sir Arthur O'Neale, sonne to old Tirlough
> Lenogh that had been O'Neale, came in unto me with some 30
> horse and foot, a man I had directions from the state, to labour
> to drawe to our side; and to promise to be made Earl of Tyrone
> if the other that mainteyned the Rebellion could be dispos-
> sessed of the Country . . .'[50]

This Toirdhealbhach served some time with the English in Ulster, and he
was supported by Sir Henry Docwra in his efforts to become earl of

Tyrone. The poet seems unconcerned that Toirdhealbhach's efforts in England, should they succeed, could mean the undoing of the negotiations that brought Rury O'Donnell to Dublin. The poets followed the logic of the chiefs and the would-be leaders. The activities of each warrior are addressed as separate episodes, and the poets' praise of the valour, courage, leadership qualities and pedigree of each individual addressee is unaffected by political values which we might readily recognize as proto-nationalist. But the poets are very much aware of and affected by the adherence of those for whom they wrote to the traditional values of the true battling chief; the hero who puts the survival of his sept and the integrity of his territory above any other consideration; the man who supports the poets – no matter who his allies are.[51]

This is particularly true in the case of Niall Garbh [Rough] O'Donnell. He was a cousin and brother-in-law of Red Hugh. His grandfather An Calbhach O'Donnell had been Ó Domhnaill (chief of the sept) before Red Hugh's father. Niall Garbh was as entitled to be Ó Domhnaill as Red Hugh. Even Red Hugh's biographer Ó Cléirigh admitted that the power of Red Hugh's mother, Fionnghuala daughter of Séamus MacDomhnaill [James MacDonnell], lord of Isla and of the Glynnes of Antrim, who had her own army from Scotland, had an influence on Red Hugh's election as chief.[52] This occurred in 1592, though Aodh Ó Domhnaill, Red Hugh's father, was still living.[53] Niall Garbh had himself proclaimed Ó Domhnaill in the traditional way, by the coarb of Colmcille, Ó Firghil, who had inaugurated Red Hugh before. This happened while Rury O'Donnell was in Dublin on the mission referred to above.

The Four Masters explained developments thus:[54]

> 'As for Niall Garv O'Donnell, a letter arrived from Dublin to him, requesting of him to come before the Lord Justice and the Council, to receive a patent for Tirconnell, as a reward for his services and assistance to the Crown. He neglected this thing; and what he did was, to go to Kilmacrenan, and send for O'Firghil, the Coarb of Columbkille; and he was styled O'Donnell, without consulting the King's representative or the Council'.[55]

The question of Niall Garbh's priorities is raised starkly here: he had defected from Red Hugh and Hugh O'Neill to gain his own ends by allying himself with Sir Henry Docwra. According to the Four Masters, when he was to receive some recognition for those services, he instead made an effort to secure his status as a legitimate Ó Domhnaill by undergoing a traditional inaugural rite, without reference to the crown's representatives in Dublin. Within the world articulated by the poets, there is no ambiguity about Niall Garbh's behaviour. His efforts to become chief of the Uí Dhomhnaill were as logical and praiseworthy as those undertaken by Red Hugh or his brother Rury. Ó Cléirigh had no love for Niall Garbh, possibly because of his defection from O'Donnell at a crucial time. He recognized him as a warrior though, and gave the following account of him:

> 'There came to him [Aodh Ruadh/Red Hugh] likewise Niall Garbh, son of Conn, son of an Calbach, son of Maghnus, son of Aodh óg, who was called Aodh Dubh [black]. He was a violent man, hasty, unmerciful, and he was spiteful, inimical, with the venom of a serpent, with the impetuosity of a lion. He was a hero in valour and fighting. He was the head of an army and of troops in battle and war. But yet he was envious towards him like the rest, though the sister of Aodh was his wife [Nuala]. There was another bond of friendship between them for Aodh had been fostered in his boyhood by his parents. But yet it was through not real love for him he came, but it was wholly through fear'.[56]

Niall Garbh had been a trusted lieutenant of Red Hugh and, according to Ó Cléirigh, had given some thought to the enticements offered by Sir Henry Docwra:

> 'He [Red Hugh] left Niall O Domhnaill [Niall Garbh] . . . of his own family, behind him in the territory to guard it against the English, lest they should come to invade it in his absence. The English did not cease to entreat and implore, to urge and beseech Niall O Domhnaill secretly to enter into an alliance and friendship with them, and they foretold for him the kingship and chieftaincy of the territory if they were victorious, and they promised him many jewels and great wealth, and engagements and covenants, too, for the fulfilment of everything. He listened for a long time to these proposals which they were urging on him, till his ill fortune at last made him consent to join and unite with the English and be deceived and cajoled by their lying promises and by the evil counsels of envious proud people who incited and urged him to that decision. . . . However, his three brothers joined with Niall in that revolt i.e. Aodh Buidhe [yellow, sallow], Domhnall, and Conn óg'.[57]

The defection of Niall Garbh was a blow to O'Donnell. His help to Sir Henry Docwra gave the English a foothold in Ulster that they would not otherwise have had. It is easy to understand from the account of the Four Masters that Niall Garbh, Rury and Red Hugh were all more concerned with securing their position as head of the Uí Dhomhnaill, and aggrandizing their position in their traditional territories, with or without

English help, than with any other political goal. After Niall had himself proclaimed Ó Domhnaill, Rury returned to Tír Chonaill with a battalion of the English in search of Niall Garbh; and their struggles with and against the English, with and against each other were typical of the struggles between septs in *Leath Cuinn*.[58] Such internal disputes became milestones in the history of the reconquest of Ireland under the changed circumstances of the early seventeenth century. For the poets, nevertheless, as for the annalists and the biographers who are briefly looked at here, the activities of the chiefs and would-be chiefs were appraised and lauded in accordance with the political values which underpinned the independent Gaelic lordships. These writers adhered to such political values while there were chiefs to uphold the society which they were professionally trained to address.

Eoghan Ruadh Mac an Bhaird, the poet who prayed for Red Hugh going to Spain and for Rury going to Dublin (while Niall Garbh proclaimed himself Ó Domhnaill), wrote some moving poems for the erstwhile ally of the English. Niall Garbh had been abandoned by the English, even by Sir Henry Docwra who had originally supported him, but whose personal circumstances meant that he could not press his former ally's claims. Niall Garbh became implicated in Sir Cathair Ó Dochartaigh's [Cahir O'Doherty] rebellion in 1608. Whether or not he was involved was never determined by law. At his trial in Dublin in 1609, no jury could be found to convict him, though much pressure was applied.[59] He was transported to England and spent 18 years in the Tower of London, dying at the age of 57 in 1625. One of his sons Neachtain was imprisoned with him and died at around the same time.

One of Eoghan Ruadh Mac an Bhaird's poems for Niall Garbh begins 'A bhráighe atá i dTor Lonndan' ('O hostage in London Tower')[60]; a poem for Neachtain by the same poet begins 'Mairg is bráighe ar mhacruidhe Murbhaigh' ('Alas for him who is the hostage for Murbhach's host').[61]

In his poem for Niall Garbh, the poet makes use of the usual motifs associated with the loss of a patron. The fact that Niall is in the Tower means that he cannot fulfil his role as chief or warrior on his own territory. The loss of Niall Garbh is not simply a personal one for the poet. All Ireland suffers because of his imprisonment, especially the people of Donegal, and the people of *Leath Cuinn* in general. The poet does not deny or make any judgement about Niall Garbh's campaigns for the crown. He uses his knowledge of Niall's military campaigns with the crown forces to strengthen the hopes he holds out for Niall Garbh's release from the Tower, when the king examines his case:

> Ar an bhfáth fa a bhfuile i nglas
> acht go gcromadh Cing Séamas,
> ná meas nach saorfaidhe sibh,
> ar leas fraoch-mhuighe Fuinidh.[62]

(If only King James examines the reason why thou art in chains,
and the interests of the heather-plain of the west be sure thou
shalt be set free.)

The poet hopes that King James will look into Niall's case and be so
impressed with Niall Garbh's history that he will immediately see fit to
have him set free. Eoghan Ruadh uses the analogy of the Biblical Joseph
and his false imprisonment. When the king of Egypt scrutinized Joseph's
case he found the accusations to be false. He not only set Joseph free but
had him elevated to governorship of Egypt. The analogy implies that a
similar fate might be expected for Niall Garbh.[63]

No mention is made of the fact that it was Niall Garbh's mother-in-
law, the formidable Fionnghuala, mother of Niall Garbh's rivals Red
Hugh and Rury, who denounced him to the bishop of Derry, George
Montgomery, and so was responsible for his arrest.[64] Her daughter
Nuala, wife of Niall Garbh, was among the nobles who left *Leath Cuinn*
in September 1607, the 'flight of the earls'.

The poem attributed to Eoghan Ruadh Mac an Bhaird for Niall
Garbh's son Neachtain begins 'Mairg is bráighe ar mhacruidh
Murbhaigh'. It is a very gentle poem built around the conceit that
Neachtain's imprisonment is almost of benefit to Clann Domhnaill,
since it keeps Neachtain safe from rivals, and from doing those valorous and warlike deeds which would endanger his young life. The poem
could also be said to present Neachtain as a traditional hostage or
pledge, taken for the guarantee of the loyalty of the Uí Dhomhnaill – an
indicator in itself of the prestige of the hostage. The poet compares
Neachtain's imprisonment with the imprisonment of his kinsman, Red
Hugh, in Dublin Castle as a teenager, and by implication with the loss
of Red Hugh while yet so young.[65] Again, though it appears that both
families chose opposing roles in the battles for *Leath Cuinn* in the early
seventeenth century, from the poet's point of view all are heroic
members of the Uí Dhomhnaill, pursuing their destiny in a manner
which his professional training recognizes as appropriate to their status
and political duty.

The Flight of the Earls in 1607 was a devastating blow for *Leath
Cuinn*. The leaders of the chief families disappeared abroad, as it were,
overnight. The two earls, Hugh O'Neill and Rory O'Donnell, Conor
Maguire of Fermanagh, and as many of their families and retainers as
could be accommodated (99 persons in all)[66] left from Rathmullen,
county Donegal, in September. Sir Cahir O'Doherty, Sir Niall Garbh
O'Donnell and Sir Donal O'Cahan, all of whom had been enemies
of Tyrone, were killed or imprisoned within two years of the earls'
departure. Ulster was swept clean of native leaders.[67] The departure of
the earls and their followers provided an opportunity for the government to implement ambitious plantation policies which involved both

English and Scottish settlers. For the poets who recorded the departure, it was a step from which *Leath Cuinn* could not recover.

An anonymous poem – 'Mochean don loing si tar lear' ('Good luck to that ship which has gone over the sea')[68] – published by Paul Walsh in his edition of Ó Cléirigh's 'Life of Red Hugh', wishes the ship godspeed, and laments the departure of its illustrious passengers. The poet lists the principal nobles who are on that ship, namely, the families of Hugh O'Neill, and Rory O'Donnell respectively. With their departure, the honour and power of Ireland is gone.

The poem beginning 'Anocht is uaigneach Éire' ('Lonely is Ireland tonight')[69] is attributed to Eoghan Ruadh Mac an Bhaird. In this poem, Ireland is depicted as being silent and abandoned in the wake of the earls' departure:

> Anocht is uaigneach Éire
> do bheir fógra a firfhréimhe
> gruaidhe a fear sa fionnbhan fliuch
> treabh is iongnadh go huaigneach.[70]

> (Lonely is Ireland tonight: the outlawry of her native stocks fills with tears the cheeks of her men and fair women: that the land should be desolate is unusual.)

It is *Leath Cuinn* especially which suffers this huge loss. The poet suggests that it is because of God's anger with the *Gaeil* that the earls were exiled, and that God's anger can be appeased by repentance:

> Do thairrngir fáidh fada liom
> a fhearg re huaislibh Éirionn
> nach maithfidhe le Dia dháibh
> go dtia a n-aithrighe d'éunláimh.[71]

> (A prophet foretold long ago God's anger against the nobles of Erin, that they should not be forgiven by Him till they should all do penance.)

A letter written by Hugh O'Neill and Rory O'Donnell to Philip III of Spain in December 1607 echoes this sense that the misfortunes of the Irish at this time owed something to God's plan for their mortification:

> 'Although God was pleased to choose us as instruments for an enterprise of such importance [the war against Elizabeth which ended in 1602] . . . , yet he permitted that we be abandoned and deprived of all help and assistance, almost to the point of utter destruction, for when we had lost most of our

brothers, kinsmen, principal people and vassals, and when we had exhausted all our resources, the help which Your Majesty sent us and for which we had waited so many years, came to land in the province of Munster, so far from our own lands that we had to march one hundred leagues in the depth of winter, through enemy country, crossing many rivers and forced to make many bridges, in order to go to the aid of those whom Your Majesty had sent to help us. There, God permitting, we suffered a misfortune which obliged us to return to our lands and to send our brother, the Earl Odonel, who is in glory, to beg Your Catholic Majesty to be pleased to send us further help. When the news of his death in Spain became known, the English and the Irish who were helping them, closed in upon us with so many armies and planted so many garrisons in our lands . . .'[72]

An account of the travels and trials of the ninety-nine individuals who left on the ship was written by one of Maguire's followers, Tadhg Ó Cianáin. Members of the Ó Cianáin family served as chroniclers or historians to the Mág Uidhir family for several generations.[73] This author has been described as a 'simple, unsophisticated scribe, some-what naive and medieval in outlook,' and 'obviously not *au fait* with the political chicanery which revolved around his master's destination'[74]. We have seen in the case of poetic compositions how reticent the poets can be on the intricacies of the contemporary political situation. It is likely that the poets mentioned above were very familiar with the political situation of the individuals they addressed. The same may be imagined in the case of Ó Cianáin. His is a prose account. It is very detailed on the journeys taken by the group, and the physical condi-tions under which they travelled. He provides no analysis of the reasons why the leaders left as they did. His approach is factual and finishes abruptly with events that occurred in November 1608.[75] It is likely that he deliberately included no controversial material in an account which was written at a time when the fate of Ó Néill was far from decided. Besides, the earls and their company knew that they were under continual surveillance and that their households had been penetrated by spies. Tyrone's vigilance is highlighted in the following: '. . . Tyrone has taken a straight order that there shall be no access to his kitchen . . . ' This piece of information was gleaned for the earl of Salisbury, James I's secretary of state, by one of the many spies the government employed about O'Neill.[76] Likewise the nature of the narrative, a traditional annalistic account, did not lend itself to conjec-ture or analysis. In a similar fashion, the account by Ó Cléirigh of Red Hugh O'Donnell's career focuses on him alone. For instance on his final journey to Spain, O'Donnell was accompanied by the Franciscans Flaithrí

Ó Maolchonaire, who became archbishop of Tuam, and Fr Maurice Dunleavy, and the baron of Leitrim who became a Dominican some years after his arrival in Spain.[77] Ó Cléirigh's account gives no hint of the complicated network of contacts on which Red Hugh was depending in his mission to Spain. Nor does it give any indication of the parts played by prominent clergymen involved in the diplomatic preparation for that visit. Similarly, in Ó Cianáin's narrative, illustrative material is confined to feasts, festivities, funerals, local marvels and miracles. He begins quite brusquely:

> 'In the name of God. Here are some of the adventures and proceedings of Ó Néill from the time that he left Ireland. . . . He received a letter from John Bath on Thursday, the seventh of September . . . It was stated in that letter that Maguidhir, (Cúchonnacht Maguidhir), Donnchadha Ó Briain, Matha Óg Ó Maoltuile, and John Rath came with a French ship for Ó Néill and the Earl of Tyrconnell to Cuan Suilighe Móire [Lough Swilly] . . . They went on board the ship about mid-day on Friday. Then they hoisted their sails'.

A group from the ship, which went ashore in two boats to get water and firewood, were chased and attacked by a party led by a son of Mac Suibhne Fánaid and his supporters. These Mac Suibhne [Mac Sweeneys] were opposed to Ó Domhnaill claims on their lands in northern Donegal.[78] Again, this is a piece of information delivered without further comment as to the perfidy or otherwise of these Mac Suibhne. It is understood that they are enemies of the departing earls, with their own reasons for this enmity.

Though the earls had planned to go to Spain, the peace signed by that country with England in 1604, and its fragile continuance, meant that Spain did not wish to appear publicly to support enemies of the English crown. In fact the fleeing group never settled in Spain, but were shuffled from France to Flanders to Italy, experiencing no security in any of the sojourns they made due to the complicated diplomatic intrigue which surrounded their every move. In Italy during July 1608, Rury, earl of Tyrconnell, died of a fever he contracted in Ostia. His brother Cathbharr and two of their manservants, along with a clergyman Dr Domhnall Ó Cearbhaill, all fell ill of the same disease and within six weeks all had died. Cúchonnacht Maguidhir, lord of Fermanagh, and Séamus, son of Eimhear Mathghamhna of the Mathghamhna of Oirghialla [MacMahons of Oriel, Monaghan], also died in August 1608 of a fever they contracted at Genoa. Aodh Ó Néill, baron of Dungannon, son of Ó Néill and nephew of Tyrconnell, died of the same illness some short time after Ó Cianáin's narrative ends.[79] Such a decimation of the departed nobles must have been very keenly felt, not least by the narrator, his own traditional patron being among the most valorous of those stricken. Dispassionately Ó Cianáin records the misfortune of each loss, the holy death of each victim and the ostentatious funeral given in his honour:

> 'It may well be believed that it was not through good fortune or the best of fate that it happened to Ireland that so many of the choicest of the descendants of Míl Easpáinne died suddenly, one after another, in a foreign and strange land, far removed from their own native soil. The son of Ó Domhnaill was buried in the habit of Saint Francis, after having had a great funeral and splendid cortege following him in procession, in the same monastery of San Pietro Montorio, in the same manner as the Earl, and close to his tomb'.[80]

The earls and their followers, in this account, spent much of their time officiating at religious processions, visiting churches and monasteries and making pilgrimages. On an invitation from Pope Paul V, Ó Néill and some of the other nobles of his party attended the pope at evening prayer. 'A place of honour was selected for Ó Néill, close to the holy Father and opposite him'.[81] Ó Cianáin represents his leaders as men of substance, who were being received with due ceremony at different cities throughout Europe. Their reception at various places was determined by the diplomatic climate prevailing between England and the host city. Throughout the account, the earls and their company are met by expatriot Irishmen who are normally important clerics or military men. Their meetings are merely mentioned by Ó Cianáin, his laconic account is as a nod to the knowing:

> 'On Monday, the twenty-first of the same month, they bade farewell to the poeple of the city [Arras]. They proceeded five more leagues to a famous city called Douai. The people there received them with great respect. They alighted at the Irish College which was supported by the King of Spain in the town. They themselves stayed in the College, and they sent the better part of those with them through the city. They remained there until the following Friday. The reverend father, Flaithrí Ó Maolconaire, Irish Provincial of the Friars Minor [Franciscans], and Doctor Robert Mac Arthur met them here, having come from Flanders'.[82]

The ferment of activity surrounding the controversial earls can be understood from this outline account:

> 'The next day, the thirtieth of October, Ó Néill's son, the Colonel of the Irish [regiment], came to them with a large

well-equipped company of captains and noblemen, Spanish and Irish and of every other nation. On the following Saturday the Marquis Spinola, the commander-in-chief of the King of Spain's army in Flanders, came to them from Brussels with a large number of important people and welcomed them'.[83]

The earls had not merely fled to exile; Ó Néill's behaviour on the continent indicated that he, at least, had every intention of rallying Irish support and expertise there to his cause. No one who might possibly be of use to him was shunned: 'Then Sir William Stanley,[84] an English veteran warrior in the service of the King of Spain, came with many nobles to see them and pay them a visit'.[85]

The poets of the North lamented the deaths of the scions of their noble families. A moving elegy, beginning 'Truagh liom Máire agus Mairghréag' ('I pity Mary and Margaret')[86], is attributed to Fearghal Óg Mac an Bhaird. He is concerned with the four Ó Domhnaill brothers (family of Aodh Mac Maghnusa) who died between 1600 and 1608. The poem is addressed to the sisters in Ireland who lamented them:

> Truagh liom Máire agus Mairghréag
> ní beó blath na numhailghéag
> do chuir siad a nduilli dhíobh
> dá bhuime iad don iomshníomh.[87]

> (I pity Mary and Margaret; the flower of the modest princesses no longer lives; they have put off their leaves; they are two nurses of sorrow.)

The four Ó Domhnaill heroes are bewailed as chiefs and potential chiefs. The poet cannot understand how the sisters survive, since the land has died in the absence of her leaders:

'Four salmon from the great Boyne, four sons to Aodh, Maghnus' son, a group of dragons who divulged not their purpose, they had nothing to fear but jealousy.

Boughs of apple-trees bend not with fruit through-out fair Banba, nor hazel-trees with nuts; 'tis strange that Margaret lives.'[88]

Thus the poets continued to describe the feelings of Ireland and of her élites in their traditional way after the departure of the earls, after the death of a significant number of the nobles who departed in 1607.

Poets depending on the élites who were thus devastated found themselves without the support they formerly took for granted. Some poets had prudently taken steps to ensure that their titles to land and their possessions were legal in the new dispensation.[89] Poets were able to make use of their legal, genealogical and historical knowledge to help or hinder crown officials in their settlement and re-settlement of *Leath Cuinn*. Poets, and those with poetic training who had careers besides that of poet, contributed to literary comment on the events of the times.

Gaelic and Old English families were linked by blood and marriage to noble and aristocratic families in Scotland and England. Centuries of intermarriage and alliances created tenuous ties of all kinds between the more powerful families in the three countries. *Leabhar Cloinne Aodha Buidhe* – the book of the O'Neills of Clandeboy (Lower) – contains poems for Sir Henry (son of Sir Seán Mac Brian) O'Neill [d. 1638], and his wife Martha Stafford (daughter of Sir Francis Stafford), an English woman, and a Protestant. Sir Henry O'Neill himself may have been reared a protestant.[90] Poets such as Fear Flatha Ó Gnímh[91] and Gofraidh Mac Briain Óig Mic an Bháird wrote poems for Sir Henry O'Neill and for his wife Martha Stafford, without adverse comment on either her race or religion. Her Englishness is welcomed both by Gofraidh Mac an Bháird[92] and Fear Flatha Ó Gnímh specifically in his wedding poem for Sir Henry and Martha Stafford.[93] And in support of the marriage, the poets list the heroes of the history of the Gael, whose wives and mothers came from the nobility or royalty of England. The nobility of the blood always compensated for any complications of race, in the poets' eyes. In an area as tense as Lower Clandeboy [south-east Antrim] in this period, where several layers of settlers and planters jostled for position and possession, the poets in this particular collection evinced neither sectarian preoccupations nor xenophobia in the narrow sense.

Some of the best known names in the Gaelic literature of the first half of the seventeenth century were clerics who were also poets. *Leath Cuinn* was rich in clerics whose writings are classics of Irish literature. Such men were also closely linked to the chief families of the province by blood and traditional allegiance, and by the shared interests of the learned and political élites.[94] Writers in Irish, both secular and clerical, were closely linked socially and politically with the Gaelic and Old English élites. Ties of blood, religion and political allegiance created a complex network of patronage and dependency between the writers and their patrons or those from whom they sought patronage.

The earls Tyrone and Tyrconnell were always flanked by high-ranking clerics. In the case of the Ó Domhnaill, as part of their traditional support of the Franciscans the chief's chaplain was often a member of that order and the chief himself may have received his education among them. That was certainly the case with Red Hugh O'Donnell on his journey to Spain in 1602. These Fransiscans were among the stalwarts of the new continentally-trained Irish clergy. The seminaries established in catholic countries of Europe to train Irish priests in the manner demanded by the Council of Trent (1545–63), and administered by different religious orders, were the training grounds for many learned Irishmen, both diocesan clergy and members of religious orders, in the seventeenth century. The instruction given to students at these colleges attained the highest standards. Philosophical, theological and political teaching and discussion in the colleges were abreast of the full spectrum of orthodox and heterodox thinking of the day. The Irish students and teachers participated fully in the ferment of ideologies, political and religious, characteristic of European cities during the wars of religion in the seventeenth century. The Gaelic and Old English élites were closely linked with the different religious orders, the Gaelic favouring the Franciscans, while the Jesuits tended to come from Old English backgrounds. In some respects the continental colleges mirrored some of the less salubrious characteristics of Irish political life; for rivalries between different provinces and groups were carried from Ireland to the colleges in continental Europe.

During the first two decades of the seventeenth century, a flow of catechisms and other devotional works supportive of the pastoral norms of Trent emerged from the Irish priests (especially Franciscans) in the Spanish Netherlands. St Anthony's College at Louvain, a Franciscan college founded in 1607 for the most part through the efforts of Flaithrí Ó Maolchonaire, was the centre of printing in Irish at this time. Much of the material was translated and adapted from continental religious works. Many of the works began with a disclaimer to any fluency in the written language, especially in the standard insisted on by the traditional schools of literature. Many of those writing were trained poets, historians and genealogists, or had close family links with members of the learned and academic élites. Franciscans were impelled to provide printed matter in Irish for pastoral work by the production in Dublin in 1603[95] of a state-sponsored Irish translation of the New Testament followed by one of the Book of Common Prayer (*Leabhar na nUrnaightheadh Comhchoidchiond*) in 1608.

Aodh Mac Cathmhaoil (Mac Aingil) [Hugh MacCaughwell d. 1626] – native of county Down, and onetime tutor to the sons of Hugh O'Neill – produced memorable devotional poems along with substantial devotional literature which he provided for the press at Louvain, again with the intention that such material be used in pastoral work in Ireland. His best known work in Irish is *Scáthán shacramuinte na h-aithridhe* [Mirror of the sacrament of penance] (Louvain, 1618).[96] This work sought to highlight the importance of the sacrament of penance, and the appropriate preparation of the soul through citing 'authorities', 'reasons' and 'examples'.[97] Part of his discussion centered on refuting the claims of members of the Church of Ireland hierarchy, men like Archbishop James Ussher and Bishop Downham of Derry, who claimed that the Church of Ireland was not new, but had returned to the purity of the early Irish church.[98] Aodh Mac Cathmhaoil expended much energy in counteracting these claims specifically and generally. He contrasted the new protestant clergy with the early Irish saints, Patrick, Colmcille and

Brigid and the other holy virgins, confessors and martyrs. No favourable comparison could be made between the piety and abstinence of the early saints and the materialism and self-indulgence of the protestant clergy. Aodh Mac Cathmhaoil contrasted them, emphasizing the protestant abolition of the practice of clerical celibacy: 'Biadha bochda as trosgadh fada do-níodh ar naoimhchliar; biadha blasda, cuirthi as comhól, iarruid ar nuaichliar. A léintibh róinneadh as gan chompáin achd cruadhchlocha do chodladh ar naoimhchliar; leapa boga, Mór as Mairghrég, bhíos 'gár nuaichléir.' [Our holy clerics used to have poor food and long fasts; our new clergy demand tasty food, banquets and carousing. Our holy clerics used to sleep alone in a hair-shirt on a hard stone; our new clergy have soft beds with Mary and Margaret.][99] He laments the constraints placed on the catholic clergy because of their persecution by 'heretics'. One of the most unfortunate results of this curtailment of their ministry is the neglect of the souls of the faithful. Without their own true clergy, the Catholics are being led astray by the false doctrines of the Protestants.[100] He castigates Luther and Calvin as the principal doctors of heresy, and particularly attacks their denial of the efficacy of indulgences. He traces the history of Luther's campaign in Germany against the Friar Tetsel, who had been authorized by Pope Leo X to proclaim an indulgence for all those who supported the war against the Turks in 1517. From this, says Mac Cathmhaoil, came the cursed heresy that ruined and split Europe, and that destroyed religion in England, Ireland and Scotland. That same heresy caused the banishment of Mac Cathmhaoil himself, and others like him, from their native country.[101] He repeats the tradition that Luther was the son of Lucifer, and that indeed it was Lucifer himself who taught Luther to attack the Church. For this reason Luther was known as Luther Mac Lucifer. He continues the work which Lucifer began in heaven – Lucifer divided God's angels in heaven, Luther divided God's people on earth. Luther joined his 'father' in hell, where his followers will join him likewise for all eternity.[102] Far from being united in their faith, Mac Cathmhaoil points out that the Protestants are united only in enmity towards Catholics. In this characteristic the Protestants, says Mac Cathmhaoil, resembled pigs who fought to the death among themselves, but joined together against attacks by dogs. Mac Cathmhaoil is keen to make it clear that James I, whom he refers to as 'ár Rí uasal oirirc' [our noble illustrious king], was not a follower of Luther and Calvin, and had not denied the fundamental articles of faith of the true church. However, through heretical teachers he had been led away from the Roman Catholic Church, the church of his mother.[103]

From the late 1620s, Br Micheál Ó Cléirigh[104] and his assistants were engaged in the task of collating material from manuscripts in Ireland on the lives of Irish saints. This project subsequently led to the works now known as the *Martyrology of Donegal*[105] and the *Annals of the Four*

Masters. Material collected by Br Micheál, which was sent to his
Franciscan colleagues Fr. John Colgan and Fr. Hugh Ward in Louvain,
led to the publication of further material of Irish interest in Latin. All
three scholars were natives of Donegal. In Ireland, the printing of Irish
religious material was a concern of the anglican bishop of Kilmore,
William Bedell (d. 1642). He wanted to provide an Irish translation of
the Old Testament – a task which outlived him, but which provided a
focus for the talents of Gaelic scholars within Ireland, among whom
were Uilliam Ó Domhnaill, and Fearganainm Ó Domhnalláin.

As well as in their pastoral work, the catholic clergy exercised influence as emissaries and advisors to the chiefs and leaders. All the major
Gaelic chiefs and Old English leaders had a network of clergy in Ireland
and on the continent representing their interests. The Thirty Years War
(1618–48) provided a fertile ground for political intrigues of all kinds
and the Irish swordsmen, clerics, merchants, scholars and exiled leaders scattered throughout Europe were ever vigilant for opportunities to
reverse their fortunes in Ireland by means of a successful military
project supported by Spain or France. In the vanguard of these were the
descendants of the earls of Tír Eoghain and Tír Chonaill.[106] John O'Neill,
earl of Tyrone and Hugh son of Rury O'Donnell, earl of Tyrconnell,
were both the focus of northern Irish hopes and of English spies on the
continent. Irish ecclesiastics led by the archbishop of Tuam, Flaithrí Ó
Maolchonaire, and a group of Irish officers led by Hugh O'Neill's
nephew, Owen Roe son of Art O'Neill, encouraged both the young earls
to assume their traditional roles of leadership of the northern Irish and
to exploit the tension between England and Spain for their military
plans. While these plans failed and both earls were subsequently killed
in engagements on the continent – Tyrone in January 1641 and Tyrconnell
in 1642[107] – the plans in which Owen Roe O'Neill had been involved in
the late 1620s were in many respects revitalized in the 1641 rebellion.
Owen Roe himself played a leading military and political role in *Leath
Cuinn* in the decade of war which followed.

The wars in which Ireland, England and Scotland were involved in
the 1640s changed the three countries forever, and changed the
relations between each of those countries likewise. The 1641 rebellion
was initiated in the north, and an uneasy alliance was struck between
the Gaelic Irish and the Old English in support of the king. In this
period the divide between the Old English and Gaelic Irish was sealed
and breached innumerable times.

'I gcúige Uladh do mhusgail an chéidfhear',[108] 'And in Ulster uprose the
first man . . . '[109] With this statement the anonymous author of the mid-
seventeenth-century poem 'An Síogaí Rómhánach' ['The Roman Vision']
introduces us to his version of the part played by Ulster heroes in the series
of wars which took place throughout Ireland during the decade 1641–1652.
Pre-eminent among the Ulster heroes was the great Owen Roe O'Neill, and

the greater part of the poem is a celebration of his victories and near-victories both with and against the king's party in Ireland, against and with the Scots and against and with the Parliamentarians. 'Near-victories' because O'Neill, in the poetry, was never defeated through lack of ability; 'with and against' because O'Neill's constancy in pursuit of his objectives was assured by flexibility in regard to means.

Eoghan Mac Airt O'Neill (d. 1649) was a nephew of the great Hugh O'Neill (d. 1616), and a great-grandson of Con Bacach O'Neill (d. 1559), the first earl of Tyrone. His arrival in Ireland in 1642 was a triumph for the plotters in Ireland and the continent who had always seen the return of Irish veterans from the seasoned armies of Europe as a vital part of their strategy. He became the focus for northern loyalties, and as the military leader in Ulster he threw the support of his armies behind the papal nuncio, Giovanni Baptista Rinuccini, archbishop of Fermo. In June 1646 he defeated the Scots parliamentarians under Monro at Benburb, County Tyrone. Owen Roe's death put an end to the traditional position of Ó Néill in *Leath Cuinn*. After the upheaval of the Cromwellian confiscation, no traditional Gaelic leader ever assumed the same importance as Owen Roe O'Neill. The poem, 'An Síogaí Rómhánach', is written as a vision that appeared to the poet while he contemplated the tombs of O'Neill and O'Donnell in Rome. A beautiful woman in great distress uttered the poem as an address to God. The poem follows a pattern recognizable in many poems of this period, especially those poems written in the accentual metre which was becoming more popular among the Gaelic literati, and makes use of the *aisling* [vision] genre, which became more popular in the following century. The poet lists the depredations of Ireland's nobles and of her heroes which drew the anger of God upon them. The moral lassitude of the leaders is blamed for the defeats suffered by the Irish in *Leath Cuinn*.[110]

The poet – through the distressed *spéirbhean* [beautiful woman] – lists all the monarchs of England since Henry VIII and describes how their evil ways affected Ireland. Worst of all are the parliamentarians who beheaded Charles I and now lacerated Ireland itself. He then turns his attention to the heroes of the North who defend Ireland in her present troubles. Maguire and MacMahon are given the first mention, since they were credited with plotting the taking of Dublin Castle:

'I gcúige Uladh do mhusgail an chéidfhear,
Mág Uidhir, fuigheall na Féine
is Mac Mathghamhna amhail ba bhéas do,
an dá leómhan chródha mhéinnmhaith . . . '[111]

(In Ulster the first man stirred – ,
Mág Uidhir, survivor of the Féine,
And Mac Mahon, as was his wont,
the two brave, true lions, . . .)

This poem also praises the parts played by Hugh O'Neill, Red Hugh O'Donnell and Rury O'Donnell in military expeditions from an earlier period. The poem contains a eulogy of Owen Roe O'Neill, and a battle-roll of his victories. The poet declares that he could not do justice to half of his wonderful deeds.[112] He devotes seventy lines to a description of his victories and his personal valour. Other participants in the victories are given a few lines or a mention each.

Sir Phelim Rua O'Neill, a kinsman of Owen Roe, had led the Ulster forces before the latter's arrival in Ireland. He was MP for Dungannon, had been a law student at Lincoln's Inn and had conformed to the established church. He first captured Charlemont, a strategically vital fort in county Armagh (which he held until 1650), and was chosen commander-in-chief of the Ulster forces at a meeting of Irish leaders held in Monaghan. The Confederates at Kilkenny appointed him president of Ulster.[113] He and Owen Roe were rivals[114] but the author of 'An Síogaí Romhánach' makes no reference to this rivalry. He skims over Sir Phelim's career in one short complimentary sentence[115] and launches into the eulogy of his hero. None of the complexities of the returned continental veteran's strategies, alliances and loyalties are discussed in the poem. He is hailed simply as the champion of Ulster, and his victories are listed without analytical comment. The poet does not confine his praise to the Ulster leader or to the champions of *Leath Cuinn* but also lists many other Gaelic leaders who stood with Owen Roe and the nuncio against the Confederates. The faction who departed from the nuncio brought the anger of God and the curse of the nuncio on Ireland and were the cause of her troubles. The leaders listed by the poet are those who were alive after the death of the Ulster hero in 1649, and upon whom the poet placed all his hopes for the future of Ireland.[116] Chief among those are Major General Hugh O'Neill, nephew of the hero of Benburb, who arrived in Ireland with him in 1642; Sir Phelim O'Neill, alive yet when this poem was written; Colonel Richard Farrell, made a lieutenant general by Owen Roe and who held out until 1652.

The death of the Ulster general himself is seen by the poet as an act of God – not the victory of his enemies.[117] God called him to be with him among the saints. Other sources suggested that O'Neill had been poisoned slowly by a pair of boots with which he was presented by a member of the Plunket family of Louth.[118]

The author of a contemporary account in English of Owen Roe O'Neill's campaigns – the *Aphorismical Discovery of Treasonable Faction* – written some time between 1652–1660 by a person identified only by unclear initials,[119] echoes the sentiment of the poet:

'Some deeminge God in his divine clemencie, not to deale soe straight with this poore nation, as to bereaue them of this theire

onely champion, rather the worlde beinge not worthy of soe
good a masterpeece, lulled him asleepe, snatched him away to
some secret corner of the world (as another Elias) to keepe him
there for future better purposes, . . .'[120]

Another account of the wars between 1641 and 1647 is to be found in the
prose narrative 'Cín lae Ó Mealláin' [Ó Mealláin's Diary][121] This account
was written in Irish by a member of the Ulster party – possibly Fr.
Toirdhealbhach Ó Mealláin, from Tyrone, a chaplain of Sir Phelim
O'Neill. It is not a continuous analytical account, but rather notes taken
as aids for a future full account. His notes are understandably short and
laconic as for example the following on Sir Phelim's taking of Charlemont
fort:

'Do gabhadh Serlimont, agus tigherna an bhoile My Lord
Caulfilld, agus a roibh ann ó sin síos'.[122]

(Charlemont, the lord of that place, My Lord Caulfield, and
from there down were seized).

His introduction of Owen Roe O'Neill is equally sketchy:

'Táinic litreacha Eoghain Néill meic Airt meic an Fhir Dorcha
go Gener. Cōigidh Uladh da fhoillsiugh techt na choinne go
Caislēn na dTuath'.[123]

(Eoghan mac Airt Ó Néill's letters arrived today to the General
of Ulster, announcing his coming to meet him at Caisleán na
dTuath.)

These short notes promised a fuller account, which has not come to
light if it ever was written. Another prose account in the Gaelic of
Scotland concerning the wars in Scotland during the same period was
written by a member of the Mac Mhuirich family who were poets and
historians to the MacDonald clan, and is found in the Book of
Clanranald.[124] The hero of this account is Alasdair MacColla, who also
took part in the wars in Ireland, and is mentioned in another Irish poem
from this period 'Aiste Dháibhí Cúndún'.[125] Gaelic Scotland and Ireland
shared a common literary culture and the learned dialect of the bardic
poets, historians and so forth, was identical. In 1623 Pope Urban VIII
apppointed four Irish Franciscans as missionaries to the Western Highlands.[126] Fathers Edmund MacCann, Paul O'Neill, Patrick Hegarty and
Cornelius Ward undertook this mission from their headquarters in
Bonamargy Friary in county Antrim. In this effort they were supported
by Colla Ciotach, father of Alasdair MacColla. The 'conversions' achieved

by these missionaries were for the most part the revival of a dormant Roman Catholicism, rather than conversion from any other denomination. The efforts of the missionaries further strengthened the links between the re-catholicized members of Clanranald in the Isles and their kinsmen and clansmen in Ireland. The author of the narrative in the Book of Clanranald, Niall Mac Mhuirich (d. 1726)[127] emphasizes the part played by the *Gael* as opposed to the *Albanach* [Scot] in Montrose's campaigns.[128] Ó Mealláin's account may have become something like that of Mac Mhuirich's if it was ever written.

*

Events which diminished their leaders and undermined their own way of life are the context of many poems written by northern poets during this period. Yet much of the material surviving seems to indicate that the immediacy of their destruction was not a continual nagging element in the poets' professional productions. Using a selection of the material produced by the learned élites of Ulster during this period, we get a sidelong glimpse of the history of *Leath Cuinn*. The picture which emerges complements that which is based on sources which always refer to 'rebels', 'rhymers' and 'traitors'.[129] It is a view from a Gaelic aristocratic perspective. The complexity of allegiances and alliances, illustrated starkly in many episodes of the 1641 rebellion, were neither new nor entirely inexplicable. The surviving poetry indicates that loyalty to the crown co-existed with attachment to local Gaelic lordly families, and western Gaelic-speaking Scotland was very much part of the Ulster Gaelic world at this time. The Gaelic poetry in praise of Sir Henry O'Neill and his wife Martha Stafford indicates that allegiance to the protestant religion and an English background could be accommodated within the Ulster Gaelic *mentalité*, for in this aristocratic society distinguished ancestry was prized above all else. It further points to the ability of sections of the Gaelic literary class to adapt to the new order in Ulster after 1603. The careers of many of the more prominent individuals of the period reveal a number of layers of political, religious, social and professional loyalties, none of which could be contemplated apart from the others. Poets and writers whose profession demanded that they provide leadership or instruction in a catechetical context, like the Franciscan Aodh Mac Cathmhaoil, did indeed promote catholicism against protestantism, in the spirit of the counter-reformation. Yet his attacks in *Scáthán shacramuinte na h-aithridhe* are on what he sees as the errors of protestantism, not on the evils of Protestants.[130] He was one of Hugh O'Neill's representatives in the latter's efforts to become reconciled with James I. His participation in these dangerous and tricky negotiations did not undermine his role as catholic reformer, or compromise his status as guardian [head] of the

Irish Franciscans in Louvain. Sectarian attacks on settlers or natives, of the kind associated with some of the excesses of the 1641 rebellion, were not anticipated, much less advocated, in the learned Gaelic literature of the first half of the seventeenth century. Oppression and persecution of a more general kind, which members of any beleaguered sect or religion expected from an unsympathetic government, was a common theme in the devotional and catechetical literature of the period. Continentally-trained Irish clergy who produced devotional literature in Irish followed the pattern of their continental colleagues, drawing on the same and similar material.[131] The adaptations they made of French, Spanish and Italian originals made very few overt references to Ireland and her circumstances in a purely political sense. The focus was at all times on the standards of Roman Catholic practice expected of Catholics.

This brief survey of Ulster Gaelic literature written around the first turbulent decade of the seventeenth century, and during the subsequent decades up to the 1641 rebellion, gives us a glimpse of the world through the poets' eyes. This literature illustrates aspects of the *mentalité* of the Gaelic élites at a period when their way of life was being thrown into disarray and undermined by unrelenting pressure from rival political, social, economic, cultural and religious systems.

Companyes of the Rebells meeting with the English flyinge for their lives, falling downe before them cryinge for mercy, thirst theire Pichforkes into their Childrens bellyes & throws them into the water.

ULSTER 1641 IN THE CONTEXT OF POLITICAL DEVELOPMENTS IN THE THREE KINGDOMS

M. Perceval-Maxwell

The immediate political developments in England, Scotland and Ireland that contributed to the outbreak of the rebellion can be divided into three periods. The first is from the signing of the Scottish National Covenant in February 1638, when the Scots protested against the attempt to introduce a Scottish prayer book in 1637 which had similarities to the English one, to the meeting of the Long Parliament in November 1640 (a parliament so named because it was not formally dissolved till 1660). The second may be defined as from November 1640 to the execution of Thomas Wentworth, earl of Strafford and lord lieutenant of Ireland, in May 1641, and the final phase covered the period from his execution until the outbreak of the rebellion. During all three periods, however, there existed a basic instability in the relations between the three kingdoms over which Charles ruled. Ireland, for instance, because of the plantation policy, had for a century offered an opportunity to venturesome Englishmen for advancement in terms of place, or land or both. Thus he who controlled the government of Ireland commanded considerable influence and patronage in assisting or denying advancement. Yet the authority of the Irish governor rested ultimately upon retaining the confidence of the king in England. As a result, no sooner was a man appointed to the governorship than his rivals sought to undermine his position at court with an eye to winning the position, and thus the profits, for themselves.

Thomas Wentworth had tried to take special precautions to prevent this type of out-flanking. On taking office as lord deputy, for instance, he had insisted that no Irish issue be appealed over his head. Nevertheless, in his correspondence with his ally at court, William Laud, archbishop of Canterbury, he showed constant concern about his standing within the English council. Indeed, from the time of the initial riots in Edinburgh during July 1637, up to the signing of the Covenant the following February, the deputy's correspondence betrayed more concern about the machinations of his enemies at court than about the activities of the Scots.[1] He had, indeed, good reason to fear that the many enemies he had made in Ireland and England would attempt to undermine his position at court. Under his administration, Ireland enjoyed internal peace and the volume of trade increased substantially, but such order and prosperity was purchased at a high price. His method of government was draconian. Wherever he could, he challenged the legitimacy of land titles, whether those of the British planters in Ulster or those of Ulick Burke, earl of Clanricard, in Connacht, in order that the crown might resume the land and re-distribute it at a profit. He also used the council to settle issues that would normally have passed through the common law courts. Such policies, along with a ruthlessness in dealing with opponents, ensured that there were many who were ready to unseat him should opportunity arise.

The Scots added to the structural instability between the three kingdoms. Since the accession of James VI of Scotland to the English and Irish thrones, Ireland, and particularly Ulster, had become a source of advancement for Scots as well as Englishmen. They could not expect to be appointed to office in Ireland, but they acquired considerable estates and Scottish landowners were followed by Scottish tenants. The Scottish penetration of Ireland, although intended to reinforce English interests there, had, by the time the covenanting crisis broke, begun to undermine them. As the Scots were signing their covenant, the Scottish courtier, James Hamilton, the third marquis of that name, was attempting to procure the lands in Ulster that had originally been settled by the livery companies of the city of London but which had been forfeited because of failure to fulfil the terms under which the land had been granted. To Wentworth, this Scottish territorial ambition was as unwelcome as religious dissent. The way in which the two issues were linked in his mind is illustrated by his comment to Laud in March 1638 that, if Hamilton was allowed to receive the land, it would 'turn the English wholly out of Ulster' and the Scottish settlers would start 'the very same rebellion against the clergy and discipline of the church' as had been begun in their homeland.[2]

It was this same Hamilton who served as Charles' chief negotiator with his Scottish subjects. Ostensibly the dispute between the king and the Scots concerned the introduction of a Scottish prayer book and the role of bishops in the Scottish church. The prayer book, although drawn up by Scottish bishops, resembled that used in England and was perceived as a move to force the Scots to worship in the manner of the English. Bishops had operated in Scotland since the days of James VI, but side by side with the presbytery system. They had, however, begun to assume a more dominant role in the church, the introduction of the prayer book being symbolic of the change, and the presence of some of them on the Scottish council gave them a high political profile in temporal as well as spiritual matters. At the heart of the dispute, therefore, lay a growing concern about Charles' disinclination to consult

representative Scottish institutions in governing the country and a fear
about an anglicization of Scotland. English customs and practices were
beginning to penetrate Scotland, and they were resented just as much as
Wentworth resented the Scottish encroachment into Ireland.[3]

By November 1638 Hamilton's efforts to reach an agreement with
the covenanters had failed, largely because Charles was unwilling to
make meaningful concessions, and both sides began to prepare for war.
During these preparations Hamilton again became involved in Irish
affairs because it was apparently he who initiated the idea that his
friend, Randal Macdonnell, the catholic earl of Antrim, should launch a
flank attack upon the covenanters from Antrim's estates, which faced
the west coast of Scotland. The scheme was rightly condemned by
Wentworth as 'vast, vain and childish' as Antrim possessed neither the
resources nor the skill to deliver such an assault, but it illustrates the
way Ireland was about to be drawn into the vortex created by the
Anglo-Scottish confrontation.[4]

We do not know whether Wentworth knew that Hamilton was
behind the unwelcome plan to allow Antrim to raise an army, but there
is no doubt that the deputy associated the Scottish noble with his
primary opponents on the English council, the earls of Arundel
and Holland. The situation was particularly threatening to the deputy
because it was Hamilton, Thomas Howard, earl of Arundel and earl
marshal, and Henry Rich, earl of Holland and general of the horse, who
were primarily responsible for Charles' military preparations during
1638 and the first half of 1639. Arundel and Holland were also close to
Richard Boyle, earl of Cork, Wentworth's strongest rival in Ireland,
who had recently gone to live in England. The military duties of Arundel
and Holland, moreover, gave them new prestige on the council. Such,
indeed, was the growth of their ascendancy during the early part of
1639 that Laud was driven in March to exclaim to his friend in Ireland:
'we are undone, my lord, and there is no more to be said.'[5]

What preserved the influence of Wentworth (and Laud) on the council was the ignominious failure of Arundel and Holland to supply the
king with an effective army. Charles, realizing that his forces were in no
condition to fight, had to agree to a truce with the Scots in June 1639
under the treaty of Berwick. Let down by Wentworth's opponents, the
king turned unreservedly to his Irish deputy in an attempt to deal with
the Scottish challenge, and, unless the king was prepared to make major
concessions, which he was not, this could only be addressed by a
renewed military effort. Wentworth crossed to England in the late
summer of 1639 and by September had begun to take a leading part in
the English council's proceedings. By the end of the year the king had
granted him the earldom of Strafford and promoted him to the position
of lord lieutenant of Ireland.[6] From September till the Scots delivered a
second and greater humiliation to their king by occupying the English

town of Newcastle in August 1640, Wentworth remained the dominant figure on the council.

It will be remarked that, up to 1640, Ireland had remained peripheral to the conflict. Antrim had never been able to gather an army, let alone launch one across the sea. The Irish government did dispatch some 500 troops from the small standing Irish army to help garrison Carlisle, but this was a token force. About the only substantial consequence of the conflict for Ireland so far had been Wentworth's treatment of those Scots who had made Ireland their home since 1610. As early as January 1639 the deputy had indicated that the Scots in Ireland would have to renounce the covenant or be sent 'over to their fellows in Scotland'. To give effect to this policy, an oath (the so-called Black Oath) was devised to be taken by all Scots living in Ireland. The authorities began to impose the oath during the summer of 1639 though it became increasingly difficult to enforce once the news about the treaty of Berwick became known in Ireland. Numerous Scots returned to Scotland rather than take the oath, and it created deep hostility towards Wentworth both in Scotland and among the Scots living in Ireland, but the majority of the population of Ireland remained, as yet, unaffected by the crisis except in so far as a decline in trade hurt the economy.[7]

When Charles turned to Wentworth for leadership, in effect he turned also to the country over which Wentworth presided, and as a result Irish issues became embroiled with those of Scotland and England. Until his position within the English council was secure, Wentworth had opposed calling parliament, but by the end of 1639 he had decided to call one, not only in England but also in Ireland. If the following year's military campaign was to be effective, it had to be backed by the resources that only a parliament could provide. Moreover, instead of relying on the ineffective earl of Antrim to put pressure upon the Scottish western flank, Charles and his minister had decided to raise a new Irish army separate from the small existing standing army and this was to be paid for out of the Irish treasury with money to be raised by the Irish parliament.

The decision to involve Ireland more directly in the struggle made sense strategically, particularly because Wentworth's control over Ireland had been sufficiently rigorous that he could expect a compliant parliament, and a cooperative Irish parliament would serve as a good example to that in England. At the same time, by using an Irish army which was paid for by his Irish subjects, Charles was raising the political, and even the constitutional, bidding. If Scottish dissent could be crushed with the assistance of an Irish army, so might that in England, a possibility not lost on some of the king's English subjects. Moreover, unless very strict control was exercised, the Irish parliament could demand concessions in return for its financial support and so place an additional source of political pressure upon the king.

Initially all went well for the royal policy. Wentworth, or Strafford as he had now become, returned to Ireland and addressed parliament on 20 March 1640. Six days later the Irish commons voted four subsidies of 45,000 pounds each to pay for the new army, a sum which was to be collected over eighteen months. MPs uttered loyal declarations, and some indicated that they would like to have made the grant larger.[8] The Irish parliament was then prorogued till 1 June, by which time it was hoped that the English parliament would also have demonstrated similar loyalty against the Scots and it would be possible to introduce unpopular Irish legislation giving effect to plans for the plantation of Connacht. This legislation and that providing for the support of the new army had to be kept separate because the Connacht scheme aroused deep fears in the minds of the sixty-seven Old English MPs and those they represented. The Old English, who were solidly catholic by faith, were descendants of the Anglo-Norman settlers in Ireland. Thus their land deeds had sometimes been lost during a civil unrest, or dated from a period when boundaries had been defined vaguely. Legislation for the crown to resume land in Connacht, therefore, was perceived as a precedent for challenging all weak titles.

Strafford returned to England early in April to face the parliament there secure in the knowledge that adequate resources had been obtained to create an effective Irish army of 9,000 men that would strike at the Scots from the west.[9] Expectations that the English parliament would prove as cooperative as its Irish counterpart were quickly dashed. The Short Parliament met on 13 April and had been dissolved by 5 May. The elections had been strongly contested, which boded ill for the support of royal policy. Strafford was ill when it met, and Charles created more difficulties for himself by asking for money to deal with the Scots without explaining what was at issue in the quarrel. Sir Henry Vane, recently appointed as the king's secretary, was supposed to guide the request for subsidies through the commons, and Vane was among Strafford's most bitter enemies in the council. Strafford had wanted to restrict the number of subsidies requested to eight, but Vane, possibly deliberately in order to make them particularly unpopular and therefore to undermine his enemy, insisted on twelve. The MPs refused to grant any money before their grievances, which included the ship money tax which had never been sanctioned by parliament, had been addressed, and they even threatened to take up Scottish grievances. On the advice of the council, and with Strafford's reluctant agreement, Charles dissolved parliament.[10]

News of what had happened in England was slow to pass to Ireland. Strafford's deputy there, Sir Christopher Wandesford, did not know of the outcome of the Short Parliament till 16 May, and we may assume that it took longer for Irish MPs to hear English news and to decide how to react. This explains why there is no hint of opposition during the second session of the Irish parliament until a week after it had begun its sitting, but by 8 June the contrast between the acquiescence towards government policy during the first session and the atmosphere of the second session was striking. Not only did the plantation bill disappear into a committee, never to emerge, but technical objections were raised about the way the subsidies were being levied, which had the effect of reducing the total collected to a fraction of what had been expected. In addition, both catholic and protestant MPs challenged certain levies being collected by the established church. Worse still from Strafford's point of view, not only were Catholics and Protestants working together in parliament against the government, but, as Wandesford himself remarked, some members of the Irish council were supporting the parliamentary opposition. Faced with this general revolt against his authority, on 17 June Wandesford prorogued the session until 1 October.[11] We may presume that he hoped that by this date the king would have restored his position in both Scotland and England and as a consequence Strafford would be able to reassert direction over the Irish parliament.

As might be expected, the reduction in the size of the Irish subsidies had political repercussions in England. Charles was reported to be angry at the unexpected reduction in funds to fight the war, and Strafford perceived the act as a blow to his own position at court. It was surely not an accident that the lord lieutenant's great rival in Ireland, Richard Boyle, earl of Cork, was added to the English council on 28 June, by which time the news of the failure of the second parliamentary session in Ireland had reached the king.[12]

We can assume that the Scots were as well informed about Irish as about English affairs. They must have known that, despite the reduction of the subsidies, by July the new Irish army, whose rank and file consisted largely of catholic Irish even if most of the officers were protestant, was preparing shipping on the east coast of Ulster in order to invade Scotland. The Scottish parliament had also met in June (against the king's wishes) and a general assembly of the Scottish church was held from 28 July to 5 August. By 3 August the Scots had decided to invade England and by the last day of that month they were in possession of Newcastle. Charles' English army had once again proved unable or unwilling to resist, and he had to agree to call yet another English parliament in order to begin negotiations for the withdrawal of the Scots. The Irish army, while still a threat, could not attack Scotland on its own. It was with this military situation in the background that the Long Parliament assembled on 3 November 1640.[13]

The next period to consider is that from the opening of the Long Parliament to Strafford's execution in May 1641. During these months the dominant issue, of course, was Strafford's fate, but the attack on Strafford was a symptom of the change that had taken place in the relations between the three kingdoms and not a fundamental issue itself. From 1638 to August 1640 policy had been directed towards the preparation and delivery of military force. Initially this policy had been in effect in Scotland and England, but from early 1640 it was operative in Ireland as well. From November 1640 to May 1641 the three armies formed during the previous period remained in being, but policy shifted to finding a settlement that would permit all three armies to disband. Strafford's fate (and to a lesser extent Laud's) was a key component of these discussions as he was seen as the prime architect of the policies that had led to the formation of the armies. This was made evident as early as 28 August 1640 when twelve English peers, none of whom occupied a seat on the council, petitioned the king in order to pressure him to recall parliament. One of the 'evils and dangers' listed by the peers was the Irish army, which was seen as a threat to England.[14] Significantly, as Strafford was being executed, the Irish army had begun to be disbanded, and within a matter of weeks the Scots had withdrawn from England and the English began to disband their army.

This is not the place to review the accusations against Strafford and his trial, but some points may be made about them that pertain to the new relations that were being established between the three kingdoms. First, it was in Ireland that the formal assault on Strafford began. It will be recalled that the Irish parliament's third session began on 1 October 1640, a full month before the Long Parliament assembled, and a day before Charles began his discussions with the Scottish commissioners at Rippon. The muted criticism that had become evident during the second session now became strident. The subsidies remained in their truncated form and the bill to implement the Connacht plantation made no headway, but more importantly, by the end of the session the commons had drawn up a sixteen-clause Humble and Just Remonstrance addressed to the king in which they itemized their complaints against Strafford's administration.[15]

Perhaps the most significant of these complaints was Wentworth's failure to make good in law one of the Graces (some fifty-one royal promises made in 1628 to redress grievances in Ireland in return for money to defend the country during the war with Spain) which would have secured land titles that went back sixty years or more. Such a concealment act had been passed in England in 1624 and was of particular concern to the Old English gentry in Ireland because their titles tended to be ancient and sometimes ill-defined.[16] If the Old English, most of whom were Roman Catholics, had strong reason to support the Just Remonstrance, it should also be stressed that the other clauses reflected dissatisfaction among the population as a whole, and one third of the eighty-four men who signed a document that accompanied the Remonstrance were Protestants.[17] We may also surmise that there were more than this number (of both faiths) who sympathized with the protest.

A second point about the campaign to unseat Strafford is that, when it was launched in the English commons, it was with the close co-operation of the earl's Irish opponents. One of the first to prepare the way for the attack was Sir John Clotworthy, an English planter in Antrim of puritan sympathies who had ties with Cork and was related by marriage to John Pym, the leader of the group in the English commons most critical of royal policy.[18] Clotworthy illustrates the way that English, Irish and Scottish opponents of this policy worked together. In 1638 he had travelled to Edinburgh where he had discussions with the covenanting leaders. He then went to London, but he maintained contact with Scotland and he warned his Scottish friends of the planned attack by the earl of Antrim. Although his estate lay in Ireland, he was found a seat in the Long Parliament, and on 7 November he alerted MPs to the dangers threatening from Ireland, concluding his speech with a warning that a 'popish' army was 'ready to march where I know not.'[19]

Pym, however, did not immediately make his accusations of treason against the lord lieutenant following Clotworthy's speech, but waited till 11 November, and it looks as though the delay was connected with a need to coordinate the actions of the English and Irish parliaments. One of the first measures taken by the Long Parliament had been to secure free passage to England for petitioners from Ireland, which under Wentworth had been prohibited. On the day that Pym formally laid his charges two Irish MPs arrived in Westminster.[20] Thus it looks as though Pym waited for confirmation from the Irish parliament that it was ready to work with him before he took the decisive step.

During Strafford's trial there was a continuation of the factional struggle that had been evident during the military confrontation with the Scots. Cork's celebrated strong stance as a witness against his rival in court was matched by an energetic participation in council meetings. From June 1640, when he joined the council, to October 1640, he attended only two of the thirty meetings held. From 1 November 1640 to the beginning of August 1641 he missed only three of thirty-one sessions, and his friendship with Strafford's English foes has already been remarked.[21] When Strafford's replacement as governor of Ireland was being considered, we find both Holland and Vane among the candidates for the position, and it may be remarked that seven of the thirteen Irish MPs sent as a committee to London to discuss Irish grievances with the king also served as witnesses for the prosecution at the trial.[22] To this factional animosity was added personal hatred, particularly by the Scots. When Strafford defended himself well against the charges, a Scot reported home that the earl 'would be content to go and live the rest of his wicked life at Venice. But it is presumed that the wise English know that dead dogs bark none.'[23]

We misinterpret the nature of the process at work if we ignore this factional contest and the personal hatred that went with it. On the other hand, the presence of these features should not blind us to the larger issues that lay behind them. Perhaps the most fundamental of these was fear of religious persecution. We have seen that this is what lay at the heart of Charles' dispute with the Scots, and it has been shown how Clotworthy stressed the catholic composition of the new Irish army, but it is worth quoting John Pym himself to illustrate the nature and depth of these fears. At the beginning of his first speech to the Long Parliament, Pym remarked: 'there is a design to alter law and religion: the parties that would effect this are papists who are obliged by a maxim in their doctrine, that they are not only bound to maintain their religion, but also to extirpate all others.'[24] To Pym there was an international conspiracy to root out his type of protestantism and he associated English bishops with this conspiracy.

The religious question, in turn, when linked to the existence of the Irish army, raised the question of Ireland's position within the three kingdom structure. The English, on the whole, were slow to perceive this connection. They feared catholicism in Ireland when it appeared to be attached to an army, but they gave little thought to how that army had come into being. It was assumed that Ireland was a dependency of England and, indeed, during Strafford's trial its status had been likened to that of Jersey and Guernsey.[25] Only at the end of the summer of 1641, when some Irish lords declined to answer for their actions before the English upper house, did the issue surface in the English political mind. Immediately a search of the records was ordered to prove Ireland's dependency status, but, so far as we know, without success.[26]

The Scots, on the other hand, revealed a clear grasp of the constitutional implications of the formation of the Irish army. Their primary task from November 1640 onwards was to work out a settlement with Charles and the English parliament, and this ultimately took the form of the treaty of London, which was ratified by the parliaments of both countries at the end of the summer of 1641. One of their concerns during the negotiations leading to this treaty was that the military situation that they had just confronted should not be allowed to develop again. They recognized that it was unreasonable to forbid the king to move troops from one of his kingdoms to another, although they set an upper limit of 10,000 men to the size of such armies. At the same time, they wanted a guarantee that the king could never act on his own as he just had. They therefore insisted on a clause which declared 'it is agreed that an Act be passed in the parliament of England that the kingdom of England nor Ireland shall not . . . make war against the kingdom of Scotland without the consent of the parliament of England', and elsewhere they declared that 'we comprehend [Ireland] under the name of England'. Yet, ironically, given their desire to subsume Ireland into England, the Scots demanded that the Irish parliament ratify the treaty.[27]

This contradictory demand was explained by the diarist of the English commons, Sir Simonds D'Ewes. Ratification by the Irish parliament was necessary because the Irish parliament had, either of its own accord, or by 'some subtle practices' declared its readiness to assist the king in fighting the Scots. It had, therefore, acted as an autonomous body, and the implication of this was that it was not bound by decisions of the English parliament. Only, therefore, through Irish ratification could this part of the treaty be secured.[28]

Initially, as we have seen, Pym worked with Irish interests, catholic and protestant, in order to destroy Strafford, but as the attack developed, English fear of Strafford was increasingly tied to the fear of catholicism as personified in the army he had raised. Thus Pym's interests began to separate from those of the catholic gentry of Ireland. The leaders of the Roman Catholic Church in Europe certainly desired and worked towards a return of England and Scotland to the old faith. There were, indeed, numerous catholic conspiracies in England.[29] To some degree, therefore, we may say that Pym and his followers had grounds for their fears. Yet their responses to the threats they perceived were so extreme that they helped to create just what they feared most, a determination by Irish Catholics to use force if necessary to protect their faith, just as the Scots had done in the face of pressure from England. A few weeks after the rebellion had broken out the Irish declared that they were forced to resort to arms because the 'puritans of England, Scotland and Ireland intended the utter extirpation and destruction of the catholic religion.'[30] Almost certainly the Irish leaders were totally unconscious of how closely their words resembled Pym's own of only a year before.

The examination of Irish catholic opinion takes us into the third and final period, from May to October 1641, but to do justice to this opinion, we have to look back to when the Scots and the English were discussing the Irish army and the terms of the London treaty. On 12 November 1640, that is the day after Pym had accused Strafford of treason, an Irish Jesuit wrote from London to say 'we are tossed between hope and fear'. Parliament, he explained, had not yet addressed religious issues, but he warned that 'such measures seem to be carried from them [that] perilous times are seriously dreaded.'[31] A month later a priest writing from Ireland noted to a friend that he expected reform in the 'temporal state', but 'we stand in awe concerning matters of religion because the parliament of England is jealously bent that way.'[32]

The comments illustrate the dilemma facing catholics in Ireland, and particularly the Old English. They had two primary interests: retention of their estates and retention of their religion. They also wanted to be rid of the repressive regime established by Strafford. They, like Pym and his followers in England, valued rule under law for which the lord lieutenant seemed to have little respect. He had, moreover, deliberately denied them the security of their estates which they had been promised and the planned Connacht scheme indicated an inclination to manipulate their doubtful titles to expand New English settlement at their expense. At the same time, under Wentworth they had enjoyed tacit religious toleration. Now, as his regime began to crumble, their estates remained insecure, but there was an additional threat in that the elements in England that were prepared to strike at Strafford took a harsh attitude towards their religion. As a Scot reported from London in March 1641, the Irish Catholics had purchased their religious liberty from Strafford at a 'dear rate', and now they feared losing both their property and religion.[33] The Graces appeared to be no closer to being confirmed, and Wentworth's successor might take measures against catholic worship.

The statements made by the Scots as they negotiated the treaty of London with the English also aroused deep alarm among Irish Catholics. Not only, as we have seen, did the Scots wish, in effect, to incorporate Ireland with England, they also wanted a union of the three kingdoms with one church which was to be fashioned along the Scottish model. 'Religion,' they said, was 'the base and foundation of kingdoms...and the strongest bond to tie subjects to their prince in true loyalty.' They urged, therefore, that there should be 'one confession of faith, one form of catechism ... and one form of church government in all the churches of his Majesty's dominions.' Once this had been achieved, Catholics would 'either conform themselves or get themselves hence.'[34] The English friends of the Scots in the commons often spoke in similar terms. To cite but one example, Sir Simonds D'Ewes remarked that 'the only [way] to bring his majesty's three kingdoms into perfect unity was to consider thoroughly of reducing Ireland to the profession of the true religion.'[35]

Such expressions by Scottish and English opponents of Charles were quickly picked up by Irish leaders. Lord Maguire, for instance, who was involved in plotting the rebellion but was captured as it began, reported after his capture that in the spring of 1641 the Irish understood that 'the Scottish army did threaten never to lay down arms until an uniformity of religion were in the three kingdoms and the catholic religion suppressed.'[36] The Gaelic Irish leader in exile, Owen Roe O'Neill, wrote early in July that he was convinced that a 'great tempest' was about to burst upon Catholics in Ireland that would 'deprive them of their property, and reduce the survivors to perpetual slavery.'[37] Such leaders were not to know that the more extreme Scottish demands would be rejected by the English, and it is understandable under the circumstances why many Irish Catholics looked to Strafford's new army - 'all Irishmen and well armed' - for protection. This army, as has been pointed out already, was disarmed and disbanded almost immediately after the execution of Strafford, but the men remained in Ireland and were well trained. During the summer Charles made arrangements with Spanish authorities for the shipment of the men into Spanish service, and this, according to Maguire, caused considerable concern among the gentry of the Pale, a concern which was reflected in a resolution passed in the Irish house of commons opposing the departure of the men.[38]

It is evident that there were those in Ireland and outside who, because of the extreme anti-catholic statements being made in England, were prepared to resort to force and to use the new army if they could. Had this been known for certain in England, it would have confirmed the worst fears of those making the extreme anti-catholic statements and led in all probability to precisely the type of persecution that the Catholics feared. However, it was not known, and over the summer there were some catholic Irish leaders who became convinced that a political settlement without force was possible. At this point, we have to draw a distinction between the catholic leaders in Ireland and on the continent, and those who were part of the Irish parliamentary deputation negotiating in England with the king and the English council. The latter, as might be expected, were much more in touch with the English officials who were making the decisions than the former and therefore had much better information about the progress of the negotiations in London.

We know relatively little about the negotiations between Charles and his Irish subjects during the third period under consideration, but certain features stand out. By early April 1641 the king had agreed in principle to implement the Irish legislation necessary to secure Old English estates.[39] This was bitterly opposed by some protestant planters, who saw it as putting an end to the process whereby Protestants gained an increasing share of Irish land which could be settled with tenants of their own faith. This group of planters controlled the Irish council after Strafford's impeachment and had friends in England, and they were able to delay the preparation of the legislation in England, but they could not stop it. Thus, by the end of August the necessary bills for this concession as well as others had been prepared in England and dispatched to Ireland for passage through the Irish legislature.[40] This had been prorogued early in August as part of the Irish council's delaying tactics, but it was due to meet again in November, and with royal backing of the bills, passage could be regarded as certain.

Another encouraging sign for the Old English leaders in England over the summer had been the attitude of Robert Sidney, earl of Leicester, who succeeded Strafford as lord lieutenant a week after the execution. Before his appointment, the Old English had feared him as a representative of the puritan faction in England, and undoubtedly his connections with some of those linked to this faction helped him win the position. Leicester, however, was a diplomat and at the time of the appointment as governor of Ireland served Charles as ambassador in Paris, a post he continued to hold even after becoming lord lieutenant.

Although he did not go to Dublin, he seems to have won the confidence
of the Old English representatives in England over the summer, particularly Thomas Preston, viscount Gormanston, who commanded much
respect among the gentry of the Pale. By mid-July Gormanston let it
be known that Leicester had the support of the Irish parliamentary
deputation in England and that, on their return to Ireland, they would
acknowledge his help. Again, early in August, Gormanston reiterated
his support for the new lord lieutenant, and we know from a marginal
entry in Leicester's commonplace book that by about this time he had
concluded that the Irish parliament, under the crown, was autonomous
from the English one, an opinion that would have endeared him to most
Irish MPs and particularly to the Old English.[41] Gormanston returned to
Ireland in August, and it has to be assumed that, as the news about the
bills ratifying the Graces and the attitude of Leicester became known
among Gormanston's confreres in Ireland, interest among the gentry of
the Pale in using force diminished, and this assumption is supported by
Maguire's account of what happened as the conspiracy took shape.

While this process of settlement with the Old English was taking
place, Charles was also reaching a measure of accommodation with his
Scottish subjects. The treaty with the Scots was agreed, and without his
catholic subjects being required to adopt the protestant faith. Despite
opposition in both the English lords and commons, Charles was able to
set out for Scotland on 10 August and meet with his parliament in
Edinburgh on the seventeenth. Four days later the Scots left Newcastle.
The so-called Incident, when courtiers close to Charles were discovered
to be planning to kidnap and possibly murder the two most powerful
Scottish nobles, Hamilton and Archibald Campbell, eighth earl of
Argyll, nearly upset the negotiations. Nevertheless, despite this apparent duplicity on the part of the king, he and the Scottish nobility
ultimately agreed on the composition of a Scottish privy council
which was to rule Scotland upon Charles' return to England.[42] Even in
England, where the forces arrayed against him were more irreconcil-
able than elsewhere, he began making headway in winning a measure
of popular support. As the English army had also disbanded and the
threat from Scotland had disappeared, there were many MPs who were
willing to dissolve parliament. What upset this gradual unwinding of
the dispute was the action of the Ulster Irish on 22 October.

During the various discussions between the Irish catholic leaders
and the crown, the Ulster Irish had been virtually ignored. They too
feared for their faith, but they also had grievances related to their land,
though different ones from those of the Old English. Gaelic Irish gentry
had received considerable grants of land at the time of the plantation in
Ulster, but whereas the British landowners were allowed to purchase
Irish-owned land, the Irish landowners were not allowed to expand
their estates, even by buying the property of other Irishmen. They

complained against this discrimination at the time that other Irish grievances were being aired, but were put off with the promise that Leicester would look into the matter. No Ulster Irish participated in the parliamentary committees that conducted the negotiations in England, and although two of their leaders, Sir Phelim O'Neill and Sir Philip O'Reilly, were elected to parliament, their representation was minimal. They were in short politically isolated.[43]

The alienation of the Ulster Irish went deeper than immediate grievances in that the introduction of English and Scottish settlers into their lands remained fresh and rancorous in their memories. The new arrivals appeared in their eyes as upstarts who often showed scant respect for the ancient inhabitants, and men like Owen Roe O'Neill (c. 1583-1649) regarded themselves as disinherited by the plantation process. Yet, had they been more closely integrated into the political process, it is not inconceivable that they could have been reconciled to the post-plantation regime. Their political isolation precluded this because they could neither communicate their frustrations to a government which was insensitive at the best of times, nor detect any shift in royal policy which might dissuade them from taking up arms. They too made military plans, and Owen Roe made it plain that he regarded the new army as crucial to the use of force. Their isolation helped them in that they were saved from early detection, but unlike the Old English, about whose initial interest in force they had knowledge, they were given no reason to alter their policies.

As is well known, although the Irish rebels initially enjoyed considerable success in Ulster itself, the accompanying plan to capture the seat of Irish government, Dublin Castle, was betrayed at the last moment. As one of the leaders of the rebellion was reported to have remarked soon after its outbreak, the Scots had taught them their 'A.B.C.', but the failure to take Dublin denied the Irish the position of strength from which to negotiate acquired by the Scots when they took Newcastle.[44] Moreover, the very success in Ulster and the subsequent treatment of the protestant settlers there seemed to justify the paranoia of the anti-catholic extremists in England and Scotland. The outbreak of the rebellion therefore transformed the developing politics of accommodation. In Ireland the parliamentary confirmation of Old English land titles was once again postponed and by 1642 a majority of the Old English gentry had joined the Ulstermen in arms. In Britain, Charles and his opponents were agreed that new Scottish and English armies had to be formed if the Irish rebellion was to be suppressed, but neither the king nor the English parliament would entrust the other with control of such armies. It required a civil war in England, in which parliament gained Scottish support, to determine the nature of the military command, and since Oliver Cromwell won that struggle, it was he who led the army that ultimately crushed the rebellion in Ireland.

DESTABILIZING ULSTER, 1641-2

Raymond Gillespie

About eight or nine o'clock in the morning of 23 October 1641 Stephen Allen, sovereign of the town of Cavan, received a visit from Edward Aldrich, sheriff of the neighbouring county of Monaghan. In the normal course of events this would not have been unusual but this visit was not normal. Allen later described Aldrich as 'very much affrighted and dismayed'[1] – not Aldrich's normal demeanour. A Dublin vintner, who had used the wealth acquired in trade to buy an estate of over 500 acres near Clones in county Monaghan, Aldrich was well known for his pride and for his contempt of the native Irish. Hugh Mac Mahon, one of the justices of the peace for Monaghan, had been on the receiving end of this contempt. He related later how in 1640 he had met Aldrich at the Monaghan assize yet Aldrich 'gave him [Mac Mahon] not the right hand of friendship at the assize or session, he being also in the commission of the peace with him' and described the 'proud and haughty carriage of one Mr Aldrich'.[2]

The story Aldrich told Allen was enough to make him 'affrighted and dismayed'. Earlier that morning a group of Irishmen had seized the town of Clones and the strategic castle of Shancock, killing Arthur Champion, the sub-sheriff of Monaghan, and others. Later depositions made by witnesses, including Champion's wife, made it clear who had been murdered.[3] They included Thomas Ironmonger, the clerk of the peace for Monaghan, Humphrey Littlebury, Christopher Linnes, John Morris and Hugh Williams. This murder became one of the talking points of the early months of the rising with stories being told in contemporary pamphlets of how Ironmonger's head had been cleaved from his body on a kitchen table using a hatchet. Aldrich himself escaped to Dublin in a convoy of Protestants from Cavan including the minister Faithful Tate. In Dublin Aldrich joined the government army and was killed in December fighting with the government forces at the siege of Drogheda.[4]

The implications of Aldrich's tale were indeed frightening. Within hours the entire county administration of Monaghan had collapsed. The key royal official, the sheriff, had fled and the other important

Orange banner, Loyal Orange Lodge 273, Portadown No. 1 District.

administrative officials, the clerk of the peace and the sub-sheriff, were dead. Moreover at least one of the rebels, Hugh Mac Mahon a justice of the peace, was a royal official. This pattern of the collapse of local government was repeated all over Ulster. In Cavan one of the leaders of the rising, Mulmore O'Reilly, was the sheriff of the county. In other areas the system was unable to act to restore order. In Donegal Ever Mac Swyne, a justice of the peace, wrote from Ray, in north Donegal, that he feared arresting some of the O'Donnells in that part of the country because he was not powerful enough to do so successfully.[5] In county Down, where most of the sub-sheriffs were among the insurgents, the sheriff managed to hold five sessions of the quarter sessions at which the rebels were duly indicted in their absence. However, given their inability to enforce the indictments, the juries merely issued writs against the rebels to appear at a Dublin court.[6]

This breakdown of the local government system meant also the breakdown of law and order and a consequent panic throughout Ulster. The depositions taken shortly after the rising, which provide evidence of what people believed and said in the early months of the rising rather than a record of objective reality, capture this sense of fear. Outsiders also noticed it. John Galbraith, travelling from Scotland to Dublin through east Ulster in November 1641, observed 'the most woeful desolation that was ever in any country on the sudden is to be seen here. Such is the sudden fear and amazement that has seized all sorts of people that they are ready to run into the sea'.[7] One result was a dramatic fragmentation of society into local groups for mutual protection. One of the earl of Ormond's correspondents in December 1641 reported that attempts in county Down to produce a concerted response to the rising had failed because 'we could not (by any means) draw them [the inhabitants of Down] together from their own towns either to assist one another or to oppose the enemy in any other place (were the occasion never so important) when their own particular interests did not evidently press them unto it'.[8] Local bands for protection were common. At the beginning of the rising in county Antrim Murtagh O'Gilmore 'and presently after all his sons and neighbours gathered together to defend themselves against any that should oppose them'. Meanwhile in county Louth, Brian O'Donnelly 'did keep his own tenants about him with pikes and forks and such kind of weapons as they could get to preserve themselves and their cattle'.[9] Local landlords, such as Sir William Stewart and viscount Ards, who also held military commissions endeavoured to organise their tenants into military groups. Viscount Ards' force at Comber was made up of his tenants armed with 'scythes, cornforks, staffs and a few pikes' and in county Antrim Captain Upton included many of his native Irish tenants among his troop.[10] Not surprisingly protection rackets grew up as soldiers and others offered some groups protection in return for payment.[11]

The outbreak of a rebellion and a disintegration of social order were traumatic partly because the rising was totally unexpected. Many of those settlers in Ulster who later made depositions about their fate in November 1641 expressed their bewilderment at this turn of events. In the years before 1640 most settlers had reached local accommodations with the native Irish. At the upper social levels many native Irish had accepted positions in local and central government. The commander of the insurgents, Sir Phelim O'Neill, was a justice of the peace and was on visiting terms with Sir Toby Caulfield, seizing Charlemont on the pretext of calling on Sir Toby for dinner. Sir Phelim's involvement with government was even greater for he was also a member of parliament, as were Philip O'Reilly, the leader of the rebels in Cavan, and Rory Maguire, their commander in Fermanagh. All three almost certainly knew the murdered Arthur Champion, sub-sheriff of Monaghan and MP for Enniskillen.[12] At the lower social levels there is also evidence of ties of intermarriage, trust, as evidenced by bonds of debt, and landholding between native and newcomer. William Skelton, one of Sir Phelim's tenants at Kinnard, deposed that before the rising natives and newcomers 'differed not in anything...save only that the Irish went to mass and the English to the protestant church'.[13] Other more practised observers of Irish society agreed. Richard Bellings, an Old English Catholic and later secretary to the Confederation of Kilkenny, felt that 'the colonies (setting aside their different tenets in matters of religion) were as perfectly incorporated and firmly knit as frequent marriages, daily ties of hospitality and the mutual bond between landlord and tenant could unite any people'.[14] Most settlers knew their attackers and indeed some rebels inquired of their victims by name and in their claims for losses many, such as John Gourley an Armagh merchant, included lists of debts owed to them by the Irish.[15]

The accommodations between native and newcomer meant that the fear of a native Irish rising which had been ever present in the early days of the Ulster plantation had almost evaporated by the 1630s. The last serious plot, in the eyes of the Dublin government, had been in 1615 and although there were some scares in 1625, coinciding with the threat of a Spanish invasion, rumour and threats of rebellion had largely disappeared by 1630.[16] Men were much less worried about being prepared for a rising than they had been before. In 1630 individual settlers were less well armed than they had been ten years earlier. Whereas in 1619 one Ulster settler in eight owned a musket there was only one between thirty-three in 1630. Even garrisons were poorly equipped. While Newry, Carrickfergus and Londonderry might seem well supplied in 1631 with 120, 20 and 20 muskets respectively the effectiveness of these was limited by a shortage of gunpowder. They did, however, have a rather better supply of pikes with 140, 220 and 250 respectively.[17] By the 1630s settlers were beginning to abandon the heavily fortified castles which they had constructed in the early years of the settlement in favour of Jacobean style manor houses. Sir Toby Caulfield's new house at Castlecaulfield was constructed with almost no defensive features at all and with large windows.[18] The folly of this innovation in the light of later events was well expressed by a Kerry gentleman begging refuge in the earl of Cork's castle: 'my house I built for peace having more windows than walls'.[19]

While close relations between native and newcomer made the outbreak of rebellion in 1641 surprising, there were other prevailing circumstances which were more likely sources of disturbances in 1640 and 1641. The harvests of both those years had been bad and the poor harvest had been compounded by a shortage of labour to gather what had grown since many Scottish settlers in Ulster had fled to Scotland to escape the penal legislation being imposed on them by the Dublin administration. A large army, raised by Dublin for service against the Covenanters in Scotland, was also quartered on Ulster.[20] The result was an economic crisis. As Edward Chichester wrote from Belfast to the earl of Ormond in May 1641:

> the repair of the army hither hath been so on laid with number that the poor people have not the bedding or merchandise to supply them and by that occasion are so much impoverished that they can no longer subsist and the plantation which was here begun and brought to some perfection is now so much ruined...the inhabitants [of Belfast] have spent their whole years provisions and have not wherewith to furnish themselves with necessary victuals to maintain them and their families.[21]

Food riots and civil disturbance were therefore a likely source of disorder and in May 1641 viscounts Ards and Clandeboy wrote to the lords justice in Dublin explaining that recent disturbances in county Down were the result of a shortage of food, seed corn and the quartering of the army in the area.[22]

A rather different potential source of disturbance lay in Scotland. There the presbyterian Covenanters, resentful of Charles I's attempts to impose ecclesiastical innovations on Scotland, had bound themselves together in a National Covenant and had gone to war against England in 1639 and again in August 1640. The attempts by the Irish lord deputy Thomas Wentworth, earl of Strafford, to neutralise support for the Scots from Scottish settlers in Ireland by forcing them to abjure the Covenant and swear an oath of loyalty to the king (the Black Oath) had provoked rioting in Ulster. On one occasion James Forsythe, the rector of Killinchy in county Down, while reading the burial service over a corpse, was pushed from a grave by a crowd including women 'with their laps full of stones and men armed with swords'.[23] The possibility of an invasion from Scotland seems to have been real and rumours were circulating in Ulster that this would happen. Some English settlers in Fermanagh certainly believed that the Irish who went into rebellion were in league with the Scots to extirpate the English in Ireland.[24]

Despite the political improbability of a rebellion given the good social and political relations between native and newcomer, nevertheless the greater likelihood of disruption from other sources was sufficient to create an atmosphere of uncertainty and instability among the settler community. When the rising began they tried desperately to understand and describe the motives of their unexpected attackers. In some cases the motives were painfully obvious. Under cover of the rising planned and led by Sir Phelim O'Neill men began to take revenge for existing grievances. Some rebels stated this as their motive for the murders they committed. The murderer of John West in county Down said 'that will make an end of him, that he shall never write a mittus [a writ] to send me to Down gaol again'. From the settler side Thomas Dixon of Bishopscourt in county Down resolved a dispute between Cormack Mc Guire and Thomas' brother by murdering Cormack.[25] At least some of those who fled from their homes in the early months of the rebellion did so because they feared similar attacks. A Mr Haughton in north Antrim quickly left his house for Lisburn at the outbreak of the rising because he feared Collo Mc Knogher, with whom he had a dispute, would attack him.[26]

A second layer of violence also quickly became indistinguishable from the rising, the on-going criminal activity of theft and assault. Edward More from Cavan, for instance, was attacked on the road to Drogheda and his clothes taken. His attackers fled into the woods daring him to report them as O'Reillys.[27] Other similar events soon became the acts of rebels although they were not tied with either army. Patrick Green in Fermanagh told his employer, Edward Mayor, 'that he would possess himself of his house and estate and knocked Edward on the head with a spade'.[28] Local communities tried to control this sort of activity but with the breakdown of the local government machinery this was difficult. In one north Antrim parish the parish constable was instructed to keep a special watch on Rory Duff Mc Cormick because 'at that time all the parish where he dwelt were very suspicious of him in regard he had been arraigned at the bar at Derry before for villany and also did know him to be a man of very bad carriage'. Mc Cormick, however, assaulted the constable and escaped.[29] Some attacks with the motive of robbery were more sophisticated. The Armagh man Christopher Stanshaw claimed that the rebels had forced him to write out acquittances for debts which they owed him. At a cruder level in Fermanagh Richard and John Weston claimed that rebels threatened 'to kill them if they would not confess where their money was'.[30] Other violence was more directly related to military activity. Ransom, for instance, was a reason for taking prisoners, £18 being given for two ransoms in county Down and £30 for another. Another prisoner, who could not raise the ransom, was hanged.[31] Some violence was simply the result of giving men arms in a situation in which controls on their actions were weak. The attack on the Magees of Islandmagee in early January 1642 by a troop of Scots from Ballymoney is one example of such gratuitous violence as was the drowning of the settlers at Portadown by Toole Mc Cann in November 1641. All sides agreed that such activity was unacceptable. While the leaders of the rising had a strategic plan to gain control of Ulster and use their position of strength to negotiate with Dublin this was quickly destabilised by economic and religious pressures at local level. Native Irish commanders apologised for the actions of the 'lewd people' or the 'common sort of people' but once military action started it was impossible to bring them under control.[32] The anecdotal character of the evidence for the nature of violence in the early months of the rebellion makes it difficult to identify motivation in any meaningful quantitative way but it is clear that a wide diversity of motives was operative.

Despite the apparent chaos many settlers persisted in believing that there was an explanation for the rebellion. To find that explanation they asked the rebels to explain their motives. Some of the stories they heard confirmed their presuppositions about the unreliability of the Irish. Thomas Knowles in Fermanagh was told that the rising had been planned for two years. In Cavan, Mary Bedell was told of a seven year plot and a plot of seventeen years was revealed to one Monaghan deponent. In county Down the abbot of Newry told one deponent that the plot had been laid for eighteen years and that all the original plotters were dead. Others were less specific about the length of time the rising had been under consideration but Henry Steele in Monaghan alleged that lord Maguire and the Roman Catholic primate had been travelling through Ireland for some time to persuade men to join the rising. It is difficult to know how much weight to put on this evidence since by the admission of the plotters the plot was no older than early 1641.[33] Some of the comments may have been the result of the fertile imagination of the deponents convinced that a rising of this magnitude must be the result of careful planning. Some of the conversations may well have been genuine. Those natives who reported apparent careful planning may have been victims of a propaganda war being waged by Sir Phelim O'Neill in Ulster in late 1641.

The second set of stories which were recorded by deponents certainly did not conform to their presuppositions about the native Irish and were the result of the large number of rumours about the plot which were circulating in Ulster. Rebels in Cavan told Paul Mitchell that the plan to seize Dublin Castle on 23 October had been successful and in Monaghan Brian Mac Mahon said that not only Dublin but all

Ireland had been seized. In Armagh Turlough O'Neill claimed that
English noblemen were also involved in the plot and in Fermanagh it
was claimed that not only had Dublin Castle fallen but Edinburgh
Castle and the Tower of London had also been taken. Another type of
victory was claimed in Cavan with rumours of the death of Charles I
and the conversion of his heir to catholicism. In explaining why
the rebellion had occurred most accounts centered on events outside
Ireland. The most common reason given was that the English parliament had passed legislation requiring Catholics to attend the protestant
service or, according to other versions of the rumour, lose their land or
be executed. For this legislation they blamed the Scots who had recently
defeated the king in the second Bishops' War. Some claimed that the
London puritans had already seized the catholic queen, Henrietta Maria,
and intended to execute her. The king, it said in Tyrone, was
already dead, executed by the Scots.[34]

All of these rumours had one feature in common. The rebellion was
not against the king but in support of him against his 'evil councillors'
in the English parliament led by John Pym and his puritan faction.
These rumours gained credence when, on 6 November 1641, Sir Phelim
O'Neill produced a document which he claimed was a commission
from the king for his actions.[35] In fact the document was forged as soon
became clear when other forged commissions appeared all over Ulster,
each leader demanding his own royal document. In Fermanagh Rory
Maguire produced a parchment claiming that it was a warrant from the
king for his actions which Charles had given him in Scotland. In Leitrim
Con O'Rourke produced another document with a royal seal making a
similar claim but it was later discovered that he had manufactured it
from the seal on a patent to his lands of Mohill.[36] To judge from the
number of times these documents were mentioned in later depositions
this propaganda exercise was very effective; one Donegal rebel even
believed that the king himself was due in Ireland on 10 May 1642 to lead
the rising. There were other variants of the story, such as the version in
county Cavan which said that the warrant was from the queen, but the
loyal basis of the rising was consistently emphasised by the rebels using
the forged commission as evidence.[37]

The forged commission and the wild rumours which were circulating about events in other parts of Ireland and England were only partly
spontaneously generated. At least some were deliberately manufactured by Sir Phelim and his council for their own propaganda purposes.
Sir Phelim's decision to stage a local rising on 22 October, the evening
before the main rising was planned on 23 October, meant that he had to
fight a military campaign for which he was singularly ill equipped.[38]
Robert Maxwell, rector of Tynan, claimed that a heavily indebted Sir
Phelim O'Neill had told him that he had £8,000 to spend on the rising
which he reckoned would keep a force together for at most a year.[39]

Moreover it became clear early in the rising that the command structure was fragmenting. In Cavan, accoring to William Wate, the general cry was 'God save king O'Reilly' but in Fermanagh it was Maguire that the rebels wished to make king. Sir Phelim himself was the choice in some other areas, and one deponent claimed that O'Neill had been prayed for at mass as king of Ireland. In county Monaghan a rather unlikely contender had appeared in the person of a lawyer called Nicholas Shergill. A few even looked to Owen Roe O'Neill, then in the Spanish Netherlands.[40] In this situation Sir Phelim had to provide coherence for the movement and a conviction that the rising would succeed. This he did through the forged commission and generating favourable rumours. Richard Bellings recorded in his history of the 1640s that the 'conspirators in Ulster strove to countenance their undertakings with all the fictions and artifices imaginable' which included rumours of outside support and arms, 'at other times receiving letters, penned by themselves, in their most public assemblies, by some unknown messenger instructed in those things which they thought fit to be divulged...others mentioning the access of such and such a nobleman to their party'. Bellings also reported that O'Neill had 'among many other engines he had framed to raise the courage of his party' a machine to make gunpowder which could keep the rebels supplied indefinitely.[41] O'Neill also resorted to the use of prophecy, some of genuine antiquity, such as those of Patrick or Columkille, interpreted in the light of current events and some of dubious origin such that which predicted that Sir Phelim O'Neill would become king of Ireland and, in one extreme form, that he would drive Charles out of England.[42] The importance of these prophecies lies in their political context. Prophecy, the word of God addressed to a holy man, agreed with the royal will, expressed in the forged commission and, from a propaganda position at least, Sir Phelim's position was unassailable. The power of prophecy was such that it was not left to be the tool of the native Irish alone. Henry Jones, later bishop of Clogher, brought a pictorial prophecy, found on an old scroll discovered in the wall of the fort of Newry, predicting the Irish massacres to the London house of commons in 1642. It was solemnly considered by the committee on Irish affairs.[43] The main aim of Jones' mission was not to present the prophecy to the commons but a petition for redress of the losses suffered mainly by the clergy in the early months of the war. The prophecy proved the inevitability of the rising and hence the need for compensation for those who had suffered through neglect of its warning.

The combination of violence, rumour and inspired propaganda severely destabilised settler society in Ulster in late 1641 and early 1642. The social stability, apparent in the 1630s, collapsed under this strain. However, at a popular level this breakdown was not strictly on ethnic or factional lines. From Leitrim the story came of how Thomas Mac

Granald was hung by the rebels 'notwithstanding he was one of their own nation but he went to the protestant church which was without doubt the cause of their quarrel against them'.[44] Religious divisions which had been acceptable and accommodated in times of stability quickly came to the fore in times of uncertainty and instability. Protestant religious symbols such as the bible were foci for attacks by catholic rebels. The bible was torn up at Armagh city and urinated on by Patrick O'Cullane saying 'I would do worse to it if I could' and at Belturbet bibles and protestant books were burnt at the market cross. In Fermanagh the rebels also abused bibles, one saying 'this book hath bred the quarrel'.[45] The religious difference was not about ecclesiastical organisation but rather about interpretations of the sense of what was holy and therefore a mediator of divine will. For Protestants it was the bible which led individuals to an experience of the holy whereas for Catholics it was the mass. Rebels frequently urged settlers to go to mass and when John Cook in Leitrim did so his looted property was restored to him.[46] Attendance at mass was a sign not only of political sympathy, at best it might assure neutrality, but its real significance was that of entering the world of an elect who understood themselves to be doing God's will.

This view stemmed from the stability which a view of divine approbation conferred on a highly unstable situation. The early success of the Irish forces was seen as providential, illustrating that God was on their side. As James MacDonnell wrote from the 'catholic camp' at Oldstone in Antrim to his adversary, Archibald Stewart, 'it is folly to resist what God pleaseth to happen'.[47] In Cavan Philip O'Reilly told one deponent, John Whitman, after the defeat of the English forces at the battle of Julianstown at the end of November 1641, it was done 'by the hand of God'.[48] Religious ceremonies and the use of religious images were common during the early stages of the war. Mass and benediction for the Irish forces at the siege of Drogheda were regular occurrences. At the siege the Irish army was accompanied by a wooden image 'called Mac Kill Murragh (i.e. son of Mary)...and when it first came among them it was received with acclamations of joy like the ark at the camp of Israel'.[49] Irish soldiers going into battle carried prayers such as those to Saint Joan found at Dundalk, a devotion fostered by the Franciscans who were active in Ulster in 1641. There were also prayers with a charm-like quality, deriving from late medieval catholicism, invoking the measure of the wounds of Christ and 'Our Blessed Lady's foot'. Among the wounded of the upper social levels there were some individuals wearing St Francis's girdles. Some Protestants might scoff at the efficacy of these devotional objects but others were less sure. Even Nicholas Bernard, dean of Kilmore and archbishop Ussher's chaplain, observed of the protecting power of religious talismans 'I was slow of believing such fables yet hearing it so often protested unto me by some officers upon their own experience I could not but listen to it'.[50] Many catholic soldiers believed that if they were killed in battle they would go straight to heaven without passing through purgatory.[51] Providential involvement in the early months of the rebellion proved to be a two-edged sword. There was a real fear among military commanders that the uncontrolled looting and gratuitous violence would provoke retaliation from God. Sir Phelim O'Neill, for example, was recorded as saying that he feared God would not bless their endeavours 'because of their murders and cruelties'. Catholic priests ritually cursed some of those involved in massacres because they believed that such crimes might incur the wrath of God.[52]

Such a view of the hand of God at work on behalf of the Irish implied that God could not be at work among the settlers and therefore the settlers must be God's enemies. This view was widely expressed by the rebels. From counties Cavan, Armagh and Monaghan came reports that Protestants were not christians and one rebel is recorded as saying that the English were God's enemies. Margaret Bromley from Armagh was told that Protestants were no christians and had to be baptised at mass. The idea of baptism at mass suggests a belief that it was the mass which was central and that the sacrament of baptism had no validity without it. The most strident statement of this position came from a rebel in Seagoe in county Armagh who said that Protestants 'were all devils and served the devil'.[53] The devil's servants included witches and in north Antrim rebels identified at least one settler, Jeanette Wilson of Ballintoy, as a witch and believed that her witchcraft would be used against the Irish forces.[54] Consequently it became common wisdom among the rebels that it was no sin to kill a Protestant since they were already damned. It is this attitude which lay behind the desecration of protestant graves in counties Fermanagh and Cavan since 'heretics [were] not to be buried in holy ground'.[55]

From a settler perspective, God was indeed at work in the events of 1641 and 1642 but their experience proved that his providential intervention was to protect them. During the rising those who survived encounters with the Irish frequently ascribed their fortune to providence. Edward Philpot of Belturbet, for instance, deposed that 'by God's providence they were brought at length' to Dublin and Captain Thomas Chambers from Armagh deposed that 'by God's providence' he was brought to Dundalk. Others who endured hardship ascribed their strength to supernatural assistance. Ellen Matchet lived in hiding in Armagh for some time and 'they could not have endured and lived but that God almighty gave them still extraordinary strength and patience'.[56] A more direct instance of providential action was provided by Mary Biggot in Cavan who claimed that Turlough O'Reilly was preparing to burn the houses of Protestants in Virginia when 'it pleased God to command and work with the rebels to out-rule him so that that most imminent danger was prevented'.[57] As the war progressed into 1642 settlers felt they saw many more instances of God's providence at work for them as a sign 'for the good that God hath done his Israel' as Robert Cole from Fermanagh observed.[58] The attack by the county Antrim landlord Sir John Clotworthy on Moneymore in early 1642 was seen as a providential intevention for 'just as he was coming the rogues were going to kill one hundred and twenty poor English...but by God's providence his coming was so seasonable that he relieved and rescued all of them and cut off all those who were going to destroy them. Thus did the Lord bring on them what they intended for others'.[59] Similarly the raising of the siege of Drogheda in March 1642, which marked the beginning of the pushing back of O'Neill's force into Ulster, was due to a providential changing of the wind to allow supplies to break the boom which the Irish had built across the river. The raising of the siege provided evidence that 'God, that provides for his and will never suffer the righteous to perish, sent such a storm that their works and endeavours they had used to stop up the river were torn down...thus you see God provides for the distressed'. The settler army was viewed by the settlers as God's army and as it marched from Drogheda 'we had prayers commending them to God's protection which in the greatest expedition was seldom omitted'.[60]

The evidence of divine intervention came not just in the form of interpretation of victories. It was seen also in abnormal occurrences in the natural world. In normal circumstances these might have been ignored but in the trauma of the 1640s they were carefully recorded as supernatural evidence of the revulsion of the divinely appointed natural order at the actions of the Irish. Patrick O'Corry of Loughgall and Francis Leiland of Drumadmore both deposed that at the outbreak of the rebellion in Ulster a river turned to blood which 'pressaged a great mischief and shedding of the English blood'. Rev Robert Maxwell, rector of Tynan, also noted unusual happenings in the early days of the rising and on the night after the murder of Maxwell's brother 'a light was observed in manner of a long pillar to shine for a long way through the air' which was bright enough to read by and lasted for an hour. At Belturbet the rebels reported that since the drownings of some Protestants no fish had been seen in the river.[61]

These abnormalities were not confined to the natural world. The supernatural world was also seen as crying out against the diabolical actions of the rebels. The most spectacular example of this supernatural intervention in the natural world were the ghosts allegedly seen after the massacre of the Protestants on the bridge at Portadown in late 1641.[62] Catherine Cook deposed that about nine days after the event 'a vision or spirit in the shape of a woman appeared in that river in the place of the drowning, bolt upright and breast-high with elevated and closed hands and stood in that posture there until the latter end of Lent next following'. Other descriptions from the depositions agree with Cook's. Rev Robert Maxwell's description, although hearsay, was the most dramatic, observing that the spirits 'were seen daily and nightly to walk upon the river, sometimes singing of psalms, sometimes brandishing of naked swords, sometimes screeching in a most hideous and fearful manner'. The deposition of Elizabeth Price provided a similar description to that of Catherine Cook of 'a vision or spirit assuming the shape of a woman waist-high in the water with elevated and closed hands, her hair dishevelled, very white, her eyes seemed to twinkle in her head and her skin as white as snow which spirit or vision seeming to stand straight upright in the water divulged and then repeated the word "Revenge, revenge, revenge"'. The vision continued to appear for some time and attempts to exorcise it both by protestant and catholic clergy were unsuccessful and the Irish ascribed it to witchcraft. According to Cook it only disappeared when the settler force reached the town, when it was seen by some of the soldiers including her own husband. Whatever appeared on the river frightened many of the native Irish who, deponents said, moved away from the area as a result. Portadown was not the only example of this phenomenon. After the drowning of Protestants at the bridge at Belturbet in county Cavan, Henry Baxter deposed that there had been 'strange visions and apparitions commonly seen on the waters of Belturbet . . . and some of them a year after the English were drowned there'. In county Down Sir Conn Magennis was haunted on his death bed by the ghost of a protestant minister killed at the capture of Newry yet 'still in his presence'.[63]

Given this widespread protestant view of divine intervention on their behalf the conclusion the settlers could draw was that the catholic Irish were not in God's favour and hence were his enemies. The enemies of God were seen as the allies of the devil who had entered a pact with Antichrist. Some saw this diabolical pact manifested in witchcraft. Major James Turner, for instance, marching with a Scottish force through the Mourne mountains in May 1642 'suffered one of the most stormy and tempestuous nights for hail, rain, cold and excessive wind that I ever saw'. The soldiers of his troop 'attributed this hurricane to the devilish skill of some Irish witches'.[64] Such a view accorded with the more general European current of thought which identified the Antichrist of the book of Revelation with the papacy. This interpretation provided further validation of the diabolical contract made by the catholic rebels in Ulster which seemed to explain the rebels' actions so plausibly.

One problem remained with this explanation of the events of late 1641. If God had intervened providentially against the rebels to protect the settlers then why had he allowed the rebellion to occur in the first place and why had he held back during the initial Irish successes. The Irish made the most of this reality. According to Elizabeth Croker in county Down, viscountess Iveagh 'did bid this deponent and her distressful company call down their God and see if he would save them and their clothes and speaking other prophane words' and in Fermanagh some women were stripped, the 'rebels bidding them go and look for their God and let him give them clothes'.[65] Such taunts were not easily answered. The explanation which evolved incorporated a view of providence which was conditional on man's behaviour. Sir John Temple, for example, trying to make sense of the events of the early 1640s some years later explained that God had allowed it to happen as a punishment on the settlers for their sins

> the iniquities of the English nation which were very great in this kingdom were now full: heaven and earth seemed to conspire together for the punishment of them. God certainly declared his high indignation against them for their great sins ... and suffered the barbarous rebels to be instruments of mischief as the cruel executioners of his wrath against them.[66]

Unfortunately for the Irish they enjoyed the role of agent too much and Temple argued that God would punish them likewise for this. Temple's view of why God allowed the rebellion were shared by James Ussher, archbishop of Armagh, who in his sermon before the Long Parliament in London on 22 December 1641 spoke of the rebellion as the consequence of the sins of the settlers.[67] Those in Drogheda when Sir Phelim O'Neill's force besieged it late in 1641 had a similar view. They greeted the news of an approaching Irish force by 'a great congregation' going to church where 'we there spent time in a sorrowful confession of our sins, acknowledged God's justice in their punishment, begged pardon and implored his succouring of us'.[68] The exact nature of the settlers' sin was for some time unclear until Roger Puttock, minister of Kentstown in county Meath clarified the situation in a pamphlet of 1642: 'for our sufferings I doubt not that they have wrought much good in many of us. We were doting before on Rome and her idolatories, now her cruelties cause a great loathing of her and her doctrine. Before we were wedded to the world, now weaned from it and I hope they shall work a greater measure of grace here and glory hereafter'.[69] Thus the consensus of the 1630s on social and economic matters became a feature of the past. The violence of the rebellion and the religious fears it had aroused would not be quickly forgotten.

The months of late 1641 and early 1642 were profoundly disturbing times for Ulster people of all persuasions. There was the problem of a war which was going badly out of the control of the military commanders. Looting, revenge, and gratuitous violence came to dominate those months much to the concern of both military commanders and clergy. An economic crisis, partly natural and partly created by the political events of 1640 and 1641, made the problems even more acute. This situation was made worse by wild rumour, encouraged at least in part by Sir Phelim O'Neill and his council for their own propaganda purposes. To win they needed men to fight, to fight they needed assurance of legitimacy and of supplies. O'Neill generated both by rumour. For the settlers these rumours were profoundly disturbing. Not only had the social fabric of Ulster been rent apart by the collapse of the administration and violence but those developments were alleged to have been sanctioned by the guarantor of stability and order, the king himself. In this situation fear and instability were the factors which made men such as Edward Aldrich 'very much affrighted and dismayed'. To provide certainties they turned to the unchanging truths of religion. However the popular understanding of those unchanging truths was precisely the factor which so many commentators agreed was the main source of division between native and newcomer. It was all the more divisive because each group perceived themselves in the same way. Settlers saw themselves as God's 'Israel', guided by his providence, and the Irish as the Maccabees 'fighting for God's cause'.[70] Each side validated its understanding by interpreting the events around them within a providential framework in which only they were the favoured group. Prophecy, wonders and supernatural experiences were all pressed into service to this end. The defection of the gentry of the Pale to the Ulster cause in December 1641 and the beginning of civil war in England in August 1642 complicated this situation by adding other factions, each with its own view of providence, to make it 'a war of many parts, carried on under the notion of so many interests, perplexed with such diversity of rents and divisions among those who seemed to be of a side'.[71] There could be no meeting of minds only of swords.

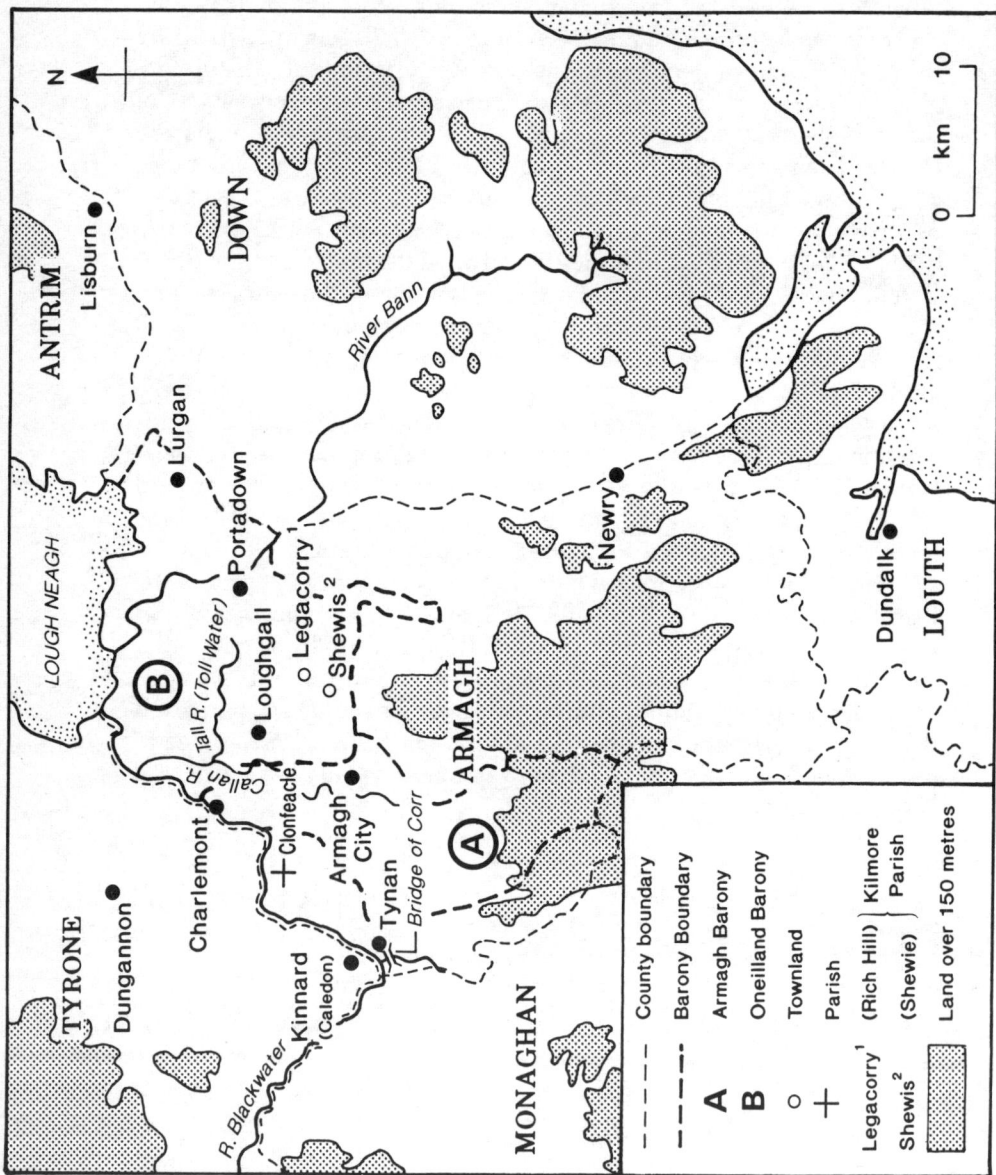

N

ANTRIM

DOWN

Lisburn

Lurgan

Portadown

LOUGH NEAGH

River Bann

Newry

Legacorry
Shewis²
Loughgall

B

Tall R. (Toll Water)

Callan R.

Clonfeacle

Charlemont

Armagh City

ARMAGH

A

Tynan

Bridge of Corr

Kinnard (Caledon)

R. Blackwater

TYRONE

Dungannon

MONAGHAN

LOUTH

Dundalk

0   km   10

County boundary
Barony Boundary
A Armagh Barony
B Oneilland Barony
o Townland
+ Parish
Legacorry¹ (Rich Hill) ⎫ Kilmore
Shewis²   (Shewie)   ⎬ Parish
Land over 150 metres

VIOLENCE IN COUNTY ARMAGH, 1641

Hilary Simms

The main evidence of violence in Armagh in 1641 is contained in the County Armagh volume of the 1641 Depositions. These are the collected accounts of witnesses, most of whom were victims of the 1641 rebellion.[1] This article is based on a detailed study of the Armagh volume of the Depositions, in which the different accounts of massacres and individual murders were compared. The evidence was carefully examined and assessed in order to quantify the extent of the violence and to get a clearer picture of what happened in Armagh over 350 years ago.[2]

In the first part of the seventeenth century the plantation of Ulster had brought many British settlers to live in the planted counties which included Armagh and it was in Armagh that the 1641 rising started. In the plantation scheme for county Armagh Oneilland barony was assigned to English undertakers, Lower Fewes to Scottish undertakers and Orior to servitors and natives. There were some exceptional areas in county Armagh where specific grants were made. Sir Turlough McHenry O'Neill was granted the Upper Fewes. Trinity College was granted half of Armagh barony and the other half went to the established church and other servitors. The barony of Tiranny was granted to the church and to natives. As the plantation progressed Oneilland barony in north Armagh became one of the areas most densely populated by English settlers. By 1630 it contained the greatest concentration of settlers in the county and this meant that by 1641 there were considerably more English than Scottish settlers in county Armagh.[3]

The 1641 Depositions mainly cover events in the period from October 1641–May 1642. The lords justice [heads of the government in Dublin] appointed eight protestant clergymen led by Henry Jones dean of Kilmore, and by two commissions in December 1641 and January 1642 they were empowered to take evidence of all robberies and murders.[4] The witnesses were encouraged to give evidence of other people's sufferings. This meant that much hearsay evidence was included as witnesses reported incidents about which they had been told. In 1652 the Cromwellian commissioners, who ruled Ireland at that time, set up a High Court of Justice whose members, including Henry Jones, collected evidence of murders for the trials of Irish rebels.[5] The Armagh volume is particularly interesting as it contains 52 depositions to the 1642 commission and 50 examinations taken by the 1652 commission.[6] The evidence is mainly given by protestant settlers but the witnesses include some Irish rebels. Only two of the witnesses were examined by both commissions so direct comparison is limited but it does reveal that the 1652 commission had a more precise approach as its evidence was to be used in the trials of the Irish leaders. However the 1652 commissioners did not use this approach to re-examine the evidence given in a 1642 deposition but rather to supplement it.

When examining the 1641 Depositions for evidence of violence in Armagh at that time, the simplest approach is to identify the different massacres and murders and look at the evidence for each one separately. One of the most notorious massacres was the drowning of a large group of people in Portadown. A number of English protestant settlers was imprisoned in Loughgall church and taken in convoy to Portadown where they were drowned in the River Bann. This is the episode used by some historians to support the theory that the Irish had planned to kill all the protestant settlers in Ulster. Undoubtedly it was the largest massacre in Armagh and in the Depositions it was the most frequently mentioned incident both in 1642 and 1652. Altogether twenty-eight people described it although some of them only gave the number of people they believed to have been drowned there. As there are so many accounts it is possible to group the evidence according to whether it is direct experience or hearsay. When this is done it emerges that only one witness, William Clark, was present at the Portadown massacre. His account is particularly important as he is one of only two people who gave evidence both in 1642 and 1652.[7] Four other witnesses were imprisoned in Loughgall church but were not taken to Portadown.[8] Five witnesses had relatives who were drowned there and eighteen gave hearsay evidence.

William Clark gives the best account of what happened. In the 1642 deposition he describes himself as a 'Brittish protestant' and says that he was 'imprisoned for the space of nine days with at the least 100 men women and children during which time manie of them were sore tortured by strangling and halfe hanging' ... 'after which time of imprisonment hee with an 100 men women and children or thereabouts weer' ... 'driven like hogs about six miles to a river called the band [Bann]' ... 'and there [the Irish] forced them to goe upon the Bridge which was cut down in the midst and then striped the said people naked and with theire pikes and swords and other weapons thruste them down headlong in to the said river and immediately they perished and those of them that asayed to swim to the shore the rebels stood to shoot at'.[9] Ten years later he was examined by the 1652 commission. Here he says that he 'with such other English as they [the Irish] could find to the number of threescore persons which belonged to the said Parish of Loughgall and putt them all into the Church there and did sett a Guard over them and from there took then to Porte of Doune [Portadown]' . . . 'and that such English as they met then [they] did take them alongst with the rest which were in all at their comeing to Porte of Doune about an hundred persons – where they were all drowned at that time'. William Clark himself 'purchased his life then by giveing unto them fifteen pounds'.[10] This account shows clearly the different approach of the 1652 commission which recorded the basic facts but did not include all the description that is in the 1642 deposition. The two accounts are very similar as regards the sequence of events and the number of people drowned and they are very good sources of evidence for this mass drowning.

When studying this evidence it is hard to understand why the prisoners were taken in convoy and then drowned as there is a large lake beside Loughgall church. William Clark said it was Manus Roe O'Cane who imprisoned him in the church. This is confirmed by Richard Newberry who described O'Cane as the captain of the Irish rebels around Loughgall.[11] John Warren who was also imprisoned in the church said that Sir Phelim O'Neill came and told them that they would be deported to England.[12] Other witnesses, who were giving hearsay evidence about this, said they heard that the convoy was intended to deport the English from Armagh and several destinations such as Dundalk and Lisnegarvey [Lisburn] were cited.[13] It is clear from all this evidence that a convoy of English protestants left Loughgall believing that they were to be deported to England. When it reached Portadown this convoy was suddenly drowned. Not one of the witnesses gives a definite reason or explanation.

There is much confusion as to who was responsible and what was the motive. One of only two witnesses who said that Sir Phelim O'Neill had ordered the massacre was in Fermanagh when it happened.[14] William Clark said he heard the Irish say that they were commanded by Sir Phelim O'Neill but added that he himself was not sure who did it.[15] Part of the confusion as to who was responsible may have arisen from the fact that the convoy came under the control of another Irish leader. Manus O'Cane was the captain of the Irish rebels in the Loughgall area and two witnesses believed he ordered the drowning.[16] Toole McCann was the Irish leader who took control of Portadown when the rebellion began and a number of witnesses said that he was responsible for drowning the convoy at Portadown.[17] Valentine Blacker gave evidence, undated, that he saw a warrant of execution written by Sir Phelim O'Neill which was given to Toole McCann three days before the mass drowning at Portadown.[18] However this was not mentioned by Toole McCann when he was examined in 1653 and he simply said that 'he never saw any drowned att Portedaune, But he heard of itt'.[19] Other convoys had been sent to Newry and Carrickfergus on Sir Phelim O'Neill's orders and had arrived safely [20] so there does not have seem to have been a general plan to massacre convoys of prisoners.

The date of the massacre is of some importance when trying to establish who was responsible. William Clark and the other witnesses in Loughgall church say it happened soon after the rebellion began or a few weeks after 23rd October 1641. Allowing for the days spent in Loughgall church it would seem to have happened about the middle of November. At that time Toole McCann was in control of the area around Lurgan and Portadown. The convoy entered his area of control and it would seem likely that even if he did not order it he and his men could not have avoided being involved in it to some degree. It would therefore seem most likely that it was Toole McCann who was responsible for the drowning of a convoy which had come into an area under his control.

One of the most disputed facts about this massacre is the number of people who were drowned in the Bann at Portadown. This is the one detail which is included in all the accounts. The totals range from 80 to 380. William Clark, the only eye-witness, said in 1642 that 100 were drowned and he repeated this figure ten years later. Similar low figures were given by the witnesses who were in Loughgall church. Richard Newberry said it was 80, Nehemiah Richardson and John Warren both said it was 100. Those who only heard about the massacre tended to give higher totals, averaging about 160. Those who deposed latest under the 1642 commission tended to be the most exaggerated. In 1644 Katherin Cook said 180 were drowned and Anthony Stratford gave a figure of 308.[21] As the eye-witness and those who were imprisoned in Loughgall church with him gave very similar totals it would seem reasonable to conclude that a convoy of about 100 British protestant prisoners were drowned at Portadown in the middle of November 1641, probably by Toole McCann and his men.

This was an horrific killing but there does not appear to have been a plan to kill them when they were first captured. This massacre obviously terrified the protestant settlers and the reports of the numbers involved grew and were used as evidence of a conspiracy to massacre protestants. Henry Jones was the leading member of the 1642 commission and used the evidence in the depositions in his 'Remonstrance'. He read this out to the English parliament in March 1642 to show how the protestant settlers were being attacked and massacred. The extracts from the depositions that he quoted were, with one exception, all based on hearsay evidence and the 'Remonstrance' shows the strong anti-Irish and anti-catholic bias of Henry Jones who was so influential in both the 1642 and the 1652 commissions.[22]

An interesting version of this massacre is given by a British officer in Sir John Clotworthy's regiment. He said that he made inquiries about the 1641 massacres and concluded that the worst one was at Portadown. He wrote: 'the most that were there drowned and murdered exceed not ninety persons' . . . 'My ground for the same is that I had the same account from an Englishman, who had the good fate to escape that day, and from some of the Irish that were spectators and liked not that inhumanity and unchristianlike murder'.[23] It is interesting to note how this total is close to that of the only eye-witness.

After Portadown the massacre at Shewie, a mile from Legacorry, is one of the most reported incidents. The main facts are that a number of protestant settlers were herded into a house and burnt alive. The evidence in the depositions contains some of the most precise information that is given about any of the massacres. This is due to the fact that two people who escaped out of the burning house gave evidence to the 1642 commission and the witnesses who gave hearsay evidence about it lived in the parish of Kilmore where it happened. Ann Smith and her daughter Margaret Clark described how they were driven into a thatched house belonging to Ann Smith along with many other English and Scots protestants.[24] The rebels were led by Jane Hampson of Legacorry who, according to another witness, was 'formerly a protestant but a meere [pure, unmixed] irish woman and lately turned to Masse'.[25] The unfortunate victims begged her to let them out but she 'being resolute to destroy them by that way sayd she would be a Blacksmith amongst them' and fastened the door, the house having already been set on fire. Ann Smith and Margaret Clark managed to escape by breaking through a hole in the wall. The rebels outside knocked them both on the head and left them for dead. They later escaped and survived to give evidence in March 1643. Unfortunately they gave no date nor could they give the exact number of those killed. They named ten people who died there and said that the others were strangers who had been brought there the previous day.[26]

A number of witnesses gave hearsay evidence about the massacre at Shewie and again the totals vary a great deal. Jane Grace who lived in the parish said that 22 were burnt alive.[27] Joan Constable who also lived in the parish heard about the burning which she said happened about Candlemas [February 1642]. She named 19 people whom she knew to have perished there.[28] Some of these were also named by Ann Smith and when the two lists are compared they contain the names of 16 adults and 10 children. Having so many names, some of them given by an eyewitness, means that there is very strong evidence of the numbers killed in this massacre. Robert Maxwell heard that, 'Att Sir Phelim's returne from Lisnegarvey some of his soldiers forced about 24 brittish into a house where they burned them alive'.[29] Although he does not say it took place at Shewie it seems likely that he was referring to it as there is no evidence of any other group being burnt alive in Armagh at the time and also Shewie is near the main road between Lisnegarvey and

Armagh. Other totals given in evidence as to the number of people who died at Shewie are 44[30], 60[31] and 90.[32] All the above evidence was given to the 1642 commission. Andrew Hutchenson of Hockley who was examined by the 1652 commission said that he was passing by Shewie one day when he saw smoke and was told that 30 people were being burnt alive in a house.[33] So although many of the witnesses are only giving hearsay evidence they tend to corroborate the eye-witnesses' accounts. It seems clear that up to 30 protestant settlers were burnt alive in a house at Shewie in the parish of Kilmore. The Irish rebels who did it were local and were possibly helped by Sir Phelim O'Neill's men who were returning after their defeat at Lisnegarvey in November 1641, or it may have happened at the beginning of February 1642. There is no evidence that this massacre was ordered by the Irish leaders and it appears that it was carried out by local Irish rebels and the only motive appears to be the fact that the victims were English or Scots Protestants.

The massacres at Portadown and Shewie were unquestionably horrific occurrences which happened during the early months of the 1641 rebellion but do not appear to have been planned or ordered by Sir Phelim O'Neill. They seem rather to have been carried out by local leaders acting independently. The massacre of a group of people from Armagh city was not a spontaneous atrocity by local rebels but was done with Sir Phelim's knowledge if not on his orders. It also differs from the other massacres in that it happened later on in the rebellion after a large Scots army had landed in Ulster to help the English and Scots settlers.

In October 1641 Sir Phelim O'Neill had no apparent plans to massacre the English and Scots settlers. He took Charlemont on the night of Friday 22nd October. When the people in Armagh city heard of this they fled to the cathedral for safety. It was strategically situated on top of a hill around which the city of Armagh was built. Some people such as Wilfred Bently and Thomas Dixon[34] came from their homes outside Armagh to shelter there. The citizens prepared to defend themselves. Thomas Chambers, a large landowner, said that he and others wrote to the British in the country roundabout 'to repayre unto us to Armagh with their Horses, Armes and families that there we might make a Head for our best advantage and strength, not only to secure ourselves, but in the best way to oppose the insurrecion'.[35]

Sir Phelim O'Neill came to Armagh with an army of several hundred[36] on Tuesday 26th October and started negotiating with the sovereign [mayor] of Armagh, Richard Southwicke.[37] Southwicke's niece, Mary Brabazon, said that 'the conditions were that all the inhabitants of the said toune should bee preserved in their lives and goods and that the said Sir Phelim alleadged that what he did was for the king's service and that he had a Commission for his doeinge what he did and there upon showed her uncle the Soveraigne as her uncle reported a great seale'.[38] This is evidence of Sir Phelim's claim to be fighting for Charles I and the catholic religion against the English protestant parliament. Sir Phelim kept his promise to spare their lives and most of them were held under some form of house arrest.[39] Thomas Dixon was told by Sir Phelim to 'go home and keep his mill and that dureing the warres he should pay no rent'.[40] Leading Englishmen were sent from other places to prison in Armagh such as Sir William Brownlow, who had surrendered his castle at Lurgan, and Nicholas Simpson, one of the knights for Monaghan.[41] John Kerdiff, a Tyrone clergyman, commented in February 1642 that 'att Armagh some of the English fared but somewhat better for thogh all their beasts abroad were taken from them yet many of them enioyed whatsoever they had within their houses'.[42] Phelim O'Neill made Thady Crawly sovereign of Armagh and he was 'very favorable unto the English then imprisoned there'.[43] However later on Turlogh Oge O'Neill's wife, 'beeing a woemen of a hautie and high spiritt thinkinge anythinge to[o] much that passed by herself persuaded her husband to take upon him the Government of the town'.[44] He was Sir Phelim's brother and while some individuals were killed in Armagh during that time[45] there is no direct evidence of any massacre before May 1642.

On 1st May 1642 a large Scots army landed at Carrickfergus and took Newry from the Irish on 5th May. On 6th May Armagh was burnt. There is a good deal of hearsay evidence of a general massacre in Armagh city but little precise detail. The evidence of the twelve witnesses who were in Armagh at the time is not very detailed. Eight of them merely say that many were killed in Armagh. Isabella Gowrley, who escaped from Armagh said that 70 people were killed when the city was burnt.[46] However, although it is hard to find precise evidence of a massacre taking place in Armagh itself, there is evidence of a large group of people being taken away from Armagh just before it was set on fire and this group was then massacred in or near Charlemont. Two of the witnesses say that there were 50 people in the group.[47] John Henderson said he and 40 others were imprisoned in Armagh and then brought to Charlemont at the beginning of May where 36, 19 of whom he named, were drowned in the Toll water. He managed to ransom himself. He also said that another group of about 20 people was taken away by Edmund Crawly just before Armagh was burnt.[48] This is corroborated by William Sym who said that he was in a group taken from Armagh to Charlemont by Captain Crawly and he [William Sym] was saved because he was a saddler and was set to work for the Irish. The rest of the group was taken away and murdered.[49]

In conclusion, it is clear that at least one large group, which was sent from Armagh to Charlemont, was subsequently massacred. Twenty-four of the group are named and other hearsay accounts have named these people as having been killed in Armagh. There is little evidence for a massacre in the city itself but this group of around 40 people was either drowned in a river near Charlemont or massacred on the road to Dungannon. Sir Phelim O'Neill was in control of Armagh at the time and must bear ultimate responsibility for this killing which happened after the taking of Newry. Sir Phelim himself said at his trial, 'that at the Newry the English and Scotch put all to the sword and not till then was any blood shed by his party'.[50] It is interesting to note that all the evidence for the Armagh massacre was given to the 1652 commission whose aim was to collect evidence for the trials of the Irish leaders. The examinations show that the commissioners tried to obtain as much detail as possible from the witnesses.

Sir Phelim O'Neill lived at Kinnard [Caledon], near Tynan, and what is unusual about the massacre at Kinnard is that it was Sir Phelim's tenants who were killed. William Skelton worked as a husbandman for Sir Phelim before the rebellion. He described how the protestants then lived peacefully on Sir Phelim's land and were on good terms with their Irish neighbours 'and differed not in anything ... save only that the Irish went to Masse and the English to the Protestant church in Tinan'. He described how the rebellion started and the Irish led by Nocher O'Hugh began robbing and then murdering the English. William Skelton named 18 people, including the nurse who worked for Sir Phelim, who were all killed one night about Christmas 1641.[51] Joan Constable was near Kinnard at the time and said that the sept of the Hughs murdered many protestants in Kinnard one night. She listed 28 people including most of those named by William Skelton. Her former servant, Rory O'Hugh, warned her the next day not to go to Kinnard, for 'she might goe above the soales of her shooes in bloud there'.[52] Michael Harrison, Sir Phelim's secretary, mentions that 'in November 1641 itt was generally reported thatt there were 20 or 30 persons cruelly murthered in Kinnard by the sayd Hughs'.[53] Joseph Travers stayed at Kinnard from October 1641 until the end of January 1642. He said a number of English there were murdered before the end of December and he reported a conversation he had with Sir Phelim on 31st December 1641. O'Neill told him that some of his followers 'have murdered my nurse and the child whom they knew my wife loved and respected and brought her out of England but I have beene revenged in them for I have hanged eight or nine of them for it'.[54] Joseph Travers then described the murder of Lord Caulfield at Kinnard which happened at the end of January 1642. Travers said that the murderers, one of whom was a Hugh, got drunk that night and murdered 21 of Sir Phelim's tenants. This account is corroborated by Major Patrick Dory who was told by an Irish soldier that 15 were killed in Kinnard that night.[55] The witnesses differ considerably as to the date of the massacre at Kinnard but it seems clear that in December 1641 or January 1642 at least 32 of Sir Phelim's tenants were murdered, as 20 adults and 12 children are named as having died at this time. It appears to have been done without Sir Phelim's knowledge or consent by some of his men including the Hughs and, again, was a spontaneous rather than a planned operation.

The violence in county Armagh that has been examined in detail so far consists of different massacres, that is to say, the killing of groups of unarmed defenceless people by Irish rebels. The attack on Lurgan was rather different and could be seen more as a battle than a massacre. There were several eyewitnesses of the events in Lurgan around 1st November 1641 and they all were examined by the 1652 commission. According to two of them Toole McRory McCann and Art Oge McGennis led the Irish rebels in an attack on Lurgan and some people were killed.[56] Other witnesses said that the rebels took Lurgan and the next day an agreement was made whereby Sir William Brownlow surrendered on promise of quarter.[57] William McGinn described the events in Lurgan as follows: 'that upon a Skirmish thatt passed betweene the forsayd party and the inhabitants of that town before the quarter given to the sayd Castle he saw dead uppon the plane John Davys; Leonard Rigg; Richard Rimholt; Doctor Thomas the shoemaker and Thomas Ward'.[58] From the different accounts of the witnesses 15 people are named as having been killed but it seems they were killed in the skirmish when Lurgan was taken and were not unarmed prisoners who were massacred.

The massacres or killing of groups of people in Armagh in 1641 and 1642 which have been examined in some detail above are those for which there is strong evidence in the depositions, that is to say, eyewitness accounts or lists of named people killed together with a number of reports and descriptions of the massacre. In this way it has been possible to establish approximate numbers of those killed in the massacres at Portadown, Shewie, Kinnard, the attack on Lurgan and the people taken from Armagh. The other massacres mentioned in the depositions are those for which there is only hearsay evidence. In order to establish how many people may have been killed in these alleged massacres different criteria have been used. If there were several witnesses who gave hearsay evidence of a massacre with corroborating details as to time and place then it was included in the total of numbers massacred. However if there was only the hearsay evidence of one witness about a massacre then it was omitted.

On this basis there are several accounts of a massacre where a group of people was drowned in or near Loughgall by the wife of Brian Kelly, a rebel captain.[59] Three witnesses gave totals for those drowned ranging from 12 to 23 and the fourth said 45. For the purposes of reaching an estimate of the total numbers massacred in county Armagh it is presumed that at least 12 and at most 45 were drowned near Loughgall by Brian Kelly's wife. Another massacre for which there is considerable hearsay evidence is where a number of people were drowned in a bog near Loughgall. Jonathan Richardson knew one of those drowned and was shown the victim's clothes afterwards by Tirlagh O'Donnell who told him that 16 had been drowned. Michael Harrison gave a figure of18.[60] The other two witnesses simply gave the totals of people drowned there which are '30 or 40' and 100.[61] In this case it is worth noting that the witness with most detail gave the lowest total of 16.

A number of witnesses describe hearing of the drowning of a large group of people at the bridge of Corr which is on a tributary of the Blackwater which runs between Tynan and Kinnard. The totals given of those drowned vary a great deal and are as follows: 38, 60, 120 and 144.[62] Two accounts say this massacre happened at the beginning of May 1642 after Newry was taken. Thomas Chambers was staying in Tynan at that time and said that 20 people were taken from Tynan and drowned in the river a mile away.[63] There is no way of knowing which is the correct figure for those drowned but again it is interesting to see that the lowest total of 20 is given by a witness who was staying nearby at the time. Another alleged massacre was the disappearance of a large number of people from Armagh somewhere in county Tyrone near the Armagh border. Michael Harrison who lived in Clonfeacle parish in that area said that in May 1642, 150 people were taken from county Armagh and placed in small groups among the Irish creaghts [semi-nomadic herdsmen] in Tyrone. This was ordered by Sir Phelim O'Neill and 'the cause of theire removall was for feare they should joyne with the English'.[64] They were all murdered the next night except for one who was saved by Harrison. John Parry confirms that Harrison saved one person and Thomas Chambers gives the same details as Harrison including the total of 150.[65] Like the drowning at the bridge of Corr this alleged massacre of 150 is said to have happened in May 1642 after Newry was captured by the Scots army.

As well as massacres of groups of people there was a large number of individual murders. Individual in this context is taken to mean one or a few people killed in an incident which was not part of a massacre. The most notable person to be killed was Lord Caulfield. He was shot by Edmund Boy O'Hugh on Sir Phelim O'Neill's land at Kinnard. This murder was witnessed by William Skelton.[66] Sometimes people were listed as having been murdered when they may have in fact escaped. Humphrey Stewart listed William Taylor and his family among those drowned at Portadown whereas William Clark, the only eyewitness of that massacre said that he himself escaped from it together with William Taylor.[67] Although evidence of individual murders was often given by eyewitnesses, in many other cases there is only hearsay evidence. In order to estimate the total number of individuals murdered all the depositions and examinations in the Armagh volume have been care-fully read. All possible references to identifiable people who died as a result of the rebellion have been collected together. All references to dead bodies which were not named have been excluded as in some cases they could have been named in another deposition. This evidence was then graded according to the best evidence for each murder as follows: [a] if the witness saw the murder being committed; [b] if he/she saw the body; [c] if he/she was a spouse or relative of the victim; [d] if he/she heard about the murder from reliable sources i.e. if the source of information could be named; and [e] if he/she heard about the murder as a rumour or a common report. When the evidence of individual murders was graded in this way there are 40 murders in category [a], 12 in [b], 36 in [c], 39 in [d] and 97 in [e]. In other words there is eyewitness evidence of 40 individual murders, a further 12 bodies were identified, 36 murders were reported by relatives and spouses. These first three categories provide very strong evidence of murders and together total 88. A further 39 murders were reported by witnesses who heard of them from reliable sources. However by far the largest number, 97, is in the category of rumour or common report. There is also evidence that 30 people died as a result of the rebellion and 12 of these died in prison.[68] This attempt to assess the evidence of individual murder does reveal a high proportion of reported murders for which there is only hearsay evidence.

The numbers killed in the massacres are only an approximation. As it is impossible to obtain exact figures for each incident it may be useful to add up the highest totals and the lowest totals. For the Portadown massacre the lowest total was 80 and the highest was 380. At Shewie the lowest was 22 and the highest was 90. At Kinnard the lowest was 18 and the highest was 30. At Lurgan there is only one total of 16. The massacre of people from Armagh city was at least 36 and at most 50. If the figures for alleged massacres are added up the lowest total is 198 and the highest is 439. As regards individual murders there is strong evidence [categories [a]–[d]] that 127 were murdered and it could be assumed to be the lowest total. The highest total for individual murders is reached by adding on the 97 in category [e] which brings it to 224.

The following table illustrates this more clearly:

Type	Lowest	Highest
Portadown	80	380
Shewie	22	90
Kinnard	18	30
Lurgan	16	16
Armagh	36	50
Other Alleged Massacres	198	439
Individual Murders	127	224
Deaths as Result of War	30	30
Totals	**527**	**1259**

To sum up, the lowest total of people recorded in the depositions as having been massacred or murdered is 527. The highest total including all hearsay evidence and rumour is 1259. So an examination of all the evidence shows that on the lowest estimate less than 600 people died as a result of the violence in Armagh from November 1641 to May 1642. Allowing for all the rumours and the highest totals the greatest number that could be said to have died in county Armagh is less than 1300 people. There is no doubt that a large number of people were massacred and murdered, some in the most appalling and cruel ways. However the estimated totals, given above, are far below the figures given by some of the witnesses. Elizabeth Greene said that the rebels drowned over 4,000 people in county Armagh alone.[69] Robert Maxwell estimated that 154,000 were killed in Ulster[70] and this last figure has been one of the most frequently quoted totals by some historians. Considering that some of the worst violence in Ulster at this time took place in county Armagh even multiplying the highest total for Armagh by nine in order to get an estimate for the nine counties of Ulster would still bring the total for Ulster to less than 12,000. This admittedly hypothetical figure gives one some idea of the degree to which Robert Maxwell was exaggerating.

Having looked at the violence in Armagh it is interesting to examine the background of those who gave evidence to the commissions. Most of them were British protestants who settled in Armagh during the Ulster plantation and had been living there for less than thirty years. Two-thirds of the witnesses lived in the barony of Oneilland which was, according to the Book of Survey and Distribution from the mid-seventeenth century, the most fertile barony in county Armagh.[71] In the Ulster plantation it was allotted to the English undertakers. A further quarter of the witnesses lived in Armagh barony where most of the land was held by Trinity College Dublin.[72] Loughgall was the parish where the largest number of witnesses lived, 15 in all. In the first months of the rising there were not many attacks on Scots. Some of the Irish leaders issued instructions that the Scottish people were to be left alone.[73]

The witnesses had a wide range of occupations. Of 69 men who gave evidence 12 were gentlemen, 5 were army officers, 3 were husbandmen. The others included tanners, tailors, tallow chandlers, merchants, innkeepers and clergymen. Eighteen gave no occupation. The occupations of the individuals who were killed showed a similar diversity. They ranged from gentlemen to clerks, yeomen, smiths and servants and included a cooper, a hatter and a surgeon. What is clear is that the Irish were not attacking any one social class. The 1642 commission took evidence of what the victims claimed to have lost in lands and goods. Forty-six deponents gave totals of their losses and some of them were very wealthy. Six of them lost under £100, 29 lost between £100 and £1000, 5 lost between £1000 and £2000, and 4 lost over £2000.

There is not so much evidence about the Irish who attacked the English planters. The Armagh volume of depositions contain only six examinations of Irish prisoners by the 1652 commission. These prisoners had taken part in the 1641 rebellion and among them were Sir Phelim O'Neill, two of his captains and three ordinary soldiers. Their evidence was mainly about the rebellion and various murders. One of the captains, Phelim O'Quin, described how Sir Phelim O'Neill 'gave every head of creatts orders to keep about to be upon their guard'.[74] There is little personal information about these Irish witnesses. Most of the information about the Irish came from the English witnesses. What is clear from their accounts is that on the whole the English recognised the Irish who attacked them and were usually able to name them. In the Armagh volume of depositions there are approximately 100 names of Irish rebels who are said to have robbed, stripped and expelled the English from their homes. Like their victims they came from all classes, including gentlemen such as Manus O'Cane, labourers, servants and one priest.[75]

It appears that the British and the Irish knew each other quite well in October 1641. The rules of the Ulster plantation originally forbade the English undertakers to have Irish tenants. It proved impossible to keep the Irish off English land and the Irish rented land there as subtenants. Leases were for a year or less and the Irish tended to pay higher rents than the English tenants.[76] Many of the rebels listed in the depositions are yeomen and labourers living in the barony of Oneilland. There was a tendency for the Irish to attack those neighbours who were English. For example Manus O'Cane who lived in Grange near Loughgall robbed Edward Saltenstall of Grange and then Nehemiah Richardson and Richard Warren of Loughgall.[77] There also is evidence of a closer relationship between the Irish and their victims. Nine deponents were owed money by the Irish. It may have been rent that was owed but this is only specified in one case. Thomas Chambers was owed £90 in rent and interest by Thady Crawley.[78] Where the evidence included a motive for any murder there was often a previous relationship between the murderer and the victim. Sometimes it was a debt or sometimes the English were attacked by their Irish servants.[79] These unequal relationships between the English and the Irish, whether it was that of creditor and debtor or master and servant must have been a motivating factor in the Irish joining Sir Phelim O'Neill.

Further evidence in the depositions would support the theory that the local rebels were economically rather than politically motivated. The evidence given to the 1642 commission indicated that the robberies and murders happened separately. The robberies seem to have occurred at the beginning of the rebellion between the end of October and the beginning of November 1641. The massacres started in mid-November 1641 at Portadown. William Skelton described the rebels' attacks around Kinnard where at first they only 'pillaged and plundered then beginninge first with the best of their estates as their cattell and corne, then their household stuff at another tyme; and lastly with their clothes and lives'.[80] Some of the Irish, when they first attacked the English, went to extreme lengths to obtain money. Jane Grace said that the rebels 'sett them in the stockes in frost and snow untill they confessed mony'.[81] James Gibson was half-hanged and had his ears cut off to confess the same.[82]

Another way of obtaining money was for the rebels to promise safe convoy to the English. Often the rebels were paid money to provide safe convoy but did not fulfil their promise.[83] However William Clark did escape after paying £15.[84] When all the money had been taken the Irish rebels took everything else of value including their victims' clothes. A number of witnesses described how they were stripped and driven out naked into the cold and wind whence they managed to escape to Dublin. Mrs.Gowrly said that 'she was stript of her clothes seven severall tymes after she gott other clothes and at length they left her not soe much as her smock or hairlace'.[85]

Although the Irish rebels who attacked the English settlers sometimes treated them in the most appalling and humiliating ways curiously enough there is very little evidence of rape. There are only two references to it in the Armagh volume of depositions. In one case the rebels took possession of an English gentleman's house and there they regularly forced their attentions on the servant girls. In the other case a girl in Armagh who 'being a pretty woman they [the Irish] took to themselves to keep and to use or rather abuse as a whore'.[86] In the Armagh volume of depositions nearly 30 women gave evidence but none of them said that they had been raped.

In some cases previous relationship between the English and the Irish was an advantage for the English as some of the Irish helped them to escape. Anthony Workeman was saved by Edmund Roe McArdell who 'had been bred and brought up in this examinant's father's house'.[87] Thomas Jukes was saved by a former servant.[88] Altogether ten people escaped with help of the Irish rebels. There were other reasons as to why many of the witnesses were not killed. Ten of them were preserved in order to use their skills. William Sym was a saddler, Richard Miles a shoemaker and Simon Hasleton a tanner. They were all made to work for the Irish and believed that they owed their lives to their trade.[89] Twenty witnesses were imprisoned by the rebels. William Brownlow and Francis Sacheverall, two of the undertakers in Oneilland, were released through an exchange of prisoners.[90] Others were released when they obtained a pass from the Irish leaders.[91]

This closer examination of the evidence in the 1641 depositions reveals a more complex picture than was previously described by some historians. There does not seem to have been a conspiracy by the Irish to exterminate all the British protestants living in Armagh. The first attacks on the English consisted of robbery rather than murder. There were some massacres in the first months of the rebellion and some of them happened after the arrival of a Scots army in Ulster. The massacres often were carried out by local rebels apparently spontaneously rather than as part of a general policy of extermination. Most of the English witnesses lived in Oneilland, the most thoroughly planted and the most fertile barony in county Armagh. Much of the violence was concentrated in the area around Loughgall in Oneilland. The Irish did not come from another area but were living among the English, contrary to the rules of the Ulster plantation. Sometimes the English sublet land to the Irish. In other instances they had Irish servants. These unequal relationships between the English and the Irish must have played a large part in the motivation of the local Irish who fought in the rising led by Sir Phelim O'Neill. He had political reasons for leading this rising but many of his followers in Armagh saw the opportunity for monetary gain.

As the rising in Ulster proceeded so did the proliferation of exaggerated accounts of the atrocities. The 1641 depositions were the main source for these. Historians tended either to believe them or to discount them entirely. In the nineteenth century P.F.Moran, the noted historian and cardinal, described the 1641 depositions as 'little more than a series of contradictory statements and exaggerated hearsay reports'.[92] M.Hickson made a detailed study of them and concluded that 'not less than 25,000 could have been murdered'.[93] The truth, as so often is the case, would appear to lie somewhere in between. Earlier in this article the figure of 1300 people was established as the maximum number killed in county Armagh according to the 1641 depositions. This figure includes all rumours and hearsay evidence. The real total is probably nearer the minimum figure which is less than 600 people. This has to be compared with the figures for the population of British settlers in Ulster at that time. Recent research has concluded that 34,000 British people were living in Ulster by 1640.[94] This would suggest that there may have been 5,000 British settlers in county Armagh and on this basis using the figures calculated above at least 10½% and no more than 25% of them were killed in 1641–2. Other research would indicate that there were about 1000 British males in county Armagh in 1630.[95] If this is multiplied by three to include women and children this would suggest a figure of 3,000 British settlers living in Armagh in 1641 and using the above totals of people killed would mean that at least 17½% and at most 43% of the British population in County Armagh died in the violence of 1641–2. It should be noted that this maximum total which suggests that nearly half the British settlers were killed does include all hearsay evidence and rumours of murders. There is no escaping the fact that large numbers of British settlers were murdered and massacred at that time but it was not the planned annihilation of British protestant settlers as depicted by some historians but a series of uncontrolled massacres and murders carried out by local Irish leaders and their men.

THE 1641 REBELLION AND ANTI-POPERY IN IRELAND

Aidan Clarke

The study of English anti-popery has become sophisticated of late, and it might be supposed that simple transference would allow the Irish experience to be comparably treated. The proponents of anti-popery in Ireland were Englishmen, after all, many of them recent arrivals. But the English findings have been increasingly specific to a country where there were relatively few Roman Catholics and the fear of popery was of a shadow rather than a substance; what seems to call for explanation is why the response was so disproportionate to the threat, and the study of anti-popery has become yet another access route to the understanding of the English mentality, a way of approaching how the English looked upon their own religion and the anxieties they entertained about their situation.[1] The validity of this approach is perhaps supported by the absence of an equivalent contemporary obsession in Ireland where Catholics were a large majority of the population, where the threat was real and the fear proved to be justified, but where the view that catholicism was a papally directed international monolith ceaselessly plotting the overthrow of protestantism was fervently embraced only after the outbreak of rebellion in 1641. Associated as it was with attacks on both protestants and protestantism, the rebellion had all the marks of the universal popish plot that had been so often foretold. That reading was to endure, aided hugely by its incorporation in Sir John Temple's *History of the rebellion*, published in 1646 and regularly reprinted thereafter, which became the authoritative protestant text, and by its canonization in the special order of service with which the Church of Ireland commemorated each October 23 for almost two centuries.[2] The actualisation of the fear of catholicism is the fulcrum of the theme of this essay: whereas anti-popery in England was at worst neurotic polemics and at best an exegesis on the hidden meaning of current events, the Irish rebellion demanded explication and brought forth a new literature of post facto anti-popery which dealt with what had happened rather than with what might happen. The two most authoritative and coherent of the early responses, the first of which was both celebrated and seminal, the second unpublished and unknown,

139

Woodcut, friars watching drownings, frontispiece, Sir John Temple, *The Irish Rebellion*, 6th ed. (Dublin 1724).

were written by some of the same authors at an interval of about eighteen months, in March 1642[3] and the late summer of 1643[4] respectively. Together, they provide an opportunity to observe anti-popery dogma being put to the practical test of elucidating real events.

The antecedents to the appearance of full-blown anti-popery in Ireland in 1642 can only be stated tentatively because, odd as it may seem, there has not been much disposition to look at early modern Ireland this way round. The traditional emphasis has been on finding the links between the survival of catholicism and resistance to English rule, and on investigating the conditions which caused protestantism to fail, rather than on the character of protestantism itself. There have been two governing assumptions, both confessional: the first, which derived from the continuing protestant tradition, was that an evangelical and expansionist thrust was inherent in the protestant religious impulse, and anti-catholicism was its natural expression; the second, common to both catholic and nationalist traditions, simply took it for granted that protestantism was a cloak for avarice, national or personal, and its attitude towards catholicism part of an easily penetrated rhetoric of self-justification.[5] In neither case was there any obvious need to single out a specifically anti-catholic motif for analysis, and the recent lively reconsideration of the course of the reformation in Ireland has been more concerned with finding new answers to old questions than with reformulating the questions themselves.[6]

The socially disintegrative consequences of the reformation released religious dissenters from the obligation to obey political authority and committed catholic dissenters to an alternative loyalty to the leader of their church. At first sight, these consequences would appear likely to have had particular force in Ireland where, uniquely, religious dissent was not a minority phenomenon, but the condition of the vast majority. Ireland was, moreover, the weakest strategic point in the English defence system: it invited attack because it was not securely under government control and it was especially vulnerable to catholic attack because it was presumptively disobedient, disloyal and without the will to defend itself. It was, in short, a country where both of the perils associated with religious dissent, internal revolt and external intervention, might have been expected to present themselves in extreme and urgent forms. Local circumstances, however, complicated the matter. Most starkly, Irish disobedience was longstanding, and had little to do historically with religious difference: for centuries before the reformation, Ireland had been in a state of arrested conquest which had produced a shifting patchwork composed of areas under firm government control, areas of domination by settlers whose connections with the Dublin administration were vestigial, and areas where the native Irish continued to rule.[7] More subtly, the Tudor effort to bring Ireland under full control, though it developed in the reformation decade of the

1530s and in the context of the international problems caused by Henry's divorce, was animated by secular humanist principles. Its starting point was a view of Irish society as primitive and anarchic: in social terms, nomadic, pastoral, communal, and without fixed land ownership or rules of inheritance; in political terms, tyrannical, lacking the protections of law or due process, and without fixed rights of succession; a society, in summary, that was inherently instable, endemically warlike, and wholly oppressive. In a word, a word which acquired its modern meaning very largely in this context, the Irish were barbarous. It followed that if Ireland were to be brought into a satisfactory relationship with the crown, the Irish must not merely be subdued, but changed. The outcome was a programme of 'civil reform' which was essentially a process of modernisation, intended to induce the Irish to jump the gap in social evolution which separated them from civilisation by introducing tillage agriculture, individual landholding, primogeniture inheritance and, above all, the rule of law.[8]

It proved unexpectedly difficult to assimilate the introduction of the reformed religion to this programme. Protestantism was brought to Ireland by members of that transitional generation which experienced the reformation. Those of them who had not been born and bred as Catholics themselves were familiar with an older generation which had been, and they had well-formed ideas about what catholicism was. In Ireland they recognised the religion practised by the long established colonial community to be catholicism as they understood it. But they found the religious practices of the native Irish entirely alien and unfamiliar, deviant in both substance and form, and they withheld recognition from it. It was their considered view that the Irish were not only not authentically catholic, but that they were not Christian. In short, to the perception of the Irish as barbarians was added a view of the Irish as pagans.[9] That did not invalidate the civilizing thrust: the entire classical tradition demonstrated that paganism and civility were perfectly compatible. By contrast, an uncivilized protestant was a contradiction in terms: as an informed religion, protestantism presupposed civility. Thus civil reform must prepare the way for religious reform. Although this conclusion was never candidly given official status; although individual Protestants dissented from it and worked to convert the Irish; although lively disagreement surrounded the question of whether the appropriate strategy was coercion or persuasion, paralleling a secular debate on the relative merits of conquest and conciliation; and although the legal status of the established church as the sole church of the community was unambiguous, the practical outcome was that the protestantization of the Irish was treated as a second-phase objective.[10]

The classic post-reformation difficulties first emerged within the colony. The cardinal fact of early modern Irish history was that when

England became protestant, the descendants of the pre-reformation
settlers – the 'Old English', as they began to call themselves – remained
catholic. Historically, this group had constituted the English interest in
Ireland since its beginnings; in the immediate past, they had not merely
acquiesced in the renewed conquest, but to a significant extent
promoted it and supplied its rationale; contemporarily, they made up a
very large part of the political community of Ireland and possessed
substantial property and power in most parts of the country outside
Ulster. Their relations with the incoming 'new English' settlers were
competitive and unfriendly. They not merely rejected protestantism,
but embraced the revitalized catholicism of the counter-reformation.
Nonetheless, they insisted that their loyalty and obedience were
unaffected by their religious beliefs.[11] To the government they posed in
an urgent form the most basic question in the catechetics of anti-popery:
could they be loyal, though catholic? The question was highly political
in its framing, for the means of coercing them did not exist and a crisis
was at hand as Gaelic Ireland fought the Tudor advance in the 1590s.
The ambiguities of the situation were neatly profiled when the Irish
leader Hugh O'Neill sought to neutralize the catholic colonists by
securing papal agreement to excommunicate those who supported
Queen Elizabeth. Clement VIII, who was well acquainted with catholic
divisions in Ireland, refused to oblige: by limiting his support to a bull
of indulgence for those who assisted O'Neill, he ruled in effect that the
conflict was a political one in which catholics might properly disagree.[12]
In practice, colonists took both sides, depending on circumstance as
much as opinion perhaps, but the more prominent and influential of
them did loyally support the government, which in return withdrew all
pressure to conform religiously.

A crude anti-catholicism was part of the baggage of the English
settlers, but it changed in character. The later arrivals, particularly those
who came to fight in the Nine Years War, represented the beginnings of
a generational shift, from protestants who had had direct experience of
catholicism to those who had little or none. They were the products
of that well-charted new formation which taught them to believe that
in the Roman Catholic Church Christianity had degenerated into an
erroneous and superstitious organization, characterised by clerical power
and lay ignorance. This church allegedly aimed at worldly dominion,
with it co-existence was impossible, and it would be defeated only after
a titanic struggle between the forces of good and evil. This was an
indoctrination which did not prepare its votaries to see, as their
predecessors had seen, an incompatibility between native Irish norms
and the profession of catholicism. Catholicism rather than barbarism
was a sufficient explanation of what they found offensive in Ireland.
But if their view was simple, the situation in which they found themselves was not: in Ireland they served side by side with Catholics and

encountered shades of difference for which their prejudices had not equipped them. The native Irish were locally regarded as doubtfully Christian, let alone catholic, but they claimed to be fighting for catholicism and gained the support of Spain, predictably seeking a 'backdoor' to subvert the security of protestantism in England. The colonists were indubitably catholic, but many of them were loyal to protestant England to the point of being willing to fight for that country.

The successful outcome of the war appeared to resolve these ambiguities. In 1603, when James I inherited the first English government to have uncontested control over Ireland, it was a natural assumption that the Irish could no longer resist the civilizing process initiated by the Tudors and his agenda was largely set by unfulfilled objectives. Among them, the advancement of protestantism was prominent, for in the estimation of church leaders the time had come to make spiritual progress. It might not yet be possible to think in terms of conversion, at least of the adult cohort, but the first step, of suppressing catholic worship and insisting upon outward conformity, was urgently necessary.[13] The emphasis is significant: unequivocally, the church saw itself confronted by catholicism, not paganism. Although the generational shift no doubt contributed something to this difference of perception, the church leaders were older men who had good reasons to change their minds. The abortive Spanish involvement in the Nine Years War had shown that though Ireland might seem like a savage backwater whose inhabitants were more like indigenous Americans than Europeans, it was nonetheless part of the international, papally directed web of catholicism. That point was underlined and made urgent by the systematic preparation in continental seminaries of priests for the Irish mission. Their anxiously observed return to Ireland in conspicuous numbers after 1603 strongly affirmed both Ireland's connection with the catholic world and the subversive non-national character of catholicism itself. In short, in both temporal and spiritual spheres, the face of catholicism in Ireland was now unmistakably irredentist.

The attempt to expel the catholic clergy and to enforce church-going was shortlived. Presentment for recusancy was a formal process requiring institutional structures that existed only in areas of established settlement, so that it was the colonial Catholics rather than the native Irish who suffered from the government's resolve. They carried their protests to court in the aftermath of the gunpowder plot (1605), and prevailed.[14] It was a staple of the literature of anti-popery to allow no distinctions between one kind of catholic and another, all being puppets of the same master, but political reality spoke differently; James acknowledged the existence of a precarious loyalty that might be forfeited by severity and allied himself with those who believed that the propagation of protestantism was the proper business of the church rather than the state, a matter of conversion rather than coercion.[15] Though he was to denounce the catholic colonists as 'half-subjects', and contemptuously dismiss the intellectual dishonesty with which they reconciled their temporal and spiritual allegiances,[16] their conduct defied his logic and he needed to keep his share of their loyalty until he could do without it. Obedient subjects in peacetime, but presumptively undependable if trouble came, the Old English were assigned an inter-mediate status, superior to the Irish, inferior to their protestant fellow colonists. Before long, the clergy too were being pragmatically sorted into the acceptably non-political seculars and the seditious, trouble-making, Rome-running regulars.[17] In Ireland, it was a routine political necessity to know the enemy with precision and commonsense.

The Church of Ireland was not a consenting party to the opportunist policies of the government, but it was not immune from criticism and its negative stress on the suppression of catholic worship was signifi-cant.[18] The regular calls of its leaders for state action to compel church attendance disregarded not merely the realistic limits of secular power but the inadequacy of ecclesiastical provision. Undermanned and under-resourced, the church was scaled to provide only for the spiritual needs of the New English settler community, and did so unsatisfactorily: it was manifestly incapable of assuming its statutory role as the church of the entire community and servicing the policy it demanded. Though it set about overhauling itself, relying heavily on the importation of bishops and clergy from England and Scotland, the process of self-definition on which it simultaneously embarked provided both a suggestive gloss on its sense of mission and an indirect comment on the Church of England. When articles of belief were adopted in 1615, fifty-five years after the Church of Ireland had been established by law, the opportunity to maintain unity by simply adopting the Church of England's Thirty-Nine Articles was not taken, primarily because the Church of Ireland had become attached to a more severe interpretation of the doctrine of predestination. Instead, Convocation incorporated all but one of them into a set of one hundred and four articles which defined a significantly different position in a number of respects. Both churches held that the destiny of every human being was determined by God before birth, and was unaffected by anything the individual did during this earthly life. Some were selected for salvation, and these were the elect. The English articles did not go beyond that point, dealing with the theology of grace in language so vague that some were able to interpret it as meaning universal redemption. The new Irish articles treated the doctrine of election in detail and stated the corrollary without ambiguity: the rest of humanity were the reprobate, doomed to eternal punishment. The Irish articles also included an explicit denial of the power of the pope to depose kings and discharge subjects from their obedience, and they identified the pope as 'that man of sin' foretold in the Bible – Anti-Christ.[19] These variations may have owed something to contemporary English debates, but they were entirely consistent with an uncompromising local tradition that extended back to the 1560s and had been reinforced by the migration of both English dissidents and Scots crypto-presbyterians. The most significant variation, because of its local implications, was the emphasis upon the damned, which both reflected and encouraged the belief that the Irish as a race were reprobate, incapable of responding to the call because God had condemned them in their entirety.[20] This was a doctrine which excused the clergy and reassured the laity, who had little to gain from official policy for when everyone was protestant no one would be privileged. The application of the predestinarian model provided an escape from that predicament. The conclusion that the Irish were beyond redemption gave ecclesiastical sanction to the identification of the elect of God with the élite of colonialism and generated a sense of spiritual superiority which reinforced the conviction of cultural and social superiority which the settlers already felt.

It is plain that a considerable change had taken place in a short time. Less than a generation before 1615, the received view had been that the Irish were barbarians and pagans, not susceptible to conversion until they had been civilized. Now, the Irish were seen as catholic reprobates, not susceptible to conversion because God had consigned them to damnation. This was far from being a change without a difference. Barbaric pagans were a separate entity; Catholics, barbaric or otherwise, were part of an international organisation and parties to a conspiracy against protestantism, and it followed that there was no significant difference between one Catholic and another. The original assumption had provided no rationale for dealing with the catholic colonists, the Old English, who were manifestly not barbarians. The new approach resolved that problem: since there was no salvation in the Church of Rome,[21] they were manifestly reprobates. They might not be inherently incapable of salvation, for their origins were English, but they were followers of Anti-Christ, their claims to loyalty were without credence, and their conduct was an outstanding example of the innate papist capacity to dissemble.

The situation was an uneasy one. The government had no alternative but to accept, with ill grace, that the suppression of catholicism was impracticable and to draw pragmatic comfort from the declared loyalty of the catholic colonists and, indeed, from the apparent conformability of some of the Irish. The church denied the premises of public policy, stating the alternative in the words of Christ: 'Compel them . . . to come in'.[22] This tension was containable in time of peace. When war broke out, with the arch-enemy Spain in 1625 and with France in 1626, the catholic colonists deliberately exploited the government's difficulties to compel it to define its attitude towards them. In direct negotiations with the English government they undertook to provide for the defence of Ireland in return for certain concessions (known as the 'Graces'), including the suspension of the collection of recusancy fines.[23] The request was token, for the fines had been exacted rarely in the past and suspended altogether since the Spanish marriage negotiations some years previously, but its significance as a proposal to have toleration placed on a formal footing was unaffected. When Charles I accepted the condition as negotiable the suppressed conflict between church and state was forced into the open. The transaction raised in an acute and practical form the issue that Charles's conduct was soon to present to many of his English and Scottish subjects in a much less distinct way: the issue of how to deal with a king whose actions seemed contrary to the interests of the church of which he was supreme governor. The initial response was prudently private: in November 1626, the new archbishop of Armagh, James Ussher, convened a meeting of the episcopacy to approve a trenchant statement which accused Charles of putting religion and the souls of the people up for sale and making the state a party to the damnation of those who died in the superstitious and idolatrous Church of Rome.[24] When the negotiations were transferred to Ireland, so that the king's terms could be discussed by a representative assembly, the bishops published their declaration and reinforced it with sermons and private entreaties. Their remonstrations not only addressed the immediate issue, stressing the falsity of catholicism and the error of supposing that toleration would bring stability, but extended also to an unequivocal condemnation of recent leniency.[25] They were characterized, moreover, by a vehement apocalyptic thrust. Ussher publicly warned that divine punishment must follow[26]: privately, the archbishop of Cashel, Malcolm Hamilton, one of the king's chaplains, exhorted Charles, with much apposite Old Testament allusion, 'to have a special care for the suppression of idolatry in all your Majesty's kingdoms, but in special in Ireland where it reigns as a sin that rent the kingdom of David in sunder'. Reminding him how the idolatrous rebellion of a few had occasioned the wrath of God against all the Israelites, the archbishop went on to ask, 'what shall we then fear against the whole kingdom of Ireland, where all the realm is full of altars not to the worship of God but to Baal'.[27] In the luxuriant literature of anti-popery, Hamilton's remonstrance is unexceptional, but its context makes it remarkable. It required an unusual sense of purpose for a royal chaplain to remind the king of the disobedient Saul's admission to Samuel: 'I have sinned, for I have transgressed the commandment of the lord . . . because I feared the people and obeyed their voice'.[28] That allusion was well chosen to convey the essence of an intervention which was undertaken by church leaders because they believed that the king's intentions were not merely mistaken, but sinful. Some prudent softening of this emphatic resistance was provided by Ussher who formally exhorted the assembly to meet the needs of the king without insisting on the suspension of recusancy fines; defending the refusal of the bishops to make themselves 'accessary to the drawing down of God's heavy vengeance upon the people', he appealed for a united colonial front based on the recognition that the aims of the Irish, to transfer the 'throne of the English to the power of a foreigner' and to regain their ancient possessions, made them the common enemy of all the English in Ireland, whatever their religion.[29]

The episcopal initiative succeeded, within its narrow limits: the suspension of recusancy fines played no further part in the negotiations, but some of the civil disabilities attaching to catholicism were remedied, subsidies were granted, and the whole episode underlined Ussher's thesis that the Old English, though catholic, had a place in the colonial system.[30] His antithesis, that catholicism had not, became correspondingly more difficult to sustain. The doubt that Charles's conduct had raised was not easily dispelled, for its roots lay less in opportunism than in the revised view of catholicism that had become fashionable with his accession: debased, degenerate and idolatrous as it was, it was nonetheless a part of the true church descended from the church of Christ which it had defiled. Correlative revisions of protestantism brought new emphases in doctrinal teaching, which were interpreted as evidence of catholic tendencies because they favoured free will against predestination, and liturgical innovations legitimated by medieval usage were introduced.[31] In 1634, these developments were abruptly imported into Ireland: the Irish articles were superseded by the Thirty-Nine Articles and the chief substance of the English canons was introduced.[32] The effects were deeply unsettling. Membership of the established church ceased to be compatible with the beliefs of the Scots in Ulster. For others, the new dispensation was, at best, repugnant to local tradition; at worst, part of a sinister plan to 'draw us back again into Popery'.[33] Suspicion was fostered from within by the absence of any interference with catholic worship and buttressed from without by allegations in England that these innovations stemmed from the manipulation of the king by men whose objective was to recover England for Rome. To the accustomed papist threats, external and internal, was added a third, unforeseen possibility: that of betrayal from above.

In Ireland, that fear centred on the lord deputy, Thomas Viscount Wentworth, and the venom with which covert papist purposes were ascribed to him[34] may have owed something to the fact that the accustomed threats had lost much of their urgency. It is difficult to explain in any other terms the shocked surprise which greeted the outbreak of rebellion in 1641, and the unanimity with which contemporaries agreed that it was unexpected.[35] In the earlier years of the century, the settlers had dramatised their situation, 'with the sword in one hand and the axe in the other',[36] and worried that the Irish 'studie nothing els daie nor night but our overthrow';[37] as the years of peace extended, confidence grew and the sense of security was disturbed only by anxiety about the Irish abroad. At home, control seemed assured, the Irish appeared to have come to terms with their situation, and the routines of daily life involved a degree of normal intercourse from which menace seemed absent.[38] In Sir John Temple's picturesque phrase, the hatred of the Irish towards the English seemed 'deposited and buried in a firm conglutination of their affections and national obligations passed between them'.[39] In hindsight, it was easy for the colonists to believe that they had been tricked by popish guile, but the excuse itself confirms the impression that they had indeed dropped their guard and were as unready for the rebellion mentally as they were defensively. The means by which Charlemont fort in county Armagh was surprised on the first evening of the rebellion bear neatly on the point: Sir Toby Caulfield, who commanded it, assumed that the Irish leader, Sir Phelim O'Neill, had called for dinner. The centrepiece of the conspiracy, the surprise of Dublin Castle, was discovered that evening and the rising was confined to Ulster until late November when the Irish felt ready to return to the original intention of capturing Dublin and prepared the way by entering into an alliance with the Old English of the pale. Calling themselves the 'Catholic army', the two groups settled down to a preliminary siege of Drogheda while their union generated a corresponding set of alliances between native Irish and catholic colonists throughout much of Ireland and rebellion became widespread.

When the plot was revealed in Dublin on October 22 it was alleged that the intention was a general massacre of Protestants. That information reached London at the same time as news of the outbreak in the north; the two were conflated, and it was reported that a general massacre had actually taken place. As news and refugees reached Dublin in the weeks that followed, it became clear that ill-treatment was widespread, that atrocities were being committed and, above all, that there was a very general expropriation of the settlers. Among the priorities that quickly emerged was the need to meet the demand for some procedure to ensure that these losses were officially recorded so that compensation might be made in the future, and in December a commission composed of eight clergymen was set up to collect statements of loss and issue certificates of value. Five of the eight were Trinity graduates, three of them (like Sir John Temple before them) former fellows of the college[40]: all were refugees from rural livings. As they set to work they found that their role was admirably suited to the gathering of information of all sorts and they quickly became quasi-official inquisitors into the course of events, the identity of the rebels, the names of the dead, the circumstances of their deaths, and much more besides. [41]

In March 1642, the commission's head, Dr Henry Jones, dean of

Kilmore in the plantation county of Cavan and sometime prisoner of the rebels, travelled to England to seek aid from parliament for the relief of his fellow ministers and to press for urgent assistance in the defence of the colony. The house of commons heard him in person and approved the printing of his appeal. In the form in which it was published, over the names of all the commissioners, Jones's address served as an introduction of some 4,000 words to a set of 78 extracts from the 637 refugee statements or depositions which had already been taken.[42] Although these excerpts contained an ample number of atrocity stories, the prime concern of the commissioners was to disclose 'the minds and intents of these conspirators, and their adherents' and their conclusion was emphatic: the rebellion was *'a most bloudy and Antichristian combination and plot hatched, by well-nigh the whole Romish sect, by way of combination from parts forraign, with those at home, against this our Church and State; thereby intending the utter extirpation of the reformed Religion and the professors of it'.*[43] It had originally been intended, in collusion with 'correspondents' in England and 'a like party' in Scotland, that the Tower of London and Edinburgh Castle should be surprised at the same time as Dublin Castle[44], a purpose providentially thwarted. There were two aims: the first involved *'setting up that idoll of the Masse, with all the abominations of that whore of* Babylon'[45], including an inquisition, 'like that in *Spain* ', which would 'in time thorowly accomplish' 'what the Sword cannot, for the present, effect'[46]; the second was to introduce 'another form of rule ordered and moderated by themselves, without dependence on his Highnesse or the Kingdom of England'.[47] When that had been achieved, they would 'with the assistance of *Spain* and *France*, set footing in *England*, and after that in *Scotland'*; later still they would place their forces at the service of the king of Spain against the *'Hollanders* '.[48] Bulls from Rome guaranteed pardon 'of all sins of what sort soever that shall be therein committed, tending to this great work', and provided for the excommunication of those who did not join. 'Devillish' in design and 'diabolicall' in practice, the rebellion was part of a tightly controlled international conspiracy, led by the pope, locally managed by priests, friars and Jesuits, and involved 'all of the Popish Nobility and men of quality'.[49] In almost every respect the *Remonstrance* fitted comfortably into the anti-popery genre: the conspiracy the commissioners reconstructed after the event did not differ from the conspiracy that had long been foretold. They did, however, note one discordant detail: although the design was for the extirpation of Protestants, 'their generall profession is for a generall extirpation, even to the last and least drop of English blood', and those of the English who were 'of the Romish sect' were not exempt.[50] The commissioners recorded the point without comment, but they were to return to it.

Some eighteen months later, after the outbreak of civil war in

England, and after prolonged negotiations had resulted in a truce between the king and the confederate Catholics, the commissioners prepared a sequel to the original remonstrance which they presented to the Irish council. No overt reference was made to the circumstances in which they did so, but there can be little doubt that the intention was to provide support for those (among them, Sir John Temple) who were opposed to the truce and to the official policy of converting it into a peace. It is likely that this intervention produced dissent among the commissioners themselves, since only four of them signed the submission. All four were graduates of Trinity College Dublin.[51] Their discourse, as they called it, was modelled on the original hurried *Remonstrance*, being similarly composed of an introduction to a selection of the depositions taken since its publication in March 1642, but it was very much more ambitious. There were more than twice as many depositions, and the introduction was almost ten times as long.[52]

The opening made it clear that the commissioners had solved the problem which had puzzled them earlier and been led to a very much more complex explanation of what had taken place. By abandoning the convention that papists were all alike, they were able to re-define the two aims of the rebellion, which now appeared to have been 'first *the extirpation of the English nation*; and secondly the abolishment of the *Protestant reformed religion*'[53], to treat these as distinct from one another, and to explore the relationship between them. The evidence pointed to a clear conclusion: 'the *Irish* are more frequent in expressing hatred to our nation, & the old *English* to our *Religion* though both to both', they observed.[54] The source of this difference was equally clear: the Irish 'according to the restlesse disposition of a people once broken, but either never truly maistered or at least haveing (through the noble indulgence of gracious princes, and a free nation abhorring that which might but resemble tyranny) long felt a loose raine, have now at last resolved to cast that rider who to his owne great cost hath hitherto civillized, man'd and pampered them, and to return to their pristine wildnes'.[55] The benefits that conquest had brought to Ireland had been of two kinds, they explained: 'an happy freedom from the former tyranny of numerous *Tanists, and Domineering Grandies* ' and 'a most blessed reduction of a desperately seduced people from their pernicious Idolatry to the saving touch of God's word'. Both had been spurned. On the one hand, the preference of the Irish for 'that idle freedome and barbarous riotousness which they deem the only generousness' had kept them from civility; on the other, 'their wilful intoxication with *their Mother's cup*' had kept them from the true religion.[56] Even at the time of the original conquest it had been observed that 'what through pride and sloth' none of the Irish, great or inferior, were 'addicted to merchandize or sea traffick abroad, nay indeed (not even yet) to manufacture at home.'[57] Subsequent attempts 'to have melted or subdued their feritie [wildness] and love of barbarisme' through the enjoyment of wealth, honour, freedom, civility, good laws, trade and religious reformation had failed.[58] The Irish were still characterized by deep dissimulation, foul promiscuous uncleanness, beastly drunkenness, proud idleness, profound and beloved ignorance, and abominable idolatries.[59] The leading Irish despised frugality, industry, and improvement, as 'better beseeming (in their esteeme) clownish persons and men borne to care and toyle'; they called the English 'churles'[60] and the Old English 'clownes'[61] and their way of life was insidiously corrupting. Not only did those of them who had been educated, even to the point of conforming to protestantism, relapse when they returned to their native parts, but some of the English living among them also succumbed – 'of soe dangerous consequence is too neere and common conversation with an idle and uncivillized nation'.[62] That the intent was to revert to 'the pristine *Chaos* of Barbarisme and lawlesse tyranny'[63], rather than simply 'to have the kingdome cleare to themselves'[64], was evident in their determination to get rid of English breeds of sheep and cattle, 'of the very fashions of the English', and of such 'mute and senselesse remembrances' as glass windows, napkins and trenchers.[65] But it was principally shown, of course, in the match between their conduct and their words: they had already 'layd all wast and ruinous, hath turned a pleasant land into a desolate wilderness, hath raked up the civill and frugall indevours of good common-welths-men, for the flourishing and happy state of this kingdome into ashes and barbarisme'.[66] The root of the plot lay in this cultural intransigence, in 'a kind of fixed and even congenite [innate] naturall desire to withdraw themselves from the English obedience when opportunitie shall give way'[67], and the aim of the chief conspirators was to regain the 'enjoyment of their ancient barbarous tyranny over the meaner inhabitant, with the ruine of the protestant and *British* inhabitants and ejection of the English laws and government for ever'.[68]

There had been undeveloped hints of this reading of the rebellion in the *Remonstrance*, which had noted a link between the 'prophanation of holy places, and Religion' and the 'wasting and defacing of all Monuments of civility'[69]. However the commissioners had originally taken it for granted that the aim of independence subserved an international catholic purpose as a prelude to the invasion of England. They remained reluctant to discount this danger but they now saw Irish intervention in England quite differently, as a possible outcome of the rebellion rather than as its underlying motive: conceding that the evidence that invasion had been intended was little more than 'the vapouring flashes and braggs of some few', they warned that it would be prudent to expect some attempt to exploit English differences, since the hopes and aims of the rebels might 'grow more pregnant and swell higher'.[70] Their alternative secularized interpretation of the rebellion's origins was documented from the depositions, supported by a reading of Irish history and elucidated with reference to human experience. In no society, the commissioners observed, are the majority of people devout, still less so the greatest and most active men within it. In recent times, religion had been 'the usuall pretence of warr and bloodshed, not onely in Christendome, but even between the Turke and Persian', but the real causes were secular: the love of glory and victory, rivalry, real or imagined indignities, greed, and empire.[71] The leaders of the Roman Catholic Church were not exempt from this characterization: their religion was 'indeed meere policie to rule the Christian world, preserve their gotten glory, power and wealth, and destroy all gainesayers'[72], while the catholic cause itself was passingly defined as 'the manifestation of the popes crowne and monks belly'.[73] To dismiss the pope's spiritual pretensions in this way as a mask which concealed a lust for worldly dominion was a stock motif of anti-popery writings, but the revised secular context in which the popish plot had now to be set raised difficult problems of interpreting its nature as well as its connections with the rebellion.

Their radical reassessment of the fundamental character of the rising did not seem to the commissioners to be at odds with their original view that international catholicism was involved and the abolition of the reformed religion was intended: 'we will not rob him (*who makes warre with all that receive not his mark*) nor the fiery spirit of his zealous clients, of the glory of having an hand in soe holy a warr (or massacre rather, as they intended it wholely, and for the most part it proved)'. The pope, Spanish, French, Scottish and English catholics were all implicated[74]: Spanish South American policy was the model and the Spanish Jesuit Mariana had provided the primer, 'preached in their pulpetts and practised by their swords, being indeed but that bloody and cursed doctrine for our destruction, which they generally hold'.[75] In the revised reading, however, the role of religion was to attract support by hiding the real objectives, and it was this stratagem which provided the key to the perplexing conduct of the Old English: 'whom love of barbarisme could not degenerate, zeale to their religion and hatred to ours, wonderfully fomented from *Rome* and other parts, and dayly stirred up by their priests and friars have drawne on to joyne in this'.[76] The plot, that is to say, was now seen to have had primary and secondary origins: it began with a small group of 'deep, wily, and working heads'[77] who wished to return to 'their ancient barbarism'[78] and were linked with a few colonists who were infected with 'base degeneration or conceited sweetnes of the ancient Irish tyranny'. The Old English in general, however, had no thought of submitting 'to a government in the hand of the meere [pure, undiluted] Irish'. The secondary plot in which they became involved was a response to rumours of imminent danger to themselves and their religion from the English parliament, falsehoods of which they were the more easily persuaded by their priests and friars because the nature of their own religion was to 'force conscience through fear of death'. 'Zeal to their superstition'[79] thus prompted them to support a movement whose true ends included their own ultimate destruction, for they too were the objects of Irish hatred, and Irish claimants to their lands were waiting to dispossess them while they enjoyed the courtesy of Polyphemus, 'of being last devoured'.[80]

Below the social level at which the plots were hatched the same 'jugling'[81] was practised, and rumours of impending religious oppression were used by the clergy to inflame the common people. Weak, credulous and deferential as they were, it was nonetheless necessary to delude them also: the way had been prepared by the imposition of an unusual period of abstinence, 'a mimick fast for fare longer time than iust for successe for the gunpouder treason', and the friars in particular worked upon their congregations 'with that kind of clamourous, noisefull, and threshing oratorie, which they use', 'while the more wiley heads laugh both at their theatricall provokeing of sweat in a pulpit, and the meaner peoples being soe taken withal'. The prominence of the friars was accounted for not only in stock terms of 'their various subordinations of all from the lowest novice to the highest generall unto the Pope, their dependencie upon him for their being & his prime intendment of [reliance on] them for his ends', but also, more imaginatively, as an attempt to outdo the 'sublimate [exalted] Jesuits' whose absence seemed otherwise unaccountable. The pope's own direct contribution to the cause was the grant of full remission of sins to those who died in it, whose bodies *should not be cold before their soules ascended up into heaven*, being freed from all purgatorian flames'.[82]

From two premises, that religious devotion was exceptional and that the Old English were more prone to it than the Irish, it followed that even a fully fledged popish plot was not adequate to the purposes of the conspirators. Secular incitements were also required. It was in that category that the commissioners placed the claims made by the rebels to have a commission from the king, or sometimes the queen, for what they did. Though that falsehood was forged in the 'friars mint' to excite the ignorant multitude, it appealed to a sentiment that was neither necessarily religious nor compatible in any way with the real aims of the rebellion.[83] More widespread and similarly dishonest was the pretence that the aim of the rebellion was to recover lost liberties: 'the juste vindicateing their deare country from oppression, and asserting their ancient and due liberty and freedome'. This appeal was subtle in its misrepresentation, for it placed real objectives in a false framework: using Scotland as a model, it aimed to redress the injustices of expropriation, to end 'the neglect and oppression of the natives' and to take the administration of law and justice out of 'the hands of strangers', without breaking the connection with England.[84] The commissioners were in no doubt that the suppression of the intention to become independent doubled the dissimulation for it disguised the nature of the freedom the leaders wanted to restore, which was the traditional freedom of the ruling Irish to tyrannize at pleasure over the estates and fortunes, the wives and daughters, and even the lives of their meaner subjects: 'Such freedome noe doubt is the miserable inslaveing of the nobility or gentry to their owne passions, and of the miserable people to their unbridled lusts and rapine, altogether inconsistent not onely with Christianitie but even with humane society itself'.[85]

In examining the course and conduct of the rebellion, the commissioners felt able to deal more confidently with the incongruity which had puzzled them earlier. Expressions of hatred of protestantism, and indeed of God, were graphically itemised: the destruction of bibles, and 'saying it was hellfire that burned, when our bibles were in the fire'[86]; the razing of churches; the denial of Christian burial; the disinterment of corpses to purify consecrated ground; and enforced conversion to catholicism. Horrific as most of these things were, they fitted the stereotype and could be understood with the aid of the book of Revelation: 'all of which we the lesse wonder at when we remember that *the dead bodies of the martyrs slaine by the Beast, shall lye in the streets of the great citie which is spiritually called Sodom & Egypt where also our Lord was crucified, & that they will not suffer their bodies to be put in graves'*.[87] Enforced conversion, however, was not what it seemed. 'But above all to shew that (what ever they pretend) religion onely is not their quarrell', the commissioners wrote, 'it is scarce credible, how many they have murthered after they have perswaded them betwixt hopes and feares to joyne with them in their religion and goe to church.[88] The Irish explained with gallows humour that to end the lives of their converts before they relapsed was mercifully to save their souls.[89] The commissioners believed that hatred was the motive and concluded that the unpurgable crime was to be English.[90] The setting in which they placed their litany of affronts to God and protestantism was the larger one of 'an earnest desire and utmost indeavour utterly to extirpate our name & nation, our profession & all the very prints and footsteps of civilitie or religion'.

There was one further dimension to be explored. The explication of the dynamics of what had actually happened in Ireland was incomplete without an explanation of why the Irish, 'wicked to God' as they were[91], had been used by God 'this way to afflict us, by delivering of us into these mens mercilesse hands'. Shortly before his death in the early summer of 1642, Roger Puttock, a member of the original commission, had suggested an answer, almost in passing, in a brief pamphlet in which he had welcomed the hardships of Protestants in Ireland as a sign that God was not prepared to tolerate the permissive policies of recent years, when 'We were doting . . . on Rome and her Idolatries'.[92] In

July 1643, Daniel Harcourt, who was a member of a related commission specially appointed to take depositions in Ulster[93], had no doubt that it was the recent pursuit of 'policy without piety' that accounted for God's wrath.[94] The commissioners were of the same apocalyptic mind. The Irish, unwittingly, 'were the rod of Gods anger'. 'The true fountaine whence all our sufferings issued' was squarely acknowledged to have been 'our sins' and these were itemized frankly as ingratitude for God's gifts, covetousness, neglect of the poor, *'deep securitie* while all Christendome almost was on flame', dissension and strife, 'too little hatred of Idolatrie or grief for it', and insufficient zeal in propagating the truth. Their intention, of course, was 'to justifie God in his proceedings', not to 'justifie our enemies'[95], but their attitude towards the Irish contrasted with that of the distraught Harcourt, whose intransigence was conveyed in an allusion to the error of the Israelites in failing to uproot the Canaanites, and perhaps also with that of Puttock, who had called upon Wentworth to root out catholicism by force in 1632.[96] The commissioners professed to wish that vengeance should be confined to the guilty, denied that they had any desire for the utter ruin of the Irish, and hoped instead for their reclamation 'by meet and compatible meanes to true civilitie and the right worship of Almightie God'. The message that they set out to transmit to future generations in the 'Discourse' had two aspects: it was an exemplary warning of the true character of the Irish, 'their cunning and divellishnes in contrivement, closenes and secrecy in concealement, crueltie and perfidiousnes in executeing their designes'; but it was also a demonstration of *'God's* wonderfull hatred of sinne in permitting it soe farre for our punishment; his goodnes in discovering it, so strangely preventing it in the height they intended, with many of his gracious and almost miraculous deliverances of many of us, and bringing already in part *their wickednes on their owne pates* [heads]'. [97] Thus those who had been punished, with God's connivance, and been killed 'onely as protestants' were transmuted: 'we may be bold to say (to the perpetuall infamie of the merciless rebells and their bloody Doctors) that this kingdome hath in a few months yielded as many *British martyrs* as it did in farre more of the best times afford *Irish Saints'*.[98] Sir John Temple's message, three years later, was precisely similar, designed as it was to bear perpetual witness against the Irish, extol the protestant dead, and encourage living Protestants to dwell less upon the disaster that had befallen them than upon the fact that they had survived it.[99] The 'Discourse', however, may well be the more authentic colonial voice, addressed as it was to a local rather than an English audience and seeking as it did to explain a complex reality in terms of its context rather than appealing for support in the terms most likely to elicit it.

There are ragged edges in the commissioners' reinterpretation. They never squarely addressed the relationship between the Irish plot and the popish plot. They never explicitly stated that the clergy, like the Old English and the common people, were dupes, though the image of the 'wilely heads' laughing at the friars as they sweated in the pulpit suggests that they thought so. Certainly, they never implied that the clergy were familiar with the true motives of the rebellion. The impression they leave is of an arrangement of mutual convenience, in which the native Irish leaders exploited a church that was very ready to seize the chance that they had created and to provide the chief 'promoters and dispersers'[100] of a rebellion which outdid the Tartars in ferocity and the Turks in irreverence[101] and conjoined catholicism with barbarism.

At the very outset, the commissioners found the popish plot that their formation and professional predilection had prepared them for, and they described it in a form which owed so much to anti-popery typology that they failed to notice the curious absence of Jesuits. On closer acquaintance, they discerned the Irish plot that was one of the staples of their colonial ethos and they presented it in terms borrowed from a tradition of settler commentary that stretched back to Giraldus Cambrensis in the twelfth century. This tradition had reached its peak when the paradigm of barbarity and civility supplied the key to understanding what was involved in the Tudor conquest. As the commissioners uncovered the plots, one after the other, they found that the key still worked: the international apparatus of the pope and his minions was relegated to an opportunist rather than an instrumental role; it yielded pride of place to a local and secular demonology which construed the rebellion as an atavistic rejection of everything the colony stood for, and subsumed the rooting out of protestantism in the eradication of civility.

A

SERMON

Preached in

Chriſt's-Church,

DUBLIN;

On the 23d. of *October*, 1698.

Being the Anniverſary Thankſgiving for putting an End to the IRISH REBELLION, which
broke out on that Day, 1641.

BEFORE THE

Houſe of Lords.

By *NATHANAEL* Lord Biſhop of *WATER-
FORD* and *LISMORE*.

DVBLIN:

Printed by *Andrew Crook*, Printer to the Kings Moſt Excel-
lent Majeſty, for *Samuel Adey*, Bookbinder in *Copper-Alley*,
and are to be ſold by the Bookſellers of *Dublin*, 1698.

Title page, *1641 Sermon*, Nathanael Foy, 1698 [National Library of Ireland].

1641 AND THE QUEST FOR CATHOLIC EMANCIPATION, 1691–1829

Jacqueline Hill

The significance of the 1641 rebellion for those who championed the catholic cause in the eighteenth century can hardly be in doubt. From mid-century on, one campaigner after another took up the subject, with a view to combatting prevailing protestant perceptions of the rebellion – that it had revealed Irish Roman Catholics to be both disloyal and barbarous, capable of planning and (in part) perpetrating the most extensive, cruel and unprovoked massacre of their protestant neighbours. John Curry, Charles O'Conor, Fr Arthur O'Leary – to name only some of the more prominent protagonists – all felt the compulsion to campaign on this issue, and some became almost obsessed with it.[1] These catholic revisionists deployed various counter-arguments denying that the rebellion had been unprovoked, or that more than a tiny fraction of the numbers allegedly massacred had been killed, and their arguments have (in general if not always in detail) been endorsed by modern scholarship.[2] However, the persistence of the revisionist campaign into the nineteenth century suggests that stereotypical views were difficult to eradicate. Nor was the campaign confined to Ireland. In Britain, Edmund Burke threw his weight behind it;[3] and so, after the union, in the Westminster parliament, did Henry Grattan. The Dubliner Mathew Carey, sometime proprietor of the *Volunteer Journal*, who emigrated to the United States in 1784 and became a leading publisher there, devoted much effort in the 1810s to compiling a refutation of what he felt were the grossest errors in existing (protestant) perceptions of the rebellion.[4]

All this, plus the fact that the last great goals of the emancipation movement – admission to parliament and to the higher levels of the public service – were only achieved after unprecedented popular agitation in Ireland, might seem to indicate that the campaign had no effect, and that the significance of the rebellion was unchanging. Both assumptions would be wrong. Influential sections of the protestant community in Ireland and in Britain proved capable of modifying their views of the rebellion. Nor, despite appearances, was the crusade to

159

alter protestant thinking on the rebellion invariably at the centre of catholic strategy. Indeed, the changing importance of 1641 can serve to illuminate the varying nature of the catholic question itself in the era after the Williamite revolution. This can best be illustrated by breaking the period 1691–1829 down into three main sub-periods, 1691–1746 (from the treaty of Limerick to the Jacobite rising in Scotland, 1745–6); 1747–82 (from the rising to the winning of Irish legislative independence); and 1783–1829 (from legislative independence to emancipation), and looking at each separately.

I   1691–1746

By contrast with later periods, these years saw no significant new efforts to modify protestant prejudices about the rebellion, and little was added to those works which, published before the Williamite revolution, had set out to give catholic versions of events in the 1640s. Those works themselves were not revived: no new edition appeared, for instance, of the earl of Castlehaven's *Memoirs*, which had first been published in 1680, and which was highly critical of the conduct of the lords justice at the outset of the rebellion.[5]

An obvious explanation for the failure of the Catholics to campaign on this issue might be sought in their defeated condition following the Williamite victories. This was the age, *par excellence*, of the penal laws, most of which were introduced between the 1690s and the 1720s.[6] It was also the quintessential age of the anniversary service, a tradition which, in respect of 1641, was inaugurated in 1662. In that year the Irish parliament decreed that 'all and every person and persons inhabiting within this realm of Ireland shall yearly, upon the twenty-third day of October, diligently and faithfully resort to the parish church or chappel accustomed', for a service of thanksgiving. 23 October commemorated the day on which the alleged plan to extirpate the Protestants had been revealed, thus (according to the act) saving many from 'a conspiracy so generally inhumane, barbarous and cruel, as the like was never before heard of in any age or kingdom'. Prayers for the day called on Protestants to repent of their sins – for which they had indeed deserved to die – and to justify God's goodness in preserving so many of them from massacre by 'a thorough reformation of [their] lives'.[7]

It has recently been argued that during Charles II's reign (1660–85) the authorities in Ireland regarded this commemoration with a certain ambivalence; but in the aftermath of the Jacobite defeat they enthusiastically endorsed it, and the day was routinely marked by the viceroy, or lords justice, proceeding in state to Christ Church cathedral, where prayers for the day would be read, and an appropriate sermon delivered (and subsequently published). Such occasions lent themselves to hyperbole: the bishop of Waterford and Lismore, Nathanael Foy, preaching before the house of lords in 1698, contended that 'the Romish Church' shared many of the characteristics of 'the Heathen' – save that in 'Blood and Cruelty', the former had outstripped the latter:

> In proof of which, if all the Annals, and Records of Time were Cancel'd, all the Monuments of Papal Cruelty defac'd, save the Memory of this day, this single day were sufficient to convince all Mankind, that have not abjur'd their Sense, and Reason, how much the One has out-done the Other.[8]

The gentry, townspeople and members of local corporations usually attended church on that day, and there is some evidence that Presbyterians, as well as members of the established church, observed the anniversary. There was also a popular dimension: in a typical description, *Faulkner's Dublin Journal* for 21–4 October 1732 recorded that 'the Night concluded with Ringing of bells, Bonefires (sic), Illuminations [the practice of decorating buildings with coloured lights], and other Demonstrations of Joy'. Thus the commemoration was an important one for Irish Protestants. It served to maintain morale by reinforcing the idea that providence was on their side; while by demonising Catholics it also helped to justify the confiscations and penal legislation which had been implemented following the Cromwellian and Williamite conquests.[9]

If ever, therefore, the Irish Catholics were crushed and unable to speak up for themselves, it would appear to have been during this period. Perhaps because this has seemed so obvious, catholic attitudes in the half-century after the treaty of Limerick have received little detailed study.[10] However, there are signs that some Catholics, at least, were prepared to speak up for their cause, and that they did so with relative impunity. Fr Cornelius Nary, for instance, parish priest of St Michan's in Dublin, has been described by his biographer as 'by far the most considerable catholic figure in the first half of the century', who spoke out 'fearlessly and ... trenchantly for catholic rights and beliefs'. He not only managed to publish a number of important religious works, but also engaged in controversy with various members of the established church. The works reveal that Fr Nary's understanding of 'the catholic question' was very different from that of the generation which was to follow him. Nary's approach was to engage Protestants in debate as to points of theology ('to lay before them the dangerous conquences of their errors and the desperate state of their souls').[11] He was prepared to discuss the infallibility of the church, the supremacy of the pope, the invocation of saints, and other points on which Catholics and Protestants differed. Not only does this cast doubt on the picture of Catholics as utterly crushed and cowed,[12] it raises another issue. A question often asked about the age of the penal laws is, did the protestant élite either expect or want to bring about the wholesale conversion of catholics?[13] The proposition that Catholics might have seen a possibility of converting the Protestants seems, at first sight, preposterous: to take only one of the penal laws, the bishops' banishment act of 1697 would, if strictly enforced, have placed the very existence of the Irish catholic church in doubt.[14] And yet Fr Nary acted as if conversion was both desirable and possible.

The paradox may be resolved if the wider European situation is taken into account. In Ireland the Roman Catholic Church had suffered a serious setback following the defeat of the Jacobites and the rejection by the Irish parliament of much of what the Williamite leaders had conceded in the treaty of Limerick (1691). But elsewhere the prospects for the counter-reformation looked far brighter. The effects of war and a string of princely conversions to Rome during the seventeenth century had transformed the confessional map of Europe. At the beginning of the century something like half the population of Europe had been protestant; by the end, the figure was more like twenty per cent, and protestantism had been largely pushed back to the northern fringes of the continent.[15] In this unstable climate, there were still many churchmen (on all sides) who expected and hoped for the triumph of their own faith over others. For their part, rulers did not yet habitually distinguish between civil and religious allegiance. Even 'enlightened' thinkers, while they might deplore persecution on purely religious grounds, were nonetheless prepared to see 'toleration' severely restricted in the interests of the safety of the civil state:[16] they were still a long way from welcoming diversity, or supporting what we might call 'pluralism'. Thus the task of conversion, of attempting to shift people from one confession to another, still had many supporters, as it had done ever since the reformation.

For all those living in dominions under the English crown, the issue of confessional allegiance was further complicated after the Williamite revolution by the Jacobite claim to the throne. Recent scholarship has largely rescued Jacobitism in England and Scotland from the obscure position it used to occupy, and has stressed (at least for the early part of the period, before the Hanoverian accession) how likely it must have appeared that a Stuart restoration would take place.[17] England in the 1690s had yet to become firmly established as a major European power; James II, and later, his son, James [III], had the backing of the Vatican and of Europe's leading power, France. And given that it was still generally taken for granted that states took their religion from their rulers, a Stuart restoration was believed to mean that catholicism would revert to being the official religion of the state. Not surprisingly, in Ireland, few Catholics were willing to take the oath to abjure the Stuarts, which involved denying the Stuart title to the throne.[18] Against this broader background, Fr Nary's activities in Dublin do not seem odd or misplaced. Confessional stability could not be taken for granted in early eighteenth-century Ireland – on either side. And if the triumph of protestantism seemed likely to be short-lived, why spend time and trouble trying to change protestant perceptions of the 1641 rebellion?

Such considerations help explain why perhaps the most popular catholic work published in this period, Hugh Reily's *Ireland's case briefly stated* (1695), was an out-and-out Jacobite tract.[19] Reily had been James II's clerk of the council in Ireland, and had gone with him into exile after the battle of the Boyne. His book did contain a defence of the catholic record in 1641, arguing that they rather than the Protestants had been the principal victims of the rebellion:

> The Catholicks suffered in much greater Numbers, but dying as it were dumb, like so many Sheep brought to the Slaughter, their Blood made no great Noise, at least in *England*; but the Protestants fell, as I may say, with so many speaking Trumpets in their Mouths, that every individual seemed an hundred ...[20]

Reily's eloquence, however, was directed not at protestant opinion (he did not trouble to hide his conviction that protestantism was a false religion), but rather at the exiled (perhaps soon to be restored) Stuart dynasty, in order to recall these monarchs to their obligations towards their faithful and wronged Irish catholic followers.

II 1747–82

By the mid-eighteenth century, circumstances were changing. Contrary to what might have been expected, the altered succession to the English crown in 1714 (which involved setting aside more than fifty claimants with better titles) to ensure that the monarchy would be protestant had proved relatively successful. True, there had been risings in support of the Stuarts in 1715 and 1745–6, and Vatican recognition of the Stuart claim was not to cease until the death of James [III] in 1766. Nor did the first two Hanoverian kings, George I and II, enjoy the sort of popularity that would come to the English-born George III towards the end of the century.[21] But events in the 1740s had shown that even in Scotland, where Jacobite allegiance was most active, the existing regime commanded much support, while in England, the quite widespread cult of Jacobitism produced very few adherents who were prepared to go out and fight to restore the rival dynasty. Against this background, it was inevitable that some Irish Catholics should begin to reassess their position, and their relations with what looked increasingly like a permanent protestant dynasty with its corresponding confessional state. A fresh approach seemed necessary; something beyond the offer in 1727 of a simple oath of allegiance to George II (an offer which in any case carried little conviction, since it had still not been accompanied by an offer to abjure the Stuarts).[22]

Any approach by Catholics anxious to seek accommodation with the protestant regime, however, would have to overcome considerable obstacles, not all of which were on the protestant side. For Jacobite sympathies were more than mere habits of thought. Catholic bishops were nominated by James [III]; the Vatican still approved the Stuart claim; many Irish Catholics had taken service in the armies of foreign powers, such as France, which also backed the Stuarts.[23] And it was of little use to invoke overseas precedents for 'toleration', because Irish and British Protestants tended to look to conditions in France (where remaining Protestants still languished following the withdrawal of toleration in 1685), rather than to certain parts of the German empire, where the Peace of Westphalia (1648) had been rather more successful in guaranteeing the rights of the different Christian churches. But one area where progress perhaps could be made if there were to be a rapprochement between the Catholics and the state concerned the appalling public image of Irish Catholics, which was preserved and cherished in anniversary sermons and protestant histories. The 'massacre' of 1641 had taken its place alongside the 1572 massacre of St Bartholomew's Day in France as evidence of the inveterate malignancy of Catholics towards Protestants. Hence the importance attached to setting the record straight on 1641.[24]

The fact that the early work was mostly published anonymously reflects the controversial nature of the exercise. The campaign opened with the publication of *A brief account from the most authentic protestant writers of the causes, motives, and mischiefs, of the Irish rebellion ... 1641* (London, 1747). Its author was Dr John Curry, whose family had lost its land in the various seventeenth-century confiscations. Medicine was one profession not barred to Catholics, and after qualifying on the continent, Curry returned to his native Dublin to practise. His approach was to be much copied by others: to avoid (where possible) relying on direct catholic testimony, and instead to point out inconsistencies or contradictions in the protestant record, and to take extracts from the more reasoned protestant accounts, as likely to carry more weight with a protestant readership. The method (especially when compounded, as in this case, by the author posing as a Protestant) was not fool-proof; there was always the chance that the author's real identity would be discovered by some alert Irish Protestant. In this case, the Dublin antiquarian, Walter Harris, responded with *Fiction unmasked: or, an answer to a dialogue lately published by a popish physitian, and pretended to have passed between a dissenter, and a member of the Church of Ireland; wherein the causes, motives, and mischiefs of the Irish rebellion and massacres in 1641 are laid thick upon the protestants* (Dublin, 1752). But the risk of being exposed was probably outweighed by the advantage of offering those Protestants who might be supposed to have an open mind (especially, perhaps, those in England) a more dispassionate version of the rebellion than that contained in Sir

John Temple's notorious account, *The Irish rebellion: or, an history of the general rebellion raised within the kingdom of Ireland ... together with the barbarous cruelties and bloody massacres which ensued thereupon* (London, 1646: reissued 1679, 1713, 1724, 1746, 1766, and 1812).

It might be expected that the revisionist exercise would be assisted by the European Enlightenment, which by mid-century was entering its mature phase. But the Enlightenment was marked generally by anticlericalism and, frequently, by anti-catholicism; and since there was also a very strong didactic strain in the works of the leading *philosophes*, the result was decidedly mixed. On the one hand, writers from the protestant tradition became more sceptical of the supernatural elements in the contemporary tales of massacre; stories of ghosts rising from rivers, and spirits shrieking for revenge, were firmly discounted as superstitious fancies.[25] On the other hand, no less a figure than the Scot David Hume drew on conventional accounts of the rebellion to convey the pernicious effects of irrational religious enthusiasm, and he was quite prepared to repeat the standard allegations that the Irish Catholics (urged on by their priests) had attempted a 'universal massacre' of the Protestants.[26]

Thus the task of defending the catholic record was a slow and frustrating one for the 'Hanoverian' Catholics and their supporters, such as Burke.[27] Bearing in mind that their ultimate aim was to obtain relief from the penal laws, however, there was one fortuitous and important factor working in their favour. This was the ever-increasing need of the British government for military recruits. Armies in Europe were becoming steadily larger, and by the 1770s eyes were beginning to turn to the untapped sources of manpower in the Scottish Highlands and in Ireland. Catholics were not permitted to bear arms in England, Scotland, or Ireland, so if this resource were to be used beyond informal and small-scale levels, some sort of relaxation of the penal laws would be necessary, as Robert Donovan has shown.[28] Moreover, the worsening relations between Britain and her American colonies in the early 1770s helped to bring about a change of heart in British government circles towards the new catholic subjects in Quebec, who (by contrast with the Americans) appeared to be a docile and deferential people. The Quebec act of 1774 recognised the rights of the Roman Catholic Church in respect of its property, and allowed it to levy tithes on Catholics; an oath of allegiance was introduced to allow Catholics to swear loyalty to George III (and hence serve on the governor's council) without also acknowledging the royal supremacy over the church. All this was intended to foster catholic loyalty in Quebec; some even envisaged the use of Quebec Catholics to fight the Americans, should relations with the colonists reach breaking point.[29]

It was no accident, therefore, that the 1770s also witnessed the first significant improvement in the status of Irish Catholics, although not to the extent of those in Quebec. An oath of allegiance was introduced in 1774 to allow them to swear their allegiance to George III – without recognising the royal supremacy. (The terms of the oath did not meet with Rome's approval, and few Catholics proved willing to take it until 1778). In 1778 Catholics who took the oath were allowed to take long leases and inherit land on the same terms as Protestants. And in 1782 freedom of worship was conceded, and the laws preventing Catholics from buying land and teaching school were repealed. All this had also been facilitated by the death of James [III] in 1766, and the failure of the Vatican to endorse the claims of the young pretender.[30]

At the same time, it would be a mistake to suppose that anti-popery had disappeared, or that the concessions of the 1770s and early 1780s were perceived by Protestants as leading inexorably towards the relax-ation of the entire penal code. Indeed, the catholic spokesmen themselves had not presented their case in such terms. They talked not of rights, but of the evil economic effects of preventing Catholics from buying and selling land, and the loss to Ireland of industrious citizens who were forced by the effects of penal legislation to make their careers abroad.[31] Meanwhile, despite occasional self-questioning about the value of such events,[32] the annual protestant commemoration of the 1641 rebellion, as enjoined by the act of 1662, continued – with government support. On 23 October viceroys still frequently proceeded in state, accompanied by leading office holders, civil and ecclesiastical, to hear morning prayer; and dignitaries of the established church still preached at Christ Church on the occasion. Although subtle changes no doubt crept into these homilies over the years, the overall thrust of the sermons preached in the 1760s was comparable with those preached in the 1690s:

> The Annals of every Age – since the first Establishment of Papal Usurpation – the Records of every Country – where it has gained firm Footing – are stained with the bloody Marks of its Tyranny. – To shew, that in these Imputations we do no Injustice to the Maintainers of it; need we go farther? than to the History of that dreadful Tragedy, which was in Part acted, but, by God's wonderful Providence, disappointed of its full Execution; Our Deliverance from which, we are this Day Assembled to commemorate.[33]

Admittedly, the custom of publishing such sermons was falling into abeyance. And, notwithstanding David Hume's unfortunate comments, the tone of protestant accounts of the rebellion period was changing. No longer was it being suggested that the outbreak had been entirely unprovoked; no longer were Temple's grossly inflated and literally incredible figures for protestant victims of massacre being uncritically accepted, despite the appearance of a new edition of that work in 1766.

But contemporary accounts in Ireland and Britain were still marked both by anticlericalism and aversion to the 'superstition' and 'absurdities' of the catholic religion.[34]

III   1783–1829

By the 1780s the 1641 rebellion, though far from forgotten, was becoming more marginal. John Curry died in 1780, having published his last great work on the subject in 1775.[35] The state drew back from the annual commemoration, apparently without attracting adverse comment: the last viceroy recorded as having gone in state to Christ Church on 23 October was the duke of Rutland in 1784.[36] (There are occasional later references, especially during the period of the French wars, to flags flying from the Bedford tower at Dublin Castle on 23 October, and to the firing of the Phoenix Park guns).[37] Dublin's lord mayor and corporation kept up the tradition of a public procession to church and a dinner for many years after 1784, but the significance of the anniversary was shrinking – in 1788 the *Dublin Chronicle* (which enjoyed a considerable circulation throughout the whole country) described it as 'the anniversary of the deliverance of *Dublin* from the intended massacre' (emphasis added).[38] Meanwhile, though evidence has been found for only one parish, there is some suggestion that the commemoration was losing its appeal at the local level. At St Werburgh's parish, Dublin, records show that the bells were rung for 23 October only twice (1786 and 1792) in two seven-year periods (1782–8, 1792–8).[39]

These developments were in keeping with the significant relaxation in the penal laws which had taken place by 1782, and which had been accomplished without provoking significant opposition among Protestants. Prospects for additional relief, however, were less promising. Further relief would inevitably raise the question of extending political rights to Catholics: and this was an issue of great sensitivity which posed fundamental questions about the nature of the British (and Irish) constitution. It was thus more than simply an Irish issue. This was presaged by the controversy aroused in Britain over the Quebec act, during which the elder William Pitt, now earl of Chatham, argued that if the king sanctioned a quasi-catholic establishment in Quebec, this would compromise his coronation oath, and undermine 'all the safe-guards and barriers against the return of Popery and of Popish influence, so wisely provided against by all the oaths of office ... from the constable ... to the sovereign'.[40] That position had much support in Britain, although the anti-catholic Gordon riots of 1780 served, in some degree, to discredit this hard-line protestant position.

In view of this sensitivity, it was understandable that in Ireland, the Catholic Committee, which had been labouring since the 1760s for the relaxation of the penal laws, should take a cautious and deferential approach. Even Fr Arthur O'Leary, perhaps the most uninhibited of the catholic spokesmen during the 1780s, who was beginning to apply the language of natural rights to catholic claims, was prepared to concede that further relief might require Catholics to be excluded from various political rights.[41] When certain of the Volunteers (originally formed to defend Ireland from the threat of invasion during the American war) did raise the question of extending the vote to Catholics in 1783–4, it aroused such hostility among Protestants that the issue was dropped for the remainder of the decade.[42]

What transformed the prospects for Catholics obtaining political rights was not so much the campaign of Wolfe Tone and the United Irishmen in 1791 as the conversion of the British government in the winter of 1791–2. Down to this point, while a good deal of the pressure for relaxation of the penal laws in the 1770s had come from government, Irish Protestants had retained the comforting sense that they were in control of events. Accordingly, the government's change of policy – designed to keep the Irish majority firmly on the side of counter-revolution in the ideological war with radical reformers – caused a major shock to the Irish political system.[43] In principle, the resulting backlash might have involved the regeneration of the 23 October tradition. In practice, however, it was the Williamite tradition that came to the fore as the focus for protestant resistance. It was the Williamite revolution that was invoked in 1792 by Dublin corporation in order to rally Protestants behind the existing 'protestant ascendancy', and it was a Williamite victory (the battle of the Boyne) which was to form the centre of the Orange Order's cult of loyalty from its foundation in 1795.[44] Why was this?

Two main reasons may be advanced. First, the efforts to rescue the Catholics from the most exaggerated charges arising from the early protestant accounts of the rebellion had had an effect, as noted above. But more important, it was the Williamite revolution which was generally regarded as forming the foundation of British and Irish constitutional rights. Admittedly, there were important – and increasing – differences among observers as to what those rights actually were. For Dr Price and other English radical reformers, the revolution was the foundation for extensive popular rights, including, crucially, the right to change the system of government. For Edmund Burke, the revolution was much more conservative.[45] Burke also challenged what was, for most Protestants in Britain and Ireland, still a fundamental plank of the revolution: that it had created an unalterably protestant constitution.[46]

For the Irish Protestants opposed to political rights for Catholics, the revolution had indeed given the constitution a firm and permanent protestant character. The monarchy, parliament, the established church, the benches of justice, the army, the electorate – all must be and must remain protestant.[47] Clearly this was a defensive stand; but it was far from being a merely defensive stand. The reasoning that lay behind Dublin corporation's confident elaboration of the basis for 'protestant ascendancy' was that the Williamite revolution represented the verdict of divine providence on the clash between an 'arbitrary and unconstitutional Popish tyrant' and 'our ancestors'. The 'great ruler of all things decided in favour of our ancestors, he gave them victory and Ireland became a Protestant nation enjoying a British constitution'. In this way, the defenders of the protestant constitution were signalling their view that the revolution represented a victory not just of one religion over another, but also of a [protestant] people over the monarchy. Their warning against tampering with the constitution was therefore aimed as much, or more, at the British government, as at their catholic fellow-countrymen – towards whom they adopted a (relatively) conciliatory tone, addressing them as 'Roman catholics', rather than as 'papists'.[48]

Such opposition proved only temporarily capable of halting the British government's determination to extend political rights to the Irish Catholics. In 1792 and 1793 these were granted very extensive political rights, with the major exceptions of admission to parliament and to the higher levels of the public service. In view of such gains, the Catholic Committee decided to disband.[49] However, it soon became apparent that the mere repeal of penal laws would not necessarily produce the expected benefits. In the absence of more general reform of the political system, it was frequently possible for Irish Protestants to block the exercise of these new rights. And the bearing of arms by Catholics was bitterly resented, especially in Ulster, where the Orange Order was established following local sectarian clashes in county Armagh in 1795.[50]

The reason for the emergence of 12 July as the focus for the Orange cult is not immediately obvious. A number of Williamite anniversaries had been observed during the eighteenth century, and 12 July was by no means the most prominent. 1 July (the battle of the Boyne, Old Style), 12 July (the battle of Aughrim), and 4 November (William's birthday) were all celebrated. None of these enjoyed the formal legislative and liturgical status of 23 October and 4 November, though William's landing in England on 5 November 1688 was commemorated along with the gunpowder plot in prayers for that day.[51] Press reports make it clear that the July anniversaries were populist occasions, marked by the firing of guns, bonfires, dinners, and 'the usual demonstrations of joy'.[52] The fourth of November was something more. From early in the century, the day had received state recognition. Except for a controversial period around the time of the Hanoverian accession, it was customary for the viceroy, when resident, to hold a formal reception in the morning, and then to take part in a procession from Dublin Castle to

College Green, round the great equestrian statue of King William (erected by Dublin corporation in 1701), and then to St Stephen's Green, accompanied by leading office holders and members of the nobility and gentry, their carriages decorated with orange and blue ribbons and cockades. A regiment of cavalry often took part in the procession, and foot soldiers from the garrison lined the streets; the guns in the Phoenix Park were fired, and the soldiers responded with volleys of small arms fire. Occasionally, in a tradition stretching back to the beginning of the century, there was a performance of the play *Tamerlane* at the Theatre Royal in the evening.[53]

The day was thus already a major event in the Dublin anniversary calendar when it was further embellished during the 1770s by becoming 'sacred to the glorious institution of the Volunteers of Ireland', as one newspaper put it.[54] What this meant in practice was that from the time of their formation in 1778 down to 1792, it was customary for the Volunteer corps of Dublin city and county, often in the presence of the earl of Charlemont, the general in overall charge of the Volunteers, to parade under arms to the statue and fire off their guns in honour of the anniversary, thus coming near to eclipsing the viceregal procession later in the day. This was not merely an occasion for military display: from 1779 to 1785 it was the practice on 4 November to hang the statue's pedestal with placards proclaiming the Volunteers' current political demands.[55]

It might have been supposed, then, that if the Orangemen wanted to choose the Williamite anniversary with the highest public profile, they would have picked 4 November. And it might have been politically advantageous to have chosen a day that was still so publicly patronised by the state. On the other hand, the Orangemen's attitude towards a government that had undermined so much of the legal basis for 'protestant ascendancy' was ambivalent.[56] In any case, 4 November, though it was clearly identified with the celebration of constitutional rights, did not commemorate any of the Williamite military victories. It therefore gave no direct opportunity, at the popular protestant level, for vicarious triumph over popish king and rebels.[57] Moreover (although the subject requires further investigation), outside Dublin the military anniversaries probably enjoyed greater popularity than 4 November. What gave 12 July the edge over 1 July was that by conflating the old and new style dates, 12 July could stand for both the main Williamite victories, the Boyne as well as Aughrim.[58]

Meanwhile, what of 1641? The 1798 rising, which more nearly resembled a civil war than the union of hearts envisaged by the United Irishmen, put new life into the 'massacre' tradition and its literature. Sir Richard Musgrave's *Memoirs of the different rebellions in Ireland* (1801) claimed that repeated rebellions showed that Protestants and Catholics could not live together in Ireland on equal terms, because Irish

Catholics (and their priests) were different from those elsewhere: more implacably hostile to Protestants and more contemptuous of the rule of law.[59] His views were taken up by some of the staunchest opponents of catholic emancipation in the Westminster parliament, such as Dr Patrick Duigenan.[60] As the emancipation campaign progressed, some Protestants saw only the Orange Order standing between them and the danger of another 1641.[61] Proponents of emancipation, not surprisingly, felt obliged to defend the catholic record in 1641: according to the veteran patriot Henry Grattan, the rebellion was not inspired by religion, but by real grievances over land, persecution of priests, and the unsettled state of high politics in England, Scotland and Ireland.[62]

Despite these signs, however, the revived massacre tradition remained essentially marginal to the fate of catholic emancipation. Dr Duigenan's diatribes on the history of Ireland did not prove popular in the Westminster parliament, and the Orange Order was viewed with a good deal of suspicion on account of its 'conditional' loyalty.[63] Besides, catholic spokesmen had also shifted their focus from 1641 to the Williamite revolution; some claimed that the treaty of Limerick had secured them the right to vote.[64] Thus the final phase of the emancipation campaign from the 1790s down to 1829 was dominated by a protracted debate over the nature and significance of the 'glorious' revolution. Hadn't the revolution, as argued by Chatham in the 1770s, given the constitution a fundamentally protestant character? And wasn't this character necessary to safeguard not merely protestant rights and liberties, but those of all the king's subjects, by preventing churchmen acquiring too much power? Or could politics and religion be safely separated, as contended by the Whigs from the late eighteenth century on, and by successive catholic spokesmen in Ireland, from O'Conor and Curry to Daniel O'Connell? If so, why was the Vatican so reluctant to recognise such a separation, except on its own terms? The issues were thrashed out in the British parliament again and again after 1800, but the Whigs made only slow progress, and it was not until 1821 that there appeared a majority for the Whig-catholic position in the house of commons. Even then it took the mobilisation of the catholic masses and, above all, O'Connell's election for county Clare in 1828, to induce the government to persuade the king and the house of lords to grant emancipation in 1829.[65]

A BRIEFE

DECLARATION

OF THE BARBAROVS

And inhumane dealings of the
Northerne *Irish* Rebels, and many others
in severall Counties up-rising against the
English, that dwelt both lovingly and
securely among them.

VVRITTEN TO EXCITE

The *English* Nation to relieve our
poore Wives and Children, that have escaped
the Rebels savage crueltie, and that shall arive
safe among them in *England*; And in exchange
to send aid of men, and meanes forth-
with to quell their boundlesse inso-
lencies, with certaine encou-
ragements to the worke.

By G.S. Minister of Gods word in Ireland.

Volanti calamo, dolenti ànimo.
In mundo pressuram.

JOHN 16.2.
*The time commeth that whosoever killeth you, thinkes that hee doth God
good service.*

Published by direction from the
State of Ireland.

LONDON,
Printed by *A.N.* for *Abel Roper*, at the blacke spread
Eagle against St. *Dunstans* Church in

Title page, *A brief declaration of the barbarous and inhumane dealings of the northern Irish rebels* (1642)
[National Library of Ireland].

1641 : A BIBLIOGRAPHICAL ESSAY

Toby Barnard

'I have been living in the Ireland of 1641–2 during the last week, and a very unpleasant country it is to be in.' So grumbled S.R. Gardiner in 1881, at the time (and since) England's most meticulous historian of the early seventeenth century.[1] Yet others of his scholarly contemporaries, both in England and Ireland – Sir John Gilbert, Mary Hickson, J.A. Froude, C.H. Firth and R.T. Dunlop – chose to journey back to the same bloodthirsty years. All were still fascinated by 1641: as event, as historiographical problem, and as a potent symbol. Let us consider why.

At first, publications about 1641 purported simply to tell what had happened; but, from the start, they confused the insurgents' intentions with the actuality. Later writers stood back and classified the events: whether or not they were merely a series of agrarian outrages, peasant risings or *jacqueries*, eruptions of religious or racial hatred, a long-matured conspiracy or nimble-footed opportunism; and whether they belonged to a larger British or European crisis. Successive generations have been beguiled into investigating the uprising because, siren-like, it straddles a daunting heap of evidence, within which, it has been assumed, must be concealed the answers to the perennial conundrums: why did it start? how and how fast did it engulf the island? how many were murdered, or tortured, robbed and driven from their homes? By the nineteenth century, serious enquirers, mistrustful of the standard accounts with their obvious errors, aspired to extract a kernel of indisputable historical 'truth' from the deceptive husk of legend which had hardened around the episode.[2] With their superior technical skills, and given industry and application, they could sift and evaluate the copious materials. Yet these Victorian optimists, strive as they did, could not entirely shake off the partisanship which they had detected and condemned in their forerunners. Even the most dispassionate in some, and the unionist and nationalist partisans in large measure wrote under the shadow of turbulent Anglo-Irish relations, to which views of 1641 could still add. For Protestants and unionists, the rebellion with its attendant 'massacres' had always warned of catholic perfidy and irredentism.

Roman Catholics, for their part, struggled to free themselves from a distressingly tenacious reputation for disloyalty and savagery, and blamed their protagonists for exaggerating or even fabricating what had occurred in the early 1640s in order first to introduce and then to sustain a system of subjection. As at each earlier moment when the controversies over 1641 had been publicly rehearsed – 1660–2, 1678–9, 1685–90, 1714–15, 1745 and 1766 – so in the late nineteenth century the past danced a spritely *pas de deux* with the present. In the familiar configurations, protestant steadfastness opposed catholic slipperiness; loyalty, rebelliousness; heroism, cowardice; and civility, Gaelic barbarism. Arcane wrangles over specific pieces of historical evidence often degenerated into angry tussles which spoke primarily of confessional and ethnic atavism and remembered or manufactured animosities. Thus, the regular revisiting of 1641, though it owed something to supposed improvements in historical methods, was usually prompted by, and in its turn contributed to, contemporary grudges.

The very abundance of the evidence spawned divergent explanations of the uprising. Late in 1641, a flustered Dublin administration, faced first with localized trouble in Ulster and having scotched a bid to seize Dublin Castle and with it the government of Ireland, dithered as disorder spread and manifested sinister political connotations. Activists and opportunists, among them clergy of the Church of Ireland headed by Henry Jones, sometimes with the Dublin government's approval, often on their own initiative, published lurid accounts of particular atrocities and engagements. Through these pamphlets, issued mainly in London, the beleaguered Irish Protestants advertised their plight to a wider protestant world, and solicited that support from England and Scotland which alone could save them.[3] This clear propagandist purpose from the start coloured the publications. By 1642, Jones had blended the separate incidents into a hair-raising story of a planned and comprehensive catholic rebellion punctuated with pogroms of protestant settlers and clerics.[4] These tracts, vivid in their details, plausible in their larger explanations and written by men of weight within Irish protestant society, soon entrenched a highly partisan interpretation as a factual chronicle. This view, refined by Jones and perfected in 1646 by the Master of the Irish Rolls, Sir John Temple, in his book *The Irish Rebellion*, was so willingly believed because it accorded with protestant preconceptions and expectations. Furthermore, Temple's magisterial tone was calculated to silence doubters.[5] Much that Jones and Temple reported seemed to be confirmed, either generally or specifically, by the shocked refugees who had first crowded into Dublin and Waterford, and then shipped themselves to the western seaboards of Scotland, Wales and England. Moreover, biblical and recent history had conditioned small protestant settlements to expect attack both from within and from without. The puny protestant population of Ireland, flattered to be part of God's chosen people but fearful that it might not measure up to the responsibilities, alternated between exhilaration and edginess: moods which affected its relations with catholic neighbours. When something nasty did indeed happen in the distant hinterlands, explanations were to hand: that this was part of a providential scheme in which the elect would be tested and tempered in the fire. Such modes of explanation allowed Jones and Temple to weld the fragments into a powerful history, which could simultaneously lash and cheer their fretful co-religionists.[6]

At the same time, the speed and ease with which these protestant partisans had woven together the scattered evidence to ensnare the whole catholic population, and the relevance of this to the future policies of dispossession, vengeance and discrimination, soon led catholics to impugn the published accounts as fabrications.[7] Indeed, the blatant forging of a national legend for the Irish Protestants, reminiscent of those which already memorialized the persecuted Protestants of France, the Low Countries and England,[8] made some catholic apologists suspect that Jones and his crew had not just exaggerated, but invented, much of what they described. Protestants furiously rebutted this slur, and pointed to the wealth of evidence from which Jones, Temple and the other pamphleteers had drawn their gruesome details: the depositions.[9]

Earlier rebellions in Ireland had been followed by judicial processes, chiefly to determine the ownership and extent of the lands to be forfeited by the rebels. In comparison, the inquisitions authorized by the Dublin government from December 1641 looked premature. Commissions, manned largely by the Church of Ireland clergy (who had furnished a disproportionate number of targets of the recorded violence) were to collect local testimonies on oath, first about losses, soon about deaths, which would, when the Protestants had won the war, identify and incriminate the insurgents.[10] More immediately, these materials, though still in process of compilation and only sampled by Jones and Temple, underpinned their literary edifices. Intimidated by the bulk of, and the difficulties of access to, the depositions, and by the blunt way of Jones and Temple with sceptics, few contemporaries questioned either the facts of carnage and devastation or the punishments which they merited. Those who did were brusquely ridiculed as cranks, if not fellow-travellers with the Catholics.[11] So far from the accounts being doubted, the printed details were more commonly filched, garbled and elaborated, as sensation-mongers catered to the public appetite for horror and violence. Most notoriously, the tally of alleged protestant deaths rose almost exponentially: from 154,000 in 1642, to 250,000 in 1644, through Temple's estimate of 300,000 in 1646, to reach its peak in John Milton's calculation of 600,000.[12] Such shameless disregard either for plausibility or for the evidence of the depositions themselves outraged the supposed culprits, the Catholics, and alerted the reasonable to the processes of wilful and inadvertent misrepresentation at work. The quest for an accurate figure of victims has obsessed numerous later writers. Yet, while the absurdity of the gargantuan totals has rightly been lampooned, it is less often considered why they could so readily be circulated, repeated and believed. No doubt some scribblers, anxious to catch a fickle market, plucked figures from the air, ignorant or indifferent that Ireland in 1641 was inhabited by fewer than 100,000 Protestants. Others, desperate to engage English sympathy and to disable the Catholics for the future, calculated how best to rout the Irish papists. Such unscrupulousness characterized Jones's and Temple's efforts. Indeed the former, the self-appointed official historian of the rebellion, showed the topical uses of the information when, in 1652, he abstracted the atrocities and forwarded the information to the English Parliament just as it was finalizing the coming Irish resettlement.[13] But, in addition, the discrepant and fantastic totals told of a profound English ignorance of the demography and condition of Ireland, and, as Ireland itself dissolved into separate theatres of war, of the Irish Protestants' own reliance on hearsay and rumour. The swift purchase gained by panic and collective hysteria suggested societies in Ireland uneasy in their social, confessional and ethnic relationships. Furthermore, the depositions, notwithstanding their inconsistencies, repetitions and formulaic conventions, if they do not reveal the butchery of protestant fable, show a selective (and, occasionally, indiscriminate) use of terror, ritualized abuse and murder sufficient to shock and scar the victims and onlookers. Many Protestants, in Ireland as well as in England, not knowing exactly what was going on outside their immediate environs, swallowed the apparently authentic accounts, and obeyed the imperatives (stated or implicit) of protestant vigilance and vengeance.

Catholics, though quickly realising how they were besmirched by the Protestants' calumnies, did not retaliate successfully. Catholic ripostes, as yet little studied, certainly followed the same types and tropes as the Protestants' propaganda – loyalism, religion and justice; also the Catholics tried to turn the accusations of barbarism and gratuitous blood-letting against the Protestants. Thus the alternative government erected by the Catholics at Kilkenny, as well as apeing the fiscal and administrative devices of the English parliament, collected local evidence of protestant misdeeds.[14] So originated an essentially tit-for-tat approach which would bedevil the subsequent arguments over 1641, as partisans traded insults and each denounced the other for brutality and treachery. Whatever the details collected from the catholic quarters, they were not publicized in the 1640s: an omission which itself tells of an important difference between the catholic and protestant campaigns. The Irish Protestants, although hampered by having only one printing press in Dublin devoted mainly to issuing the numerous government orders and proclamations, benefited from, and themselves added to, the explosion of print in war-time London, where, as we have seen, most of their tracts appeared.[15] Both attitudes and practical difficulties may explain why the Confederate Catholics fumbled over exploiting the presses. Throughout the 1640s the insurgent Catholics disagreed, sometimes violently, over tactics and objectives, and these confusions weakened efforts to engage backing within the larger European catholic world. Aid was certainly sought, but through patient ecclesiastical diplomacy rather than crude publicity.[16] For their part the Protestants, very far from united, all agreed that the prerequisites for a stable Ireland were to defeat and disable the Irish catholic élites, and that only English assistance could accomplish these ends. In winning succour from England pamphlets could play a vital role.[17]

Shrewd Catholics knew how their chances of political and material betterment were hampered by the grim legend, and supposed that, could they but correct the record, they might be treated more generously. Their defeat after 1649 strengthened and prolonged the protestant version and further weakened the efforts of catholic publicists. The latter, separated from the evidence collected under the auspices of the Confederation of Kilkenny and from local printing presses which might publish it,[18] could only assert their innocence, rather than demonstrate it with massive documentation. Furthermore, their apologias had to be sneaked out either from continental or London presses. Immediately after Charles II was restored in 1660, Irish Catholics, scenting a chance, sought, as part of a campaign to lift their disabilities, to neutralize the stain spreading from 1641. Thus in England their patrician spokesmen disdainfully blamed the rascal multitude for the excesses of the 1640s, denied that the Irish Catholics had started the rebellion, and stressed their unwavering loyalty to the Stuarts.[19] Here then, both in the tone and nature of the arguments, and as the ground-bass which counterpointed a busy political lobby, the pattern of catholic refutation of the protestant story of 1641 had been established. The later seventeenth century witnessed the first of the series of public tussles between the historical partisans, which continue to this day.

Two works exemplified the opposed approaches, while the reaction to them showed how easily the smouldering embers could flare up. In 1662, *A Collection of the Murthers and Massacres committed on the Irish in Ireland since the 23d of October 1641*, its author concealed behind the initials R.S., and published in London, luxuriated in atrocities by the Protestants. To a list which may have been compiled by the agents of the Confederation in the 1640s, it added cruelties by the leading Cromwellian officers during the Interregnum[20]. Since the latter, regicides and unrepentant republicans, were now marked down for punishment, Charles II's government might welcome this extra evidence of their depravity. More generally, the tract seconded the lobbying of the Irish Catholics' agents, particularly at the Stuart court, for generosity, and amplified the approach first essayed in print by a recent *Narrative* of these same crimes.[21] (It would be worth trying to penetrate the disguise of R.S., who claimed never to have participated in the uprising, to have joined Charles I at his headquarters in Oxford and to have learnt of the alleged massacres, like most of his contemporaries, from 'gazettes and pamphlets printed in London'.) The Protestants who uneasily controlled the Dublin administration needed to entrench their own version of 1641, and to this end had recently institutionalized the annual commemoration of their trial and deliverance with a church service on 23 October.[22] They lambasted R.S's booklet as a mischievous device to unsettle. All copies were to be seized and burnt, turning the tract into a rarity anxiously sought by the inquisitive.[23] Censorship might, for a time, inhibit, the public circulation of catholic accounts of their mistreatment, but the outlook embodied in the *Narrative* and *Collection*, though forced underground, proved tenacious, and would reappear whenever the protestant authorities relaxed their guard.

As the Catholics suspected, so protestant sensitivity proved: the protestant monopoly over power had been constructed in, and was now justified by, 1641 and its aftermath. Yet protestant insistence on what they had then suffered grated on English monarchs and their ministers as they explored the possibility of a *modus vivendi* with the Irish catholic majority. The extent to which the indulgence of Charles II diverged from the intolerance of his Irish protestant subjects was quickly revealed; and introduced another theme – of the potential and actual conflict between the English government and the Irish protestant élites – which would recur. Charles II and his minions could not countermand the lately instituted public celebrations on 23 October, but they did interdict judicial proceedings and publications which rehearsed the battles of the 1640s.[24]

The book which had most authoritatively established a national myth hostile to the Irish Catholics was Temple's *Irish Rebellion*. As Dr Tom Bartlett has reminded us, between its first publication in 1646 and 1812, at least ten editions were issued.[25] If originally it had assisted the orchestrated campaign of Irish protestant refugees in and around London to excite or shame the English parliament into rescuing protestant Ireland and restoring it to the refugees, the different priorities of Charles II soon made Temple's a less timely tract. A rumoured reprint of the *Irish Rebellion* in 1672 – a moment of new confessional tension as Charles II's toleration was angrily (and successfully) opposed in England and Ireland – prompted minute probes into why the Dublin government could have been so careless as to allow it.[26] In the event, the reports proved false, but the fuss showed how dangerous Temple's

history was thought to be in awakening slumbering hatreds. Its importance, both to perceptions of the past and the current political tempera-
ture, was confirmed in 1689 when the Catholics briefly recovered
Ireland's government, and condemned the book. Thereafter, with its
reputation assured, its regular re-publication offers a useful barometer
to rising protestant anxieties. In 1812, for example, it was re-published
in London 'as the most effectual warning-piece' to tell the Protestants to
'guard against the encroachments of popery'.[27]

Even a cursory look at the later editions of Temple raises questions
for further study. The successive issues, printed sometimes in London
and sometimes in Ireland, adopted different formats and were, presumably, priced to sell to different kinds of readers. Furthermore, it was
altered and embellished. By 1724, for example, the fresh Dublin edition
was tricked out with six ghoulish vignettes opposite the title-page to
make instantly clear what was contained in the text. Noteworthy, too, is
the subtle change as what had originated as the sub-title, *The History of
the General Rebellion in Ireland raised upon the three and twentieth day of
October, 1641*, was elevated into the title itself. This unequivocally
proclaimed what Temple and his associates had always contended:
that, from its start – confidently dated to the 23 October – it was a *general*
rebellion, not simply scattered affrays in Ulster and a plot to snatch
Dublin Castle; long planned; involving Old English as well as Old Irish;
and rapidly enveloping the entire island. In 1724, the Dublin publisher
puffed his edition, reckoned the sixth, because it restored 'several entire
sentences omitted in all Irish editions', and, on the basis of the fullest
London edition – of 1679 – corrected 'many other omissions, errors
and mistakes'. These passages, including new, blatantly anti-catholic
invective, need to be precisely identified; so, too, the extent to which
Temple himself, or his clever sons, inspired and aided these changes
and re-issues.

The *Irish Rebellion*, a solid chronicle, sold for more than most could
pay. In 1760, for example, the 1724 edition was to be had in Dublin for
3s.6d: a price on a par with that for a workaday copy of the Bible.[28]
Owing to its size and cost, Temple's work was aimed primarily at
institutions and the prosperous. Humbler readers were more likely to
come by their knowledge of 1641 from the flimsier and ephemeral tracts
which handily digested the grizzliest incidents from Temple and Jones.
So it was, in the tense years of 1660, 1679 and 1689, collections and
abstracts again rolled from the London presses.[29] After 1662, enterpris-
ing publishers could include, as a savoury morsel for the purchaser of
Temple, the statute which commanded the annual festivities on the
23rd of October. The placing of the two works under the same cover
was particularly happy, since the 1662 act had resulted from, and then
sought to perpetuate, the antagonistic views that Temple had most
memorably formulated.[30]

However, a further problem is sketched in one of the later editions of Temple: that printed in Cork in 1766. This was published by subscription. A long list of over 700 subscribers revealed a market, perhaps created and manipulated by the canny publishers, maybe already there at a time of new protestant apprehensions.[31] What is also notable about the Cork subscribers, and others may analyse this more exactly, is their distinctive composition. At first glance the list is an unsurprising sample of Munster's solidly prospering and literate Protestant population: the attorneys, surgeons, army officers, clergymen and petty functionaries of the many small towns. Predictably women are rare; but so too, more unexpectedly, are notables – only one peer, a peer's son and a single baronet. Similarly, while clergymen formed the largest occupational group (as we might expect) – about 8 per cent of the total – these were the parish incumbents, not the bishops. The absences from the subscribers could be explained on the grounds that the social and cultural leaders of provincial Ireland already had Temple on their shelves. But a more interesting possibility, which only further research will test, is that these grandees, travelling readily and regularly between Munster, Dublin, England and the continent, did not wish to buy a book which pandered to embarrassing antagonisms. In the later seventeenth century, it seemed, the Stuarts, impatient with or insensitive to the anxieties of the Irish Protestants, had sought to implant an imported political and religious culture which appealed little to the indigenous Irish Protestants. But now, by the mid-eighteenth century, a larger and more diversified protestant population experienced cultural and intellectual shifts. Greater wealth and new stands of civility distanced the cosmopolitan notables and periodically absent Anglo-Irish from those living more continuously, if not exclusively, in the Irish provinces. The former, seldom encountering or being threatened by the Irish Catholics, disdained the cruder expressions of anti-catholicism. In contrast, those who were surrounded by, and often had to compete directly with, a large and growing catholic presence, upheld both the outlook and the discriminatory system which Temple had advocated. Thus, the very persistence and vitality of anti-catholicism, whether in its theological or civic forms, explored and aggravated the rifts among Irish Protestants and between them and their uncomprehending English rulers.

Nevertheless, if we regard Temple as an accurate register of sectarian heat, we have to explain his sudden loss of popularity in the early nineteenth century: not otherwise a period notable for Irish indifference to the past. It could be that interest shifted to other events, such as the Jacobite defeat and controverted treaty of Limerick in the 1690s or the turbulent 1790s, as more relevant to current politics. In 1859 another collective memory of 1641 was interred, when the service for the 23 October was dropped from the Church of Ireland's calendar.[32] This decree, issued by the Westminster parliament and apparently not discussed by the Church of Ireland convocation, may turn out to be a further instance of the rigorous subordination of Ireland to England, and the wish to import an insipidly uncontentious English protestant culture. The extent to which, in defiance of this order, 1641 continued to be celebrated would again merit investigation, especially at the local level.

More generally, by the later nineteenth century, interest in 1641, far from evaporating, had moved from the regular recitation of the opposed myths to a closer analysis of the testimony on which the rival accounts depended. Even before that, however, not all who read of and ruminated on the killings drew the intended conclusions. Thus for example, a contemporary of the uprising, apparently of Old English ancestry but protestant in religion, painstakingly compiled his own catalogue of the horrors. But when in the 1660s this bulky manuscript was inherited by his brother in England, the latter quarried it for its genealogical and heraldic titbits; and, on reading of a particularly savage attack, commented, 'this was great cruelty, but let any tell me and assure me he had not been an oppressive wretch when he had power'.[33] On the other hand, the normally sceptical observer, Sir William Petty, shortly afterwards, cast a disquisition on the Restoration settlement in the form of a mock 23 October sermon, in which any ironical undertones are drowned by conventional anti-popery. Adopting many of the conventions of the already well-established genre, Petty concluded that the English in Ireland should view the Irish as the rod with which they were repeatedly chastised. He irascibly dismissed the notion that the Catholics deserved generosity: not only because they still adhered to the pope's authority, but because they were boasting that the Confederate Wars of the 1640s had been 'necessary, just and holy'.[34] The annual celebrations, attended with the solemn recital of the 1662 statute and minatory sermons, imitated rather than parodied by Petty, allowed a variety of protestant preoccupations to be aired. In 1757, for example, a Dublin preacher turned it into an occasion to urge Catholics to welcome the measures to ease their condition recently introduced into the house of lords by Lord Clanbrassil.[35] More customary however was the approach of the bishop who edified the house of lords on 23 October 1733: the protestant community should better protect itself, and serve God's purposes, by endowing and patronizing English and protestant schools. By the time this popular sermon was re-printed at London in 1735 it was supplemented with a digest of 1641 atrocities, in order, we must suppose, to remind of the continuing catholic danger.[36]

The centenary of the rebellion in 1741 ought to have stimulated interesting reflections. Yet the state sermons delivered before the lords and commons on 23 October were not published.[37] We may suspect that this omission resulted from more than the indolence of the preachers; fresh signs of divine disfavour in widespread famine induced gloomy introspection rather than celebratory zest. Nevertheless, that recollections of 1641 did survive in the localities is suggested by the county histories being compiled at this time, under the auspices of that same bishop who had admonished the house of lords on 23 October 1733. Several of these accounts, without prompting,[38] adverted to the confessional and ethnic violence of the 1640s. Remembering 1641 continued to divide Protestants from their catholic neighbours. In addition the official festivities revealed the Protestants' own divisions: not only over the uses to which the sermons of the day should be devoted. For the sizeable group of protestant 'gentlemen of Ireland', exiled temporarily or permanently in and around London, the service on the 23 October catered to their sense of distinctive identity and allowed a pleasant reunion. However, in 1713, when the sermon was preached by a clergyman who had complied with James II, many of the gentry boycotted both the service and the subsequent dinner, and instead improvised their own entertainment in a coffee-house.[39] Undoubtedly, the popularity of these celebrations waxed and waned in accord with perceptions of the local and international dangers from catholicism, and with slower transformations in protestant attitudes. Again, though, it seems probable that English and official hostility to these potentially provocative displays, which led in the 1780s to the silent abandonment of the state commemorations, ran ahead of popular protestant opinion.

Easier to track, and to link with the political controversies that engendered it, is the growing scholarly interest in 1641. Those same topics disputed in the later seventeenth century – the numbers murdered, the authenticity of the evidence, and the motives of each side – continued to obsess later enquirers. The wish which had activated the catholic pamphleteer in 1662, 'to vindicate the honest party of my countrymen', inspired the eighteenth-century intellectuals, notably Charles O'Conor and John Curry.[40] The latter appreciated that Irish protestant attitudes must change before Catholics could be freed of their religious and civil disabilities, and hoped that a dispassionate reconstruction of the 1640s would speed the change. Curry, O'Conor recalled, wrote 'to instruct, not to misrepresent; to conciliate, not to irritate'.[41] The results of Curry's labours, however, provoked intemperate protestant rejoinders, notably from the versatile hack, Walter Harris, and disappointed even O'Conor, who concluded of Curry's efforts: 'this is not history, which like every true picture should consist of shade and colouring, but is a mere justification on our side, and a disguised invective on the other'.[42] The catholic cause was better assisted by an English clergyman, Ferdinando Warner, who after examining the depositions questioned their veracity, and reduced the total of protestant victims to the impressively precise and (to Catholics) comfortingly low figure of 4028.[43]

Fresh violence in the 1790s edged the 1640s from the stage for a while, though one Protestant who memorialized the more recent rebellion implied a continuity in tactics and violence by reprinting a selection of the mid-seventeenth-century depositions for his district.[44] At another level, that of unashamed fiction, the 1640s still intrigued, and offered the setting and subject of the most interesting work to be inspired by the uprising: *Mandeville*, a novel issued in 1817, written by the English radical, William Godwin, which is subtle in its characterization and in its interlacing of the present with the past.[45] Almost immediately, from a new quarter, Philadelphia, an Irish American, Mathew Carey, in his *Vindiciae Hibernicae* circulated anew the traditional catholic grievance.[46] Such sparring, necessarily inconclusive since the combatants lacked fresh material or new methods to illumine the old evidence, paled beside the warfare joined by the partisans in the heroic age of Irish historiography, which opened in the 1860s and closed with the destruction of the Irish public records in 1922. Renewed agitation, both political and agrarian, impressed investigators with the numerous parallels between present and past. Thus in 1862 one of this new generation of historians, J.P. Prendergast, wrote: 'there is no change in Ireland. One may in the course of the morning read the events of 1641, and turn then from them to *The Times* or Saunders without any breach of continuity'.[47] At the same time a more methodical analysis of the depositions and of the attendant pamphlet commentary promised to disclose 'the truth'[48]. The truth, unfortunately, remained as elusive as ever.

The depositions, a centennial gift to Trinity College Dublin in 1741 and located there ever since, still fuelled the rows. Bound in thirty-one volumes, and accompanied by two further volumes of supplementary papers, their bulk and arrangement deterred all but the most dedicated from undertaking a systematic study. In the 1870s a genteel antiquary from county Kerry, Mary Hickson, went to work on her two volumes of research which would be published in 1884,[49] prefaced by the notorious controversialist J.A. Froude. Froude impetuously rounded on those Catholics who had intermittently asserted that the massacre of 1641 had been invented by the English and Protestants. The unchecked circulation of this notion, he protested, 'lies among the causes which have exasperated the Irish race to their present attitude'. Froude, in addition to commending Miss Hickson's researches, called for the depositions to be calendared and published, either in abstracts or *in extenso*, in the same way as the state papers. He was confident that, were the full materials to be put into the public domain, their authority would be widely accepted. Froude, then, on the slender evidence of the samples shown to him by Miss Hickson, and the latter herself on the basis of a long immersion in the sources, while allowing for exaggeration and errors, concluded that the depositions did testify to widespread massacres.[50] Others of greater weight soon demurred.

Froude's notion of publishing the depositions subscribed to a fashion of the time: the serial publication of the essential manuscript sources of history. In England, the Rolls series for medieval documents, and more generally the Historical Manuscripts Commission and the Public Record Office, initiated ambitious programmes of editing, reporting, calendaring and printing; in Ireland, too, something of the same mood encouraged the ventures of the Irish Archaeological and Celtic, and Kilkenny and South-East of Ireland Archaeological Societies.[51] However, given the nature of the relationship between England and Ireland, the main collections relating to Irish history, at least in its most public manifestations since 1169, could easily be included in the series to be published in England. In this spirit, the cultivated barrister, Prendergast, and the president of Maynooth, Dr Russell, were sent to scan and catalogue the voluminous collection of Ormonde papers, removed in the eighteenth century from Kilkenny Castle by Thomas Carte and deposited in the Bodleian Library in Oxford. The yoking together of the Protestant Prendergast and the respected Russell hinted at the difficulties that beset these schemes, and the extent to which they reflected and could in their turn add to the current political and sectarian squabbles.[52] The projected published calendar, a companion to the Irish state papers and the Carew manuscripts at Lambeth Palace, never materialized. Concurrently, the well-to-do Dublin antiquarian, John Gilbert, was employed by the English Manuscripts Commission, to inform it of and to inspect the principal Irish collections. Indefatigably Gilbert discharged his brief, his enthusiasm for the past often outstripping his instructions, so that he threatened to overwhelm the poorly funded Commission with suggestions for publications.[53] Yet despite the usual enthusiasm of his reports, one collection on which he pontificated excited him less: the depositions among the manuscripts of Trinity. In a masterly reconstruction of the commissions which had elicited the documents, and of their subsequent history and use – often imitated but seldom bettered – Gilbert implied the dubious status of much that they contained and that other collections better deserved official attention.[54] Gilbert's coolness enraged Froude, who dismissed the former's report as a mish-mash based on Prendergast and violently nationalist writers like Curry and Carey. When Gilbert blocked the project of publishing an authoritative edition, Froude saw the frustration of this design, together with the scepticism of Prendergast and Gilbert, as entirely political and religious in inspiration, and not based on a cautious appraisal of evidence that Froude himself had never consulted.[55]

Any attempt by Gilbert to confine the controversy over the status of the depositions to the scholarly sphere was defeated by Froude's role in a vicious and all-too-public row over the anti-Irish thrust of his history of *The English in Ireland*.[56] One catholic adversary of Froude so far flew in the face of the historical record as to aver: 'they rose as one man. Every Irishman, every Catholic in Ireland, arose on the 23d of October, 1641'.[57] With the expanding market, in Ireland, America, England and Australia, for popular histories of a nationalist and catholic colour, it was even more difficult for the patient editor, Gilbert, than for Curry and O'Conor in the eighteenth century, to steer between protestant and catholic hyperbole. Prendergast, also lambasted by Froude, confessed to Lecky, 'This devil, Froude, and this hell-born fury, this she-devil, Miss Hickson, are intolerable to me. I really hate their names, being the only persons I hate on earth'.[58] If the study of 1641 was still capable of provoking such passion, the chances of an agreed interpretation, even among scholars, receded. So much was shown by a fresh controversy which broke in 1886, in the unlikely setting of the pages of the *English Historical Review* . A recent English recruit to Irish history, Manchester-trained Robert Dunlop, reviewed the status and recent uses of the depositions.[59] In the main a judicious and penetrating historian, he here allowed his impatience to show, as when he began: 'few questions connected with Irish history have been discussed with greater acrimony and less profit than that of the Irish massacres'. No doubt he spoilt his case when he concluded, 'I think that Irish history will gain rather than lose when these so-called facts and the depositions containing them are consigned to the limbo of all that is worthless'.[60] Dunlop, like Miss Hickson and Prendergast, explicitly drew parallels with the conditions in which the witnesses had deposed after 1641 and those prevailing in later Victorian Ireland in order to doubt the reliability of the earlier testimonies.[61] Once again, past and present intertwined. Miss Hickson, ekeing out a penurious twilight in the protestant almshouses of Mitchelstown, took Dunlop's bait.[62] Conceding nothing in insult to her adversary – thus she dismissed Prendergast's 'ability and powers of research' as being 'greatly clouded by his strong prejudices against the Long Parliament and Cromwell' – she insisted on her role as the pioneer who, virtually single-handed, had revealed the primary evidence of the 1640s hitherto disregarded 'through carelessness, prejudice and a design to suppress facts unpleasant to the political parties'.[63]

These distant spats remind us how embattled even cool scholars can become, and how too, though they may profess the opposite, their writings and researches exhale their own times and backgrounds. Twentieth-century historians, though not entirely despairing of solving the puzzles of 1641 (a recent analysis can still ask 'What did happen in Ireland in 1641?')[64] have generally shifted to reconstructing the ideological and historiographical contexts of the earlier controversies and writings, and to mining the depositions, not for numbers and losses, but for the incidental information (which is abundant) about attitudes, social structures, wealth and indebtedness, literacy and possessions.[65]

The patient reconstruction by Gilbert of how the depositions were gathered, and the partisan purposes to which they were put for two centuries, serves as a model to his successors. Another who sought carefully to strip away the accretions of fable and fantasy from 1641 was Thomas Fitzpatrick, a schoolmaster from Waterford, some of whose work has been silently or unknowingly repeated by others.[66] The most exhaustive account of the historical treatments of 1641 was undertaken during the 1960s by the American, Walter Love, whose premature death left many of his findings unpublished.[67] Most recently, a succinct and masterly analysis by Aidan Clarke has again laid bare how the depositions were taken, and the resultant problems.[68] Otherwise, if historians are more cautious and temperate about the depositions, they continue to be bewitched by 1641, and see better how the contemporary evidence can be used to answer important questions. In particular, the genesis of the uprising, whether in local and economic deprivation,[69] in confessional and ideological opposition or as an element in instability which disturbed the three Stuart kingdoms and continental Europe,[70] currently interests historians. Equally, what the episode can still teach about collective mentalities, mass hysteria and rational or irrational panics, together with the functions of anti-catholicism and invented traditions, so strongly manifested in the history of 1641, are likely to focus continuing scholarly enquiries and arguments.[71] All in all, then, it is unlikely that Dunlop's hope – that the year and its events pass into limbo – will be fulfilled.

NOTES AND REFERENCES

Introduction

1. The Bann massacre features on the banner of Loyal Orange Lodge 273, Portadown No 1 District (I am indebted to Gordon Lucy, Ulster Society, for this reference); images depicting events in 1641–2 are to be found in [James Cranford], *The teares of Ireland* (London, 1642); [Anon.] *Ireland. Or a Book* (London, 1647); Samuel Clarke, *A general martyrologie* (London, 1651); [Anon.] *The barbarous and inhumane proceedings against the professors of the reformed religion* (London, 1655) (I am grateful to Aidan Clarke and Phil Kilroy for drawing attention to these works). A selection of contemporary images is reproduced in J. Ranelagh, *Ireland : an illustrated history* (London, 1981), 102–3. For later material, see frontispiece, Sir John Temple, *The Irish Rebellion*, 6th ed., (Dublin, 1724); the Orange Order have produced a video, 'Mini-Twelfth, Orange Pageant and Commemoration of the Drowning of Protestants in River Bann 1641', (New Way Video, Portadown, 1991); inscription in Pleasure Grounds, Portadown: 'Near this spot occurred the massacres of 1641 where many Protestants were savagely murdered by the forces of the Counter-Reformation. Dedicated to the glory of God and erected by officers and brethren of Portadown District L.O.L. No I in the 350th anniversary year 1991 as a permanent tribute and a reminder to future generations of their faith devotion and sacrifice'.
2. A. Clarke, 'The 1641 depositions', in P. Fox (ed.), *Treasures of the Library : Trinity College Dublin* (Dublin, 1986), 111–122.
3. John Wesley, *Journal*, 14 August 1747, N. Curnock (ed.), (London, 1938); *The Correspondence of Edmund Burke*, ii, L. Sutherland (ed.), (Cambridge-Chicago, 1960), 285, E.B. to Dr William Markham, *post* 9 Nov, 1771.
4. Thomas Hamilton, *History of the Irish Presbyterian Church* (Edinburgh, 1887), 59.
5. T.C. Barnard, 'Athlone 1685; Limerick 1710: Religious riots or charivaris?', *Studia Hibernica*, xxvii (1993), 61–75.
6. 1641 as a theme of storytelling at wakes, William Carleton, 'Larry M'Farland's Wake', in *Traits and Stories of the Irish Peasantry* i, (Dublin, 1843) (facsimile, Gerrards Cross, Buckinghamshire, 1990),

105 (I am grateful to Brian Earls for this reference); for examples of such stories, see A. Day, P. McWilliams and N. Dobson (eds), *Ordnance Survey Memoirs of Ireland* (Belfast, 1990 et seq.) vol 28, co. Londonderry, Cumber parish, 27; vol 16, co. Antrim, Billy parish, 52; vol 29, co. Antrim, Antrim parish, 6; vol 23, co. Antrim, Ballyclug parish, 61; vol 19, co. Antrim, Duneane parish, 107–8; 'There are many traditions relating to the troubles of 1641', vol 22, co. Londonderry, Aghadowey parish, 15; Angélique Day has drawn my attention to the extent of references to 1641 in the Ordnance Survey Memoirs.

7. *Ordnance Survey Memoirs of Ireland* vol 26, co. Antrim, Templecorran parish, 115, 122–3; vol 13, co. Antrim, Racavan parish, 102–3; vol 10, co. Antrim, Islandmagee parish, 64–6; D.H. Akenson, *Between Two Revolutions: Islandmagee, County Antrim 1798–1920* (Ontario, 1979), 139–40 contains references to works which treat of the episode; see also J. McDonnell, *The Ulster Civil War of 1641 and its Consequences* (Dublin, 1879), written 'in vindication of the calumniated Ulster Irish in the war of 1641', 51–70.

8. Robert Young, *The Ulster Harmonist* (Derry, 1840), 26–7; see also 'The New Year's Protestant Warning', in *Williamite Scrap Book; or Chronicle of the Times*, No 1 (Dublin, 1823), and the allusion in 'Up, Orangemen! Up', in *Orange Minstrel* (Belfast, 1859) 45; Ulster Society, *Lilliburlero and more songs of the Orange Tradition* ii, (1988), 'Portadown: The drowning of the Protestants from the bridge over the Bann'.

9. R. Ó Muirí (eag.), *Lámhscríbhinn Staire an Bhionadaigh* (Éigse Oirialla, 1994), 289–293; for this section Bennett draws on J. Curry, *An Historical and Critical Review of the Civil Wars of Ireland* (Dublin, 1810), 623–5; the Ulster leaders Conor Maguire, Hugh MacMahon and Owen Roe O'Neill are mentioned in the poem 'Seanchas na Sceiche' [The lore of the bush], a history of Ireland from the Flood to Patrick Sarsfield, by the east Connacht poet Antaine Ó Raiftearaí (1779–1835), C. Ó Coigligh (eag.), *Raiftearaí: Amhráin agus Dánta* (Baile Átha Cliath, 1987), 147.

10. The poem 'Una Phelimy' tells of the love between a Scots planter and an Irish girl in Antrim in 1641, Samuel Ferguson, 'Una Phelimy: An Ulster Ballad AD1641', in Charles Gavan Duffy (ed.), *The Ballad Poetry of Ireland* (Dublin, 1845), 92–5; see also Dr Drennan, 'Rory O'Moore: An Ulster Ballad', in Charles Gavan Duffy, op. cit., 91–2; for further references to 1641, see Gréagóir Ó Dúill, *Samuel Ferguson : Beatha agus Saothar* (Baile Átha Cliath, 1993), 43, 54, 102–5; John Hewitt, 'The Bloody Brae: A Dramatic Poem', in Frank Ormsby (ed.), *The Collected Poems of John Hewitt* (Belfast, 1991), 400–16, set against the background of the Islandmagee massacre, features an encounter between John Hill and the ghost of a woman he killed, Bridget Magee, from whom he

asks forgiveness; M.J. Brown (ed.), *Historical Ballad Poetry of Ireland* (Dublin, 1912) contains ten poems on personalities and events in Ulster in the 1640s; Seosamh Mac Grianna, *Eoghan ruadh Ó Néill* (Baile Átha Cliath, 1931) – discussed in Alan Titley, *An tÚrscéal Gaeilge* (Baile Atha Cliath, 1991) 334–8; Breandán Ó Doibhlin, *Iníon Mhaor an Uachta* (Baile Átha Cliath, 1994).

11.   William Johnston, *Under Which King?* (London, 1873), is a historical romance set in Ulster in the years 1685–91, with some stories of 1641; Lord Ernest Hamilton (MP for North Tyrone, 1885–92), *The Soul of Ulster* (London, 1917), is an historical essay, where he treats of 1641 on pp 35–54; his *Tales of the Troubles* (London, 1925), is a collection of stories for the most part based on accounts of the early months of the 1641 rising. (I am indebted to Alvin Jackson for directing me to these works).

12.   Social and economic processes are examined in P. Robinson, *The Plantation of Ulster: British settlement in an Irish landscape, 1600–1670* (Dublin, 1984) and R. Gillespie, *Colonial Ulster: the settlement of east Ulster 1600–1641* (Cork, 1985); the economic background to the rising is discussed in R. Gillespie, 'The end of an era: Ulster and the outbreak of the 1641 rising', in C. Brady and R. Gillespie (eds), *Natives and Newcomers: the making of Irish colonial society 1534–1641* (Dublin, 1986), 191–213; landholding in west Ulster in 1641 is examined in Kevin McKenny, 'The seventeenth-century land settlement in Ireland: towards a statistical interpretation', in J. Ohlmeyer (ed.), *Ireland From Independence to Occupation 1641–1660* (Cambridge, 1995), 181–200, (here) 186–192; see also P.J. Duffy, *Landscapes of South Ulster: A Parish Atlas of the Diocese of Clogher* (Belfast, 1993).

13.   A. Ford, 'The Protestant Reformation in Ireland', in C. Brady and R. Gillespie (eds), *Natives and Newcomers*, 64–71; see also A. Ford, 'The Church of Ireland, 1558–1634: a puritan church?', and John McCafferty, 'John Bramhall and the Church of Ireland in the 1630s', both in A. Ford, J. McGuire and K. Milne (eds), *As by Law Established: The Church of Ireland since the Reformation* (Dublin, 1995), 52–68, 100–111.

14.   Religious and economic animosities revealed in the attacks on settlers in the winter of 1641 are sketched in N. Canny, *From Reformation to Restoration: Ireland 1534–1660* (Dublin, 1987), 209–10; Irish attitudes to the English and Scots, elicited partly from Gaelic sources, are offered in Mary Catherine Kennedy, '*Eagla an Ghallsmacht* [Fear of foreign control]: the religion and politics of Irish catholics, 1620s–1670s', (unpublished MA thesis, University College Galway, 1987); on Ulster catholicism, see Oliver Rafferty SJ, *Catholicism in Ulster 1603–1983: An Interpretative History* (Dublin, 1994), 6–40; the religious dimension to the attacks is treated in B.

Mac Cuarta, 'Anti-protestantism in south Ulster 1641–2', (unpublished M.Phil. thesis, Irish School of Ecumenics, 1994).

15. A. Clarke, 'The 1641 depositions', in P. Fox (ed.), *Treasures of the Library: Trinity College Dublin* (Dublin, 1986), 111; an estimate of 34000 British in Ulster by the mid-1630s is offered by N. Canny, *Kingdom and colony: Ireland in the Atlantic world, 1560–1800* (Baltimore, 1988), 96; Sammy Wilson, Democratic Unionist councillor, said in an interview, 'it's reckoned about 150,000 Protestants' were killed in Ulster in 1641, T. Parker, *May the Lord in His mercy be kind to Belfast* (London, 1993), 139–140.

16. Based on depositions taken in 1653, between 60 and 70 Irish were killed by Scots settlers in Ballydavy, near Holywood, county Down, T. Fitzpatrick, *The Bloody Bridge and other papers relating to the insurrection of 1641* (Dublin, 1903), 105–9; about 26 were killed in Templepatrick, and another 30 in Islandmagee, county Antrim, Mary Hickson, *Ireland in the Seventeenth Century*, i, (London, 1884), 255–279; Lord E. Hamilton, *The Irish Rebellion of 1641* (London, 1920), 209–212.

17. B. Walker, '1641, 1689, 1690 And All That: The Unionist Sense of History', *The Irish Review*, xii (1992), 58.

18. Letter to Hugh Bourke OFM, 29 Dec 1641, H.M.C., *Franciscan Mss* (Dublin, 1906), 112; the Jewish Maccabee family led a revolt against Syrian domination in the 2nd century BC; Irish revolt is set in a comparative European context in J. Ohlmeyer (ed.), *Ireland From Independence to Occupation*, 1–23.

19. On Scottish involvement, see D. Stevenson, *Scottish Covenanters and Irish Confederates: Scottish-Irish relations in the mid-seventeenth century* (Belfast, 1981); R. Gillespie, 'An army sent from God: Scots at war in Ireland, 1642–9', in N. Macdougall (ed.), *Scotland and War AD79–1918* (Edinburgh, 1991), 113–132; for an Antrim perspective, see Jane Ohlmeyer, *Civil War and Restoration in the Three Stuart Kingdoms: The career of Randal MacDonnell, marquis of Antrim, 1609–1683* (Cambridge, 1993) 77–126 – she gives a bibliography of the Gaelic literary background, 292–3.

20. See J. Casway, *Owen Roe O'Neill and the struggle for catholic Ireland* (Philadelphia, 1984); R. Gillespie, 'Owen Roe O'Neill c1582–1649 Soldier and Politician', in G. O'Brien and P. Roebuck (eds), *Nine Ulster Lives* (Belfast, 1992), 149–168; *N.H.I.* iii, 293; R.A. Stradling, *The Spanish Monarchy and Irish Mercenaries: the Wild Geese in Spain 1618–68* (Dublin, 1994).

Chapter 1   The Political Background to the Ulster Plantation

I would like to express my appreciation to Dr Mary O'Dowd for her comments on a draft of this essay [J.McC.].

1. Nicholas Canny, *From Reformation to Restoration: Ireland 1534–1660* (Dublin, 1987), 143.

2.   Nicholas Canny, 'Early modern Ireland, c 1500–1700', in R.F. Foster (ed.), *The Oxford illustrated history of Ireland* (Oxford, 1991), 130.

3.   For accounts of these battles, see G.A. Hayes-McCoy, *Irish Battles* (London, 1969).

4.   Grenfell Morton, *Elizabethan Ireland* (London, 1971), 134–5.

5.   J.J. Silke, *Kinsale: the Spanish intervention in Ireland at the end of the Elizabethan wars* (Liverpool, 1970).

6.   Micheline Kerney Walsh, *Destruction by peace: Hugh O'Neill after Kinsale* (Ard Mhacha, 1986), document 56b; hereinafter cited as Kerney Walsh, *Destruction*.

7.   Nicholas Canny, 'The treaty of Mellifont and the re-organisation of Ulster, 1603', *Ir. Sword*, ix, (1969), 249–62; hereinafter cited as Canny, 'Treaty of Mellifont'.

8.   F.C. Dietz, *English Public Finance, 1558–1641* (New York, 1932), 432–3.

9.   John McCavitt, 'The Lord deputyship of Sir Arthur Chichester in Ireland, 1605–16' (unpublished PhD thesis, Queen's University Belfast, 1988), 60; hereinafter cited as McCavitt, 'Chichester'.

10. Canny, 'Treaty of Mellifont', 262.

11. Kerney Walsh, *Destruction*, documents 11, 12, 22, 22a, 22b, 22c, 22d, 30, 33, 35, 36.

12. At the very least, Tyrone's negotiations for a Spanish pension committed him to a treasonable contract which involved a promise to renew revolt at the behest of the Spanish.

13. John McCavitt, 'Lord Deputy Chichester and the English government's "Mandates policy" in Ireland, 1605–7', *Recusant History*, xx, no.3 (1991), 320–35.

14. Kerney Walsh, *Destruction*, documents 43a, 56b and 72a.

15. Soon after the flight it became public knowledge that Lord Howth had been the 'discoverer of the treason of Tyrone and his confederates'. See Chichester to Salisbury, 11 May 1608 (P.R.O., S.P.63/224/102).

16. Privy council to Chichester, 27 Sept. 1607 (*Cal.S.P.Ire., 1606–8*, 287–8).

17. Chichester to privy council, 17 Sept. 1607 (P.R.O., S.P. 63/222/137).

18. W.F.T. Butler, *Confiscation in Irish history* (Dublin, 1917), 41, footnote 12.

19. Brian Bonner, *That Audacious Traitor* (Dublin, 1975), 147–8; hereinafter cited as Bonner, *Audacious Traitor*.

20. Chichester to privy council, 11 Dec. 1607 (P.R.O., S.P. 63/222/188).

21. Ibid; Bonner, *Audacious Traitor*, 151.

22. Chichester to privy council, 22 April 1608 (P.R.O., S.P. 63/223/81).

23. *Cal.S.P.Ire., 1606–8, p.* xlii.

24: Chichester to Salisbury, 20 Feb. 1607 (P.R.O., S.P. 63/221/21).

25. Bishop of Derry to Chichester, 4 Mar. 1607 (*Cal.S.P.Ire., 1606–8*, 125–7).

26. *Annala rioghachta Eireann: Annals of the kingdom of Ireland by the Four Masters from the earliest period to the year 1616*, ed. and trans. John O'Donovan, (3rd ed. Dublin, 1990), vol. vi, sub anno 1608; Dillon to Salisbury, 25 April 1608, (*Cal.S.P.Ire., 1606–8*, 485–7).

27. Chichester to privy council, 6 July 1608 (P.R.O., S.P. 63/224/150).

28. Chichester to Salisbury, 2 July 1608 (P.R.O., S.P. 63/224/145).

29. Proclamation of lord deputy and council, 20 Feb. 1607 (*Cal.S.P.Ire., 1603–6*, 259–60).

30. Report of the surprise of the city of Derrie, 3 May 1608 (P.R.O., S.P. 63/224/92ii).

31. Bodley to Worthy, 3 May 1608 (*Cal.S.P.Ire., 1606–8*, 494–6).

32. Chichester to privy council, 2 June 1608 (P.R.O., S.P. 63/224/114).

33. *Cal.S.P. Ire., 1608–10*, pp i–liii.

34. S.R. Gardiner, *History of England from the accession of James I to the outbreak of the civil war, 1603–1642* (London, 1863–81) ii, 30.

35. McCavitt, 'Chichester', 54.

36. Aidan Clarke, 'The plantations of Ulster' in Liam de Paor (ed.), *Milestones in Irish history* (Dublin, 1986), 65–6.

37. See, for example, T.M. Healy, *The Great Fraud of Ulster* (Dublin, 1917).

38. Briefs of Remembrance by Chichester, 8 Aug.1609 (P.R.O., S.P. 63/227/114).

39. Chichester's instructions, 14 Oct. 1608 (P.R.O., SP. 63/225/225).

40. Chichester to Northampton, 31 Oct.1610 (B.L. Cotton Tit. B.x, fol. 200–1).

41. Caulfield to lord deputy, 27 June 1610 (*Cal.S.P.Ire., 1608–10*, 474–5).

42. Aidan Clarke, 'Pacification, plantation and the catholic question, 1603–23', in *N.H.I.* iii, 202; hereinafter cited as Clarke, 'Pacification'.

43. McCavitt, 'Chichester', chapter nine.

44. Ibid.

45. John McCavitt, 'Chichester, Ceannairc agus Cairlinn, 1609' [Chichester, mutiny and Carlingford, 1609], *Cuisle na nGael: The Journal of the Newry Branch of the Gaelic League* (1986), 19–23.

46. Ibid.

47. The Scots owed their high profile in the plantation scheme to the extinction of the Tudor line with the death of Elizabeth I, who was succeeded by her Scots relative, James Stuart (James VI of Scotland and James I of England).

48. Clarke, 'Pacification', 200–2.

49. For the authoritative account of the Londonderry plantation see T.W. Moody, The *Londonderry Plantation, 1609–41: the city of London and the plantation in Ulster* (Belfast, 1939); hereinafter cited as Moody, *Londonderry plantation.*

50. P.J. Duffy, 'The territorial organisation of Gaelic landownership and its transformation in Co.Monaghan, 1591–1640', *Irish Geography*, xiv (1981), 1–26.

51. Raymond Gillespie, *Colonial Ulster; The Settlement of East Ulster, 1600–41* (Cork, 1985); M. Perceval-Maxwell, *The Scottish migration to Ulster in the reign of James I*, 2nd ed. (London, 1990); hereinafter cited as Perceval-Maxwell, *Scottish migration*.

52. Philip Robinson, *The Plantation of Ulster: British settlement in an Irish landscape, 1600–1670* (Dublin, 1984), 97; hereinafter cited as Robinson, *Plantation of Ulster*.

53. Aidan Clarke, 'The Irish economy, 1600–60', in *N.H.I.* iii, 175.

54. Perceval-Maxwell, *Scottish migration*, 313–15.

55. Robinson, *Plantation of Ulster*, p.xvii.

56. The fact that many native Irish were not immediately removed from the estates of the English and Scottish undertakers also accounts in part for this passive response.

57. Treasurer-at-war's account, 1611–13 (P.R.O., A.O.I/290/1090, concordatums).

58. Kerney Walsh, *Destruction*, documents 44, 49, 52, 55.

59. McCavitt, 'Chichester', chapter ten.

60. Maurice Lenihan, *Limerick: its history and antiquities*, 2nd ed. (Cork, 1967), 138.

61. P.J. Corish, 'The rising of 1641 and the confederacy, 1641–5', in *N.H.I.* iii, 293.

62. J.J. Silke, 'Bishop Conor O'Devanney, OFM, c.1533–1612', *Seanchas Ard Mhacha*, xiii, no.1 (1988), 9–32.

63. P.F. Moran (ed.), *Spicilegium Ossoriense*, 1st ser. (Dublin, 1874), 125; hereinafter cited as Moran, *Spicil. Ossor.*

64. See note 62.

65. See note 59.

66. Moran, *Spicil. Ossor.*, 122.

67. Advertisements out of Ireland, 7 June 1613 (*H.M.C. Downshire*, iv, 128–9.

68. McCavitt, 'Chichester', 369.

69. For an account of the pirate presence on Irish coasts see J.C. Appleby, 'The Affairs of the Pirates: the surrender and submission of Captain William Baugh at Kinsale, 1611–1612', *Journal of the Cork Historical and Archaeological Society*, xci, no.250 (1986), 68–84.

70. McCavitt, 'Chichester', chapter eleven.

71. Ibid.

72. McCavitt, 'Chichester', 372.

73. Kerney Walsh, *Destruction*, document 211.

74. George White (or Thomas Doyne) to Mr John Burke, 7 Sept. 1615 (*Cal.S.P.Ire., 1615–25*, 89–91).

75. Kerney Walsh, *Destruction*, document 207.

76. Raymond Gillespie, *Conspiracy: Ulster plots and plotters in 1615* (Belfast, 1987).
77. It has been remarked of James I that 'he schemed throughout his life to avoid war', S.J.Houston, *James I* (Harlow, 1973), 68.
78. Lord deputy to privy council, 29 Sept. 1619 (*Cal.S.P.Ire.*, 1615–25, 262–3).
79. Moody, *Londonderry plantation*, 239.
80. Lord deputy to Conway, 24 April 1624 (*Cal.S.P.Ire.*, 1615–24, 484–6).
81. Raymond Gillespie, 'Continuity and change: Ulster in the seventeenth century', in C.Brady, M.O'Dowd and B.Walker (eds.), *Ulster: An Illustrated History* (London, 1989), 104.
82. McCavitt, 'Chichester', chapter six.
83. Robinson, *Plantation of Ulster*, chapter seven.
84. Nicholas Canny, *Kingdom and colony: Ireland in the Atlantic World, 1560–1800* (Baltimore, 1988), 48–52.
85. Ibid, 12.
86. Aidan Clarke, 'The Genesis of the Ulster rising of 1641', in Peter Roebuck (ed.), *Plantation to Partition* (Belfast, 1981), 29–45.

Chapter 2   Protestantism in Ulster, 1610–1641

1. Aidan Clarke, 'Varieties of uniformity: The first century of the Church of Ireland' in W.D. Sheils and Diane Wood (eds), *The Churches, Ireland and the Irish, Studies in Church History* xxv (Oxford, 1989), 107.
2. C.R.Elrington, *The life of . . . James Ussher* (Dublin, 1847), 5, 16, 32-3; C.R. Elrington (ed.), *The works of James Ussher*, xvii vols (Dublin,1847-64), xv, Letter xi, 72-5; Alan Ford, *The Protestant Reformation in Ireland, 1590-1641* (Frankfurt,1985), 76-80; R.B. Knox, *James Ussher Archbishop of Armagh* (Cardiff, 1967), 14-15.
3. John Richardson, *A short history of the attempts to convert the popish natives in Ireland* (London,1712).
4. P.J.Corish, *The Catholic community in the seventeenth and eighteenth centuries* (Dublin,1981), 3, 18-42.
5. Rosalind Mitchison, *Lordship to Patronage: Scotland 1603-1745* (London,1983), 19; Marilyn Westerkamp, *Triumph of the laity: Scots-Irish piety and the Great Awakening, 1625-1760* (Oxford/New York,1988), 20-22.
6. Clarke, 'Varieties of uniformity', 108; Knox, *Ussher*, 22-3.
7. *A religious and easy course* (B.L., Cotton MSS, Titus B.X.), fol. 263.
8. William Laud was archbishop of Canterbury from 1633-45. He tried to reverse the Elizabethan consensus which tended towards a Calvinist model of church. His reforms included recovery of church

lands, restoration of church authority, a theology of grace based on Arminianism, and conformity to the Book of Common Prayer.

9. Robert Blair, *The life of Mr. Robert Blair ... his autobiography from 1593-1636 with supplement to his life, and continuation of the history of the times to 1680*, by ... Mr. William Row, ed. Thomas M'Crie, The Wodrow Society (Edinburgh,1848), 58-9.

10. John Livingstone, *A brief historical relation of the life of Mr. John Livingstone ... written by himself*, ed. Thomas Houston (Edinburgh,1848), 76-7.

11. Ford, *Protestant Reformation*, 166-8; Knox, *James Ussher*, 175-84.

12. Not all the ministers were of such distinctive calibre: Blair, *Life of Mr Robert Blair*, 57; Livingstone, *A brief relation*, 13.

13. Christopher Hampton, *An inquisition of the true church* (Dublin, 1622 edition), Dedicatory to Sir Arthur Chichester at the second session of the 1613 Parliament in Dublin; Christopher Hampton, *A sermon preached in the city of Glasgow in Scotland on the 10th day of June, 1610* (London,1610), 16; Hugh Trevor Roper, *Catholics, Anglicans and Puritans* (London, 1987), 141.

14. Patrick Adair, *A true narrative ... of the Presbyterian Church in Ireland (1623-1670)*, introduction and notes by W.D.Killen (Belfast,1866), 16-19; Blair, *The life of ... Blair*, 70, 89-90; Westerkamp, *Triumph of the laity*, 23-6.

15. Westerkamp, *Triumph of the laity*, 30.

16. 25 June, 1621 (Bodl., Carte MSS 61, fol. 110).

17. Originally Arminianism was formulated by the Dutch theologian, Arminius (1560–1609). He argued that each person possesses free will and so is capable of responding to grace, in contrast to the Calvinist notion of predestination. Arminianism soon became politicised in England, Scotland and Ireland. Trevor Roper, *Catholics, Anglicans and Puritans*, ch. 2; Phil Kilroy, 'Sermon and pamphlet literature in the Irish reformed church, 1613-34', *Archiv. Hib.* xxxiii (1975), 117-19; Phil Kilroy, 'Bishops and ministers in Ulster during the primacy of Ussher, 1625-56', *Seanchas Ardmhacha*, viii, no.2 (1977), 289-97; Edward Warren to James Ussher, 1 Sept. 1617, Elrington, *Works* xv, Letter xxxvi; J. Ussher, 'The true intent and extent of Christ's death and satisfaction on the Cross', March 1617, Elrington, *Works* xii; Randolph Holland to J. Ussher, 18 June 1623 (Bodl., Ms. Rawlinson 89, fol. 34; also fols. 3, 8).

18. Kilroy, 'Sermon and pamphlet literature in the Irish reformed church', 110-14.

19. James Ussher, *The reduction of episcopacy* (reprint London,1687).

20. Ford, *Protestant Reformation*, 159-64.

21. Ibid, 171.

22. E.S. Shuckburgh, *Two biographies of William Bedell, bishop of Kilmore* (Cambridge,1902) 131.

23. Ibid, 300, 317.
24. Knox, *Ussher*, 87-8.
25. Ibid, 30.
26. A.B. (ed.), *A brief memorial of the life and death of ... Dr. James Spottiswood*, (Edinburgh,1811), 2-17; Raymond Gillespie, 'The trials of Bishop Spottiswood, 1620-40', *Clogher Record*, x (1987), 320-33.
27. *A treatise concerning Antichrist ... proving that the Pope is AntiChrist* (London,1603); *A sermon defending the honourable office of bishop* (London,1608).
28. W.B. Stanford, 'Towards a history of classical influences in Ireland', *R.I.A.Proc.*, vol.70, Section C, No. 3 (1970), 45.
29. *The Covenant of grace, or an exposition upon Luke 1:73, 74, 75* (Dublin,1631), 33.
30. 'The diocese of Derry 1631', *Archiv. Hib.*, v, 1 ff.
31. June–Oct. 1630, three letters from Bedell to Downame on justification, discussing their theological difference, prior to the publication of Downame's *The Covenant of grace* in 1631. This work, Downame hoped, would serve 'notably to confute the erroneous concepts of the patrons of free will, the Pelagians, the Papists, the Arminians and our new Anabaptists'. E.S. Shuckburgh, *Two biographies*, 303–10.
32. Shuckburgh, *Two biographies* , 26.
33. Ibid, 324.
34. Elrington, *Works*, xv, Letter clxiv, 485.
35. Shuckburgh, *Two biographies*, 396.
36. Ibid, 303 ff.
37. Ibid, 306.
38. Henry Leslie, *A treatise tending to unity* (Dublin, 1622), 50.
39. Christopher Hampton, *An inquisition of the true church* (Dublin, 1622), Dedicatory.
40. Bodl., Carte MSS 61, fol. 110.
41. Henry Leslie, *A treatise on the authority of the church* (Dublin,1637), 42.
42. William Bedell, *A sermon on Revelation 18. 4* (Dublin,1634), 102.
43. Knox, *James Ussher*, 184.
44. F.R.Bolton, *The Caroline tradition of the Church of Ireland* (London,1958), 11-12.
45. Elrington, *Life of Ussher*, 172.
46. David Wilkins, *Concilia Magnae Britanniae et Hiberniae*, 4 vols (London, 1737), iv, 496ff; Elrington, *Works*, xvi, Letter CC, 7-8; Thomas Carte, *A history of the life of James, Duke of Ormond*, 3 vols (1736), i, bk.ii, 78-80; Richard Mant, *History of the Church of Ireland from the Reformation to the Revolution*, 2 vols (London,1840), i, 486-505; W.A. Phillips (ed.), *History of the Church of Ireland*, 3 vols (London,1934), iii, 21; Ford, *The Protestant Reformation*, 269.

47. Knox, *Ussher*, 95–6.
48. The Black Oath was aimed at the Ulster Scots and demanded dissociation from the treasonable activities of the Scottish Presbyterians (the Covenanters).
49. Edmund Borlase, *The history of the execrable Irish Rebellion* (Dublin,1680), 96.
50. Proclamation, 22 January, 1661 in Robert Steele, *Tudor and Stuart Proclamations*, 2 vols (Oxford,1910), ii, 77; *17 &18 Chas.II*; this development is discussed in Phil Kilroy, *Protestant Dissent and Controversy in Ireland 1660–1714* (Cork, 1994) and Phil Kilroy, 'Radical Religion in Ireland, 1641–1660', in J. Ohlmeyer (ed.), *Ireland From Independence to Occupation 1641–1660* (Cambridge, 1995), 201–17.

Chapter 3   Ulster Exiles in Europe, 1605–1641

A.G.R.   –   Archives Générales du Royaume, Brussels
A.G.R. E.A.   –   Ibid, papiers d'état et de l'audience
A.G.R. E.G.   –   Ibid, secrétairerie d'état et de guerre
A.G.R. E.G.C.   –   Ibid, secrétairerie d'état et de guerre, correspondances des gouverneurs
A.G.S.   –   Archivo General de Simancas, Spain
A.G.S. E.   –   Ibid, secretaria
Parish records:
A.H.V., Brussels   –   Archives de l'Hôtel de Ville, Bruxelles
A.H.V., St. Michel et Gudule   –   Ibid., paroisse de Saints Michel et Gudule
A.H.V., St. Catherine   –   Ibid., paroisse de Sainte Catherine
References also occur frequently to Brendan Jennings (ed.), *Wild Geese in Spanish Flanders, 1582–1700* (Dublin, 1964) hereafter referred to as Jennings, *Wild Geese*, and the author's own book, Grainne Henry, *The Irish Military Community in Spanish Flanders, 1586–1621* (Dublin, 1992), hereafter referred to as Henry, *Military Community*.

1. 9 Aug 1597, *H.M.C. Salisbury MSS*, vii, 340; Richard Bagwell, *Ireland under the Tudors*, iii (London, 1890), 435.
2. 2 Nov 1605, *Cal. S.P. Ire.*, 1603–6, 345–6; for Irish in Spain and France see Micheline Walsh, 'Some notes towards a history of womenfolk in the Wild Geese', *Ir. Sword, v* (1961–2), 98; Richard Hayes, *Old Irish links with France* (Dublin, 1940),15, 54,120; David Buisseret, 'The Irish at Paris in 1605', *I.H.S.* xiv (1964–5), 58–60.
3. *Acts privy council, July 1628 – April 1629*, 113; *Acts privy council, May 1629 – May 1630*, 389; *Acts privy council, Scotland, iii (1629–30)*, 354.
4. *Acts privy council, July 1628 – April 1629*, 297. See also Raymond Gillespie, 'Harvest crises in early seventeenth-century Ireland', *Ir.*

Econ. Soc. Hist., xi (1984), 5–18. Of course the reverse was also true and particularly in the early 1620s large harvest surpluses in Ulster resulted in high immigration there from Scotland. See for example *Acts privy council, Scotland, i (1625–7),* 565, 605–6; Michael Perceval-Maxwell, *The Scottish Migration to Ulster in the Reign of James I* (London, 1973), 36, 302, 303–7.

5.   See for example A.L. Beier, 'Vagrants and the social order in Elizabethan England', *Past & Present,* 64 (1974), 10; A.L. Beier, 'A rejoinder', *Past & Present,* 71 (1976), 130–4; *Acts privy council, July 1628 – April 1629,* 419.

6.   Geoffrey Parker, *The Army of Flanders and the Spanish Road, 1567–1659* (Cambridge, 1972), 46–7; for policies pursued by other European countries, see Henry, *Military Community,* 12, 18–24, 34–43; 13 Nov. 1635, Jennings, *Wild Geese,* 285–6.

7.   For references to 'voluntary levies' see for example *Cal. S. P. Ire., 1608–10,* 272, 287, 304–5; *Cal. S. P. Ire., 1615–25 ,* 360; *Cal. S.P. Ire., 1633–47 ,* 339–40.

8.   For Mountjoy's comments see *Cal. Carew MSS, 1601–3,* 50–1; see also *Cal. S. P. Ire., 1600,* 401; *Cal. S. P. Ire., 1600–1,* 305.

9.   3 Aug 1609, *Cal. S. P. Ire., 1608–10,* 25–6; 17 Aug 1609, ibid., 272; for good discussion on this subject see Lindsay Boynton, 'The Tudor provost-marshal', *E.H.R.,* lxxvii (1962), 437–55; Penry Williams, *The Tudor regime* (Oxford, 1979), 212–3.

10. 31 Oct 1609, *Cal. S. P. Ire., 1608–10,* 304–5; 30 Sept 1609, ibid., 292; see also proposed levy to Sweden under Sir Pierce Crosbie 20 June 1631, *Cal. S. P. Ire., 1625–32,* 615, 629; 30 Mar 1627, ibid., 221–2.

11. 28 Aug 1609, *Cal. S. P. Ire., 1608–10,* 281; see also 29 Aug 1628, *Acts privy council, July 1628 – April 1629,* 115–6; 18 May 1639, Strafford *Letters,* ii, 342.

12. See grants from 20 Sept. 1611 to 20 Nov 1620 in A.G.R. E.G., reg 25/44v. to reg. 27/239; 14 Nov 1632, *Cal. S. P. Ire., 1625–32,* 676.

13. In English sources particularly, it is often quite difficult to distinguish between emigrants of the wealthier and poorer classes from Ireland. English sources tend to refer to all groups simply as 'vagrants' whereas in Spain, names and case histories were recorded. See respectively *Cal. S. P. Ire., 1608–10,* 305–6; 'Intelligence of John Danyell', 1595, *H.M.C. Salisbury MSS,* v, 440, 515; also *Cal. S. P. Ire., 1600–1,* 235; Jerrold Casway, *Owen Roe O'Neill and the struggle for Catholic Ireland* (Philadelphia, 1984), 25–6; 26 Jan. 1607, *Cal. S. P. Ire., 1606–8,* 93–4.

14. 15 April 1609, *Cal. S. P. Ire., 1608–10,* 195; 14 Aug 1616, *Cal. S. P. Ire., 1615–25,* 510; Henry, *Military Community,* 144; 3 Feb 1617, A.G.R. E.G.C., reg. 181/34–5, 46; 10 May 1619, A.G.R. E.G., reg, 26/338v.

15. For English attitudes to this group of 'masterless men' see A.L. Beier, 'Vagrants and the social order', 15; J.S. Cockburn (ed.), *Western Circuit Assize Orders 1629–48* (Camden Society, London, 1976) N. 20, N. 963; Buisseret, 'The Irish at Paris', 59; *Cal. S. P. Ire., 1603–6, 496–8*; J.F. Pound, 'Debate: vagrants and the social order in Elizabethan England', *Past and Present*, 71 (1976), 128; for the earl of Cork's estate, see 18 May 1631, *Cal. S. P. Ire., 1625–32*, 611; Hayes, *Old Irish links with France*, 120; 18 May 1630, *Acts privy council, May 1629 – May 1630*, 389.

16. Parker, *Spanish road*, 207–18; C.G. Cruickshank, *Elizabeth's army*, 2nd ed. (Oxford, 1966), 296–303, for general discussion on leave; 9 Oct 1587, *Acts privy council, 1587–8*, 255; *Acts privy council, June 1623 – March 1625*, 210; 2 July 1635, J. S. Cockburn (ed.), *Western circuit*, N. 388; for restrictions on passage between Scotland and Ulster see 25 June 1622, *Register of the privy council Scotland*, xii (1619–22), 750; Mountjoy's letter, 1 May 1601, *Cal. Carew MSS, 1601–3*, 50–1.

17. It is noteworthy that Florence Conry was nominated as Punonrostro's adviser at this time. The largest number of such records was found at Santiago de Compostella which had 252 of Irish interest. For information on these Irish communities see material collected by Micheline Walsh in the Overseas Archives, University College Dublin, Dublin 2.

18. 31 Oct. 1609, *Cal. S. P. Ire., 1608–10*, 305–6; 1 Oct. 1622, *Cal. S. P. Ire., 1615–25*, 394–5; 13 Mar. 1610, Micheline Walsh, *'Destruction by peace': Hugh O'Neill after Kinsale* (Ard Mhacha, 1986), 397; 14 May 1612, A.G.R. E.A., carton 1944.

19. For Bellewe see John Burke, *Landed Gentry*, Peter Townsend (ed.), 18th ed. (London, 1969), 437–8; O'Hagan, 7 Feb. 1626, A.G.R. E.G., reg. 30/140, 11 Mar 1626, ibid., reg. 30/139v; Barry, 13 Nov. 1635, Jennings, *Wild Geese*, 285–6. For Hugh O'Neill's influence, see 4 Nov. 1607, *Cal. S. P. Ire., 1606–8*, 632; 9 Nov. 1607, A.G.R. E.G., reg. 24/78v; 23 June 1612, A.G.R. E.A.R., reg. 447 vol. 13/58; 16 May 1613, Micheline Walsh (ed.), 'The last years of Hugh O'Neill', *Ir. Sword*, viii (1967–8) 230–1, 234; Margaret MacCurtain, 'Fondo Santa Sede', *Archiv. Hib.*, xxvi (1963), 42.

20. 14 July 1608, M. Walsh (ed.), 'Last years', *Ir. Sword*, v (1961–2), 223; 12 Oct 1610, Walsh (ed.), 'Last years', *Ir. Sword*, vii (1965–6), 146; memorial of Florence Conry to king of Spain, 9 Sept, 1610, ibid., 145; Jerrold Casway, 'Henry O'Neill and the formation of the Irish regiment', *I.H.S.*, xviii (1972–3), 485–6. John was the son of Hugh's fourth wife, Catherine Magennis.

21. For an account of the 'northern group' in the Old Irish regiment see respectively, Micheline Walsh, 'The last earls of Tyrone in Spain and Captain Bernardo O'Neill, illegitimate son of Eoghan

Rua', *Seanchas Ard Mhacha*, 13 (i), 33–58. The Irish regiment set up in 1605 under Henry O'Neill came to be known as the 'Old Irish regiment' and was always under the colonelcy of an O'Neill until it was disbanded c. 1689; 3/7 Feb. 1617, Jennings, *Wild Geese*, 153–4; June 1622, *Cal. S. P. Ire., 1615–25*, 360; see also Wentworth's views, 16 July 1633, Strafford *Letters*, i, 94; case of Richard Tyrell, 14 Nov. 1632, *Cal. S. P. Ire., 1625–32*, 676.

22.   21 June 1609, *H.M.C. Salisbury MSS*, xxi, 72; 12 May 1640, A.G.R. E.G.C., reg. 374/197. In the 1621–2 lists of captains, Patrick Daniel has been included as Old English though he was sometimes cited in English sources as Patrick O'Donnell. From Waterford, his affiliations were certainly with the Old English group. For Wentworth's policy see Jennings, *Wild Geese*, 33; 14 Nov 1632, *Cal. S. P. Ire., 1625–32*, 676; 16 July 1633, Strafford *Letters*, i, 94, 6 July 1635, ibid., i, 440; 21 Oct. 1635, ibid., i, 466.

23.   For English studies, see particularly A.L. Beier, 'Vagrants and the social order in Elizabethan England', *Past & Present*, 64 (1974), 7; Hayes, *Old Irish links with France*, 120; Tadhg Ó Cianáin, *The flight of the earls*, Paul Walsh (ed.), (Dublin, 1916); 18 Dec. 1629, Jennings, *Wild Geese*, 242; ibid., 277–80; Micheline Walsh, 'Some notes towards a history of womenfolk in the Wild Geese', *Ir. Sword* v (1961 – 2), 98.

24.   18 Dec 1610, *Cal. S. P. Ire., 1608–10*, 543–4.

25.   Parker, *Spanish road*, 29; Jennings, *Wild Geese*, 277–80; Henry, *Military Community*, 84–90.

26.   It is noteworthy that Old Irish, particularly those from Ulster, do not seem to have integrated as well as Old English. Only one of the widows in the 1635 army of Flanders list who could be identified as 'northern' in origin was in fact married to a local. For parish records, see 24 July 1627, A.H.V. (Bruxelles), St Michel et Gudule, reg. 87/187; 25 Aug 1594, ibid., St Catherine, reg. 177/55; 4 Aug 1601, ibid., reg. 177/115. See also Gráinne Henry, 'The emerging identity of an Irish military group in the Spanish Netherlands, 1586–1610', in *Religion, Conflict and Co-existence in Ireland*, Comerford, Cullen, Hill & Lennon (eds.) (Dublin, 1990), 63–4.

27.   John MacErlean, 'Ireland and world contact', *Studies*, viii, pt i (1919), 308–9; for merchants who had property, 5 July 1641, A.G.R. E.G.C., reg. 373/21; J.B. Lyons, *Brief lives of Irish doctors, 1600–1965* (Dublin, 1978), 28; Samuel Simms 'Nial O'Glacan of Donegal', *Ulster Medical Journal*, iv (July 1935), 186–9; Owen O'Sheil was personal physician to Owen Roe O'Neill during the confederate wars in Ireland.

28.   John MacErlean, 'Ireland and world contact', (above), 307; M. Walsh *'Destruction by Peace'*, 127; Micheline Walsh, *Spanish knights of Irish origin* (Dublin, 1965), i, p. vi; J.J. Silke, 'The Irish abroad,

1534–1691', in *N.H.I.* iii, 605–6; 23 Dec 1630, Jennings, *Wild Geese,* 252, 19 Feb. 1631, ibid., 255.

29. See G. Henry, in *Religion, Conflict and Co-existence* (as above) 67–9; Henry Fitzsimon SJ, *Words of Comfort to persecuted Catholics written in exile anno 1607; Letters from a cell in Dublin Castle and Diary of the Bohemian war of 1620,* Edmund Hogan (ed.), (Dublin,1881), 263–4.

30. G. Henry, in *Religion, Conflict and Co-existence,* 70–72; D. Molloy, 'In search of Wild Geese', *Éire-Ireland,* v (1970), 9; will of Captain Patrick Fleming, 10 Dec. 1637, Jennings, *Wild Geese,* 498–9; Richard Hayes, *Old Irish links with France,* 12; 16 Jan 1606, *Cal. S. P. Ire., 1603–6,* 385.

31. See Henry, in *Religion, Conflict and Co-existence,* ibid.; 29 April 1627, *Cal. S. P. Ire., 1625–32,* 227; 11 Sept. 1631, ibid., 629; see also Coke to Wentworth, 21 Jan. 1634, Strafford *Letters,* i, 364.

32. Micheline Walsh, *The O'Neills in Spain,* O'Donnell lecture (National University of Ireland, 1957), 5–7; see Henry, *Military Community,* 130–1 for further references to MacMahon, MacCaughwell and Conry. On MacCaughwell, see also Anraí Mac Giolla Chomhaill, *Bráithrín Bocht ó Dhún: Aodh Mac Aingil* (Baile Átha Cliath, 1985).

33. G. Henry, *Military Community,* 130–1; Tadhg Ó Cianáin, *The flight of the earls,* 37, 69; 'Examination of James Loache (Roche?)', 18 Dec. 1607, *Cal. S. P. Ire., 1606–8,* 358–9; for the earls' stay in Flanders, see Walsh, *'Destruction by peace',* 66–70; for oration, see *Cal. S. P. Ire., 1608–10,* 122–5.

34. 4 April 1606, *Cal. S. P. Ire., 1603–6,* 442–3; for other such reports on subversive activities by priests, see 23 April 1606, ibid., 454; 20 Mar. 1607, *Cal. S. P. Ire., 1606–8,* 439; 27 Oct. 1607, ibid., 309–10; 24 Jan. 1608, ibid., 398; end May 1608, ibid., 540–1; end Nov. 1609, *Cal. S. P. Ire., 1608–10,* 325–6; 3 June 1610, ibid., 461; 27 Mar. 1624, *Cal. S. P. Ire., 1615–25,* 474; ibid., 486, 496; 27 Sept. 1610, *Cal. S. P. Ire., 1608– 10,* 503.

35. Durley O'Conor was a friar who acted as messenger between Hugh O'Neill and the Spanish ambassador in Rome, *Cal. S. P. Ire., 1608–10,* 253; Walsh, *'Destruction by peace',* 137, 282, 364–6; Casway, *Owen Roe O'Neill,* 24–5; Brendan Jennings (ed.), *Wadding Papers, 1614–38,* (Dublin, 1953), particularly 13ff, 128ff, 145ff, 181ff. Bonaventure Magennis was nephew to John O'Neill, then earl of Tyrone. See also Donal Cregan, 'The social and cultural background of a counter-reformation episcopate, 1618–60', in A. Cosgrove and D. McCartney (eds), *Studies in Irish history presented to R. Dudley Edwards* (Dublin, 1979), 85–117.

36. For a good summary of relations between Owen Roe O'Neill and Burke and Wadding, see Jennings, *Wild Geese,* 588–90; and Cathaldus Giblin, 'MSS Barberini Latini', *Archiv. Hib.,* xviii, (1955), 105.

37.   For some correspondence of Hugh O'Neill with Spain see Micheline
        Walsh (ed.), 'O'Neill's last years', *Ir. Sword.*, vii (1965–6), 143; ibid.,
        Ir. Sword, ix (1969–70), 142; C.P. Meehan, *The fate and fortunes of Hugh
        O'Neill, earl of Tyrone and Rory O'Donell, earl of Tyrconnel* (Dublin,
        1886), 172; Walsh, 'O'Neill's last years', *Ir. Sword,* viii (1967–8), 237;
        for Philip III's view of Hugh O'Neill, see particularly Walsh (ed.),
        'O'Neill's last years', *Ir. Sword,* vii (1965–6), 136; for Robert Lombard's
        views, see C.P. Meehan, *Fate and fortunes,* 251; for Hugh as king
        of Ireland, see Walsh (ed.), 'O'Neill's last years', *Ir. Sword,* ix
        (1969–70), 145; J.K. Graham, 'An historical study of the career of
        Hugh O'Neill, second earl of Tyrone, c. 1550–1616', (unpubl. MA
        thesis, Queen's University Belfast, 1938), 397.
38.   See Meehan, *The fate and fortunes,* 333–4.
39.   Burke to Wadding, 12 April 1642, Jennings, *Wild Geese,* 589; for
        Owen's letter to Charles I, 1646, see Meehan, *Fate and fortunes,* 332;
        for other references to 'nation' see for example, O'Neill to Hugh
        Burke, 8 July 1641, Jennings *Wild Geese,* 581; Jerrold Casway,
        'Unpublished letters of Owen Roe O'Neill', *Anal. Hib.,* xxix (1980),
        222–48; for Owen's relations with England, see Casway, *Owen Roe
        O'Neill,* 42–3; O'Neill to unknown, 25 Aug 1634, Jennings, *Wild
        Geese,* 404; Burke to Wadding, 30 May 1642, Jennings, *Wild Geese,*
        589–90; for very good overview of the period just before Owen left
        for Ireland, see Jerrold Casway, 'Owen Roe O'Neill's return to
        Ireland in 1642: the diplomatic background', *Studia Hibernica,* ix
        (1969), 48–64.
40.   D. Molloy, 'In search of Wild Geese', *Éire-Ireland,* v (1970), 4–8;
        H.D. Gallwey, 'Irish wills from Barcelona', *Ir. Geneal.,* vi (1980–1),
        212–18.

Chapter 4   *The native Ulster* mentalité *as revealed in Gaelic sources, 1600–
                1650*

  1. L. McKenna, *Iomarbhágh na bhFileadh,* 2 vols (London, 1918); here-
       after *Iomarbhágh.*
  2. The extent to which bardic poetry can be used as historical source
       material is a matter of some controversy. The current debate is
       addressed in Michelle O Riordan, *The Gaelic mind and the collapse of
       the Gaelic world* (Cork, 1990), introduction, 1–20; hereafter *The
       Gaelic mind.* See also Tadhg Ó Dúshláine, *An Eoraip agus litríocht na
       Gaeilge 1600–1650 [Europe and literature in Irish],* (Baile Átha Cliath,
       1987) and Mícheál Mac Craith, 'Gaelic Ireland and the Renais-
       sance', in Glanmor Williams and Robert Owen Jones (eds.), *The
       Celts and the Renaissance: innovation and tradition* (Cardiff, 1990),
       57–89.

3. Lughaidh Ó Cléirigh, *Beatha Aodha Ruaidh Uí Dhomhnaill*, Paul Walsh (ed.), 2 vols (London [1940] 1948, 1957), hereafter *BAR*.

4. Tadhg Ó Cianáin, *The Flight of the Earls*, Paul Walsh (ed.), *Archiv. Hib.* ii (1913); iii (1914); iv (1915), hereafter *Flight of the Earls*.

5. Tadhg Ó Donnchadha (ed.), 'Cín lae Ó Mealláin', *Anal. Hib.* (September 1931), 1–61.

6. Pádraig Breatnach, 'Marbhna Aodha Ruaidh Uí Dhomhnaill', *Éigse* 15 (1973–4), 31–50, hereafter 'Marbhna'.

7. B. Ó Cuív in *N.H.I.* iii, 522–3

8. See T. Ó Concheanainn, 'A feature of the poetry of Fearghal Óg Mac a' Bhaird', *Éigse* 15 (1974), 235–251.

9. *BAR*, ii, 24–25.

10. See Micheline Kerney Walsh, *'Destruction by peace': Hugh O Neill after Kinsale* (Ard Mhacha, 1986), 13–20; hereafter *'Destruction by peace'*.

11. *BAR*, i, 339–341.

12. O. Bergin, *Irish bardic poetry*, D. Greene and F. Kelly (eds), (Dublin [1970], 1974), 31–34; hereafter *IBP*.

13. *ibid.*, st. 1, p. 31.

14. *ibid.*, st. 11, p. 32.

15. *ibid.*, st. 16, p. 33.

16. And see *ibid.*, st. 25, p. 34.

17. *ibid.*, st. 24, p. 34.

18. *BAR*, i, 345.

19. *ibid.*, i, 347.

20. 'Marbhna', stanza 1, p. 34.

21. *ibid.*, st. 14, p. 37.

22. *ibid.*, st. 60, p. 46.

23. See Tomás Ó Concheanainn, 'A feature of the poetry of Fearghal Óg mac an Bhaird', *Éigse* 15 (1973–4), 235–251; here, 235.

24. 'Marbhna', st. 67, p. 47.

25. *ibid.*, sts. 19, 20, 21, p. 38.

26. *ibid.*, st. 24, p. 39.

27. L. McKenna, *Aithdioghluim dána* (Dublin, 1939), 2 vols, i, 177–180.

28. 'Metamorphosis 1603', Pádraig Breatnach (ed.), *Éigse* 17 (1977–79), 169–180; hereafter, 'Metamorphosis'.

29. See Ó Concheanainn, 'A feature of the poetry of Fearghal Óg mac an Bhaird', *Éigse* 15 (1974), 249.

30. *Iomarbhágh*, vol. 1, viii.

31. *ibid.*, vol. 1, xii.

32. *ibid.*, vol. 1, poem no. xv, st. 26, p. 138.

33. See Seathrún Céitinn, *Foras feasa ar Éirinn*, 4 vols, David Comyn and Patrick Dineen (eds.), (London, 1901-8), ii, 156–158; hereafter *Foras feasa*.

34. *Iomarbhágh* ii, no. xv, sts 55, 56, p. 184.

35. Céitinn, *Foras feasa*, ii, 386.
36. *ibid.*, i, 208.
37. *ibid.*, i, 124 – 'Corc mac Luighdeach laochdha an fear, céid-fhear ro shuidh i gCaiseal'.
38. 'Metamorphosis', sts 11, 12, 13, pp. 173–174.
39. *ibid.*, st. 14, p. 174.
40. *ibid.*, st. 16, p. 175.
41. 'Marbhna', st. 12, p. 36.
42. L. McKenna, *Aithdioghluim dána*, i, st. 27, p. 180.
43. *BAR*, ii, 113–115.
44. *IBP*, 27–30.
45. See Michelle O Riordan, *The Gaelic mind*, 185–188.
46. *IBP*, st. 5, p. 28; and see also st. 6, p. 28.
47. *BAR*, i, 264.
48. *IBP*, st. 14,16, p. 29.
49. T. Ó Raghallaigh, *Duanta Eoghain Ruaidh Mhic an Bhaird* (Gaillimh, 1930), st. 5, p. 258.
50. John O'Donovan (ed.), *Miscellany of the Celtic Society* (Dublin, 1849), 'Docwra's Narration', 240; hereafter 'Narration'.
51. See M. O Riordan, *The Gaelic mind*, 184–193.
52. *BAR*, i, 38; ii, 24.
53. *ibid.*, i, 40.
54. John O'Donovan (ed.), *Annála rioghachta Eireann: Annals of the Kingdom of Ireland by the Four Masters from the earliest period to the year 1616* (7 volumes, Dublin, 1851); hereafter *AFM*.
55. *AFM*, sub anno 1603.
56. *BAR*, i, 55.
57. *BAR*, i, 264.
58. *The Gaelic mind*, 177–202.
59. Brendan Fitzpatrick, *Seventeenth-century Ireland: the war of religions* (Dublin, 1988), 27.
60. *Duanta Eoghain Ruaidh Mhic an Bhaird*, no. 9, pp. 118–128.
61. *ibid.*, no. 5, pp. 76–84.
62. *ibid.*, no. 9, st. 21, p. 126.
63. *ibid.*, no. 9, st. 9, p. 120.
64. Colm Ó Lochlainn (eag.), *Tobar fíorghlan Gaedhilge* (Baile Átha Cliath, 1939), 69–70.
65. *Duanta Eoghain Ruaidh Mhic an Bhaird*, no. 5, st. 1, 4, p. 76.
66. 'Destruction by peace', 190.
67. See Nicholas P. Canny, 'The flight of the earls, 1607', *I.H.S.*, no. 67 (March 1971); Brendan Fitzpatrick, *Seventeenth-century Ireland*, 22–28.
68. *BAR*, ii, 118–122.
69. *ibid.*, ii, 138–146.
70. *ibid.*, ii, st. 1, p. 138.

71. *ibid.*, ii, st. 12, p. 140.
72. *'Destruction by peace'*, 190. For a history of this motif in counter-reformation literature see Tadhg Ó Dúshláine, *An Eoraip agus litríocht na Gaeilge 1600–1650*, 180–215.
73. Tadhg Ó Cianáin, *Flight of the Earls*, iv, p. ix.
74. *'Destruction by Peace'*, xiv.
75. *Flight of the Earls*, iv, p. ix.
76. *ibid.*, 54–5, n. 1.
77. *'Destruction by Peace'*, 13.
78. *Flight of the Earls*, ii, 2–9.
79. *ibid.*, 243 n. 1.
80. *ibid.*, 242.
81. *ibid.*, 174.
82. *ibid.*, 36.
83. *ibid.*, 42.
84. Sir William Stanley was an English Catholic who had served under Elizabeth but had joined the Spanish in 1587. A note in Kerney Walsh, *'Destruction by Peace'*, 302-3, indicates that an O Conor Faly had been involved in a mutiny against Stanley around 1595, because he had been treating his Irish regiment 'like slaves'.
85. *Flight of the Earls*, ii, 52–54.
86. *BAR*, ii, 126–130.
87. *ibid.*, ii, st. 1, p. 126.
88. *ibid.*, ii, sts. 9 and 13, p. 128.
89. Breandán Ó Buachalla, 'Na Stíobhartaigh agus an t-aos léinn: Cing Séamus' [The Stuarts and the learned class: King James], *R.I.A. Proc.*, vol. 83 (1983) C, 81–134.
90. Tadhg Ó Donnchadha (ed.), *Leabhar Cloinne Aodha Buidhe* (Dublin, 1931), p. vi.
91. See Bernadette Cunningham and Raymond Gillespie, 'The East Ulster bardic family of Ó Gnímh', *Éigse* 20 (1984), 106–114.
92. Tadhg Ó Donnchadha, *Leabhar Cloinne Aodha Buidhe*, no. xxiv, ll 189–204, p. 179.
93. *ibid.*, no. xxx.
94. See Donal F. Cregan 'The social and cultural background of a counter-reformation episcopate, 1618–60', in Art Cosgrove and Donal McCartney (eds.), *Studies in Irish history presented to R. Dudley Edwards* (Dublin, 1979), 85–117, esp. 103–117.
95. B. Ó Cuív, *N.H.I.* iii, 522–523.
96. Cainneach Ó Maonaigh (eag.), *Scáthán shacramuinte na h-aithridhe* (Baile Átha Cliath, 1952).
97. *Scáthán shacramuinte na h-aithridhe*, ll. 53-55.
98. Alan Ford, *The protestant reformation in Ireland, 1590–1641* (Frankfurt, 1985), 224–225.
99. *Scáthán shacramuinte na h-aithridhe*, ll. 4288–4293.

100. *ibid*. ll. 4805–5906.
101. *ibid*. ll. 5239–5272.
102. *ibid*. ll. 5272–5334.
103. *ibid*. ll. 5456–5462.
104. Paul Walsh, *The Four Masters and their work* (Dublin, 1944).
105. John O'Donovan (ed.), *Martyrology of Donegal* (Dublin, 1864).
106. T. Ó Fiaich, 'Republicanism and separatism in the seventeenth century', *Léachtaí Cholm Cille* ii (1971), 74–87.
107. *ibid*., 81–82.
108. Cecile O'Rahilly, *Five seventeenth-century political poems* (Dublin, 1977), l. 116, p. 23.
109. 'The Irish Vision at Rome ' – an English version published in John T. Gilbert (ed.), *A contemporary history of affairs in Ireland from 1641 to 1652*, 3 vols. with appendix of original letters and documents, (Dublin, 1879, 1880), iii, 190–196; hereafter, *Contemporary history*. Another version in English by Henry Grattan Curran accompanies the edition of the poem in James Hardiman (ed.), *Irish Minstrelsy*, 2 vols, [London, 1831], with introduction by Máire Mhac an tSaoi (Irish University Press, 1971), ii, 306–339.
110. T. Ó Dushláine, *An Eoraip agus litríocht na Gaeilge 1600–1650*, 180–215.
111. *Five seventeenth-century political poems*, 23, ll. 116–119.
112. *ibid*., 23–7.
113. *Contemporary history*, iii, pp. xxx–xxxix.
114. *ibid*., iii, pp. xxxiii.
115. *Five seventeenth-century political poems*, 23, ll. 126–129.
116. *ibid*., 29, ll. 265–289.
117. *ibid*., 26, ll. 200–204.
118. *Contemporary history*, iii, 211 – Appendix 'Colonel Henry O'Neill's relation of transactions of General Owen O'Neill and his party'.
119. *ibid*., i, pp. vii–ix.
120. *ibid*., ii, 63.
121. Tadhg Ó Donnchadha (eag.), 'Cín lae Ó Mealláin', *Anal. Hib.* (September 1931), 1–61.
122. *ibid*., 1–3.
123. *ibid*., 14.
124. *Reliquiae Celticae. Texts, papers and studies in Gaelic literature and philology left by the late Rev. Alexander Cameron* (2 vols, Inverness, 1892–4), ii, 138–147.
125. *Five seventeenth-century political poems*, 46, l. 237.
126. David Stevenson, *Alasdair MacColla and the Highland problem in the seventeenth century* (Edinburgh, 1980), 53–57; Cathaldus Giblin (ed.), *The Irish Franciscan mission to Scotland, 1619–46* (Dublin, 1964).
127. Derick S. Thomson (ed.), *The companion to Gaelic Scotland* (Oxford, 1983), 186–187.

128. See also David Stevenson, *Alasdair MacColla and the Highland problem in the seventeenth century.*
129. *The Gaelic mind*, 62–118; Bernadette Cunningham, 'Native culture and political change in Ireland, 1580–1640', in Ciaran Brady and Raymond Gillespie (eds.), *Natives and newcomers: essays on the making of Irish colonial society 1534–1641* (Dublin, 1986), 148–70; Mary O'Dowd, 'Gaelic economy and society', in the same volume, 120–47; Patrick J. Duffy, 'The territorial organization of Gaelic landownership and its transformation in Co. Monaghan, 1595–1640', *Irish Geography*, xiv (1981), 1–26.
130. Tadhg Ó Dúshláine, *An Eoraip agus litríocht na Gaeilge 1600–1650*, 82–115.
131. See Bernadette Cunningham and Raymond Gillespie, '"Persecution" in seventeenth-century Irish', *Éigse* 22 (1987), 15–21.

Chapter 5   Ulster 1641 in the context of political developments in the three kingdoms

1. W. Knowler (ed.), *The earl of Strafforde's letters and despatches* (2 vols, London, 1739), i, 65-7; ibid., ii, 107; Wentworth to Laud, 27 Sept. 1637, Sheffield City Lib., Wentworth Woodhouse MS 7, ff. 45-6; Laud to Wentworth, 7 Oct. 1637, ibid., f. 57; same to same, 24 Oct. 1637, ibid., ff. 58-9.
2. Wentworth to Laud, 1 Mar. 1638, Sheffield City Lib., Wentworth Woodhouse MS 7, f. 70v.
3. For fuller treatment of Charles' quarrel with the Scots, see P. Donald, *An uncounselled king: Charles and the Scottish troubles, 1637-1641* (Cambridge, 1990), 1-42; D. Stevenson, *The Scottish revolution 1637-1644: the triumph of the covenanters* (Newton Abbot, 1973), 15-87.
4. A. Clarke, 'The earl of Antrim and the first bishops' war', *Ir. Sword*, vi (1963-4), 108-9; M. Perceval-Maxwell, 'Strafford, the Ulster Scots, and the covenanters', *I.H.S.*, xviii (1973), 533; [Hamilton] to king, 15 June 1638, Scot. Rec. Off., Hamilton MS 406/1/10775, 10488; Wentworth to Laud, 10 April 1639, Sheffield City Lib., Wentworth Woodhouse MS 7, f. 182.
5. Wentworth to Northumberland, 28 Feb. 1639, 'Papers relating to Thomas Wentworth, first earl of Strafford' in C.H. Firth (ed.), *The Camden miscellany* (London, 1895), ix, 10; Laud to Wentworth, 31 Mar. 1639, in W. Scott and J. Bliss (eds.), *The works of the most reverend father in God William Laud* (7 vols in 9, Oxford, 1847–60), vii, 550. For a more extended account of the links between the deputy's Irish enemies and those in England and Scotland, see M. Perceval-Maxwell, *The outbreak of the Irish rebellion of 1641* (Dublin, 1994).

6. C.V. Wedgwood, *The king's peace* (London, 1955), 280; Knowler, *Letters and despatches*, ii, 374; *Privy council registers preserved in the Public Record Office reproduced in facsimile* (H.M.S.O., 1968), vii, 646.
7. Perceval-Maxwell, 'Strafford, the Ulster Scots, and the covenanters', 535.
8. H.F. Kearney, *Strafford in Ireland, 1633-41: a study in absolutism* (Manchester, 1959), 260-3; A. Clarke, *The Old English in Ireland, 1625-1642* (London, 1966), 127-8; Viscount Cromwell to Conway, 31 Mar. 1640, *Cal. S.P. dom., 1639-40*, 608; *Commons' jn. Ire.*, i, 138-9.
9. A. Clarke, 'The breakdown of authority, 1640-41', *N.H.I.* iii, 274.
10. C.V. Wedgwood, *Thomas Wentworth, first earl of Strafford, 1593-1641: a revaluation* (London 1961), 280-4; C. Russell, *The fall of the British monarchies 1637-1642* (Oxford, 1991), 104-23. See also E.S. Cope and W.H. Coates (eds), *Proceedings of the short parliament of 1640*, Camden Soc. 4th ser. (Royal Hist. Soc., London, 1977).
11. Clarke, 'The breakdown of authority', 276-7; Wandesford to Ormond, 16 May 1640, Bodl., Carte MS 1, f. 194v.; *Commons' jn. Ire.*, i, 142-51.
12. John Castle to Bridgewater, 26 June 1640, Huntington Library California, EL MS 7840; same to same, 1 July 1640, ibid., 7841; Nothumberland to Leicester, 22 July 1640, B.L., Alnwick MS Mic. 286; Hawkins to Leicester, 2 July 1640, H.M.C., *De L'Isle and Dudley MSS*, vi, 293.
13. Stevenson, *The Scottish revolution*, 196-211; St Leger to Ormond, 21 July 1640, Bodl., Carte MS 1, f. 214; Wandesford to Ormond, 21 Aug. 1640, P.R.O., 31/1/1, p. 141.
14. J. Nalson, *An impartial collection of the great affairs of state, from the beginning of the Scotch rebellion* (2 vols, London, 1682), i, 437-8.
15. Kearney, *Strafford in Ireland*, 202; *Commons' jn. Ire.*, i, 162-3.
16. C. Russell, 'The British background to the Irish rebellion of 1641', *Historical Research*, lxi (1988), 171.
17. B.L., Egerton MS 1048, ff. 13-14.
18. M.F. Keeler, *The long parliament 1640-1641: a biographical study of its members* (Philadephia, 1954), 10, 136.
19. G.M. Paul (ed.), *Diary of Sir Archibald Johnston of Wariston 1632-1639*, Scot. Hist. Soc., 1st ser. (3 vols, Edinburgh, 1911), ii, 351; Donald, *An uncounselled king*, 191-6; W. Notestein (ed.), *The journal of Sir Simonds D'Ewes from the beginning of the long parliament to the opening of the trial of the earl of Strafford* (New Haven, 1923), 13-14.
20. Notestein, *The journal of Sir Simonds D'Ewes*, 29n, 534; *Commons' jn. Eng.*, ii, 27.
21. *Privy council reg. facsimiles*, xi, xii, passim.
22. J. Rushworth, *The tryal of Thomas earl of Strafford* ([London], 1700), 111, 170, 236, 401, 469; Sir John Temple to Leicester, 7 Jan. 1641,

H.M.C., *De L'Isle and Dudley MSS*, vi, 360; same to same, 4 Feb. 1641, ibid., 375; same to same, 11 Feb. 1641, ibid., 379.

23.   Andrew Honeyman to —, 3 Mar. 1641, Nat. Lib. Scot., Adv. MS 29.2.9, ff. 151-v.

24.   Nalson, *Scotch rebellion*, i, 495.

25.   J. Bruce (ed.), *Notes of proceedings in the long parliament by Sir Ralph Verney*, Camden Society, 1st ser. (London, 1845), 60, 64.

26.   C. Russell, 'British background', 179; *Lords' jn*, iv, 348.

27.   *Acts parl. Scot.*, v, 342-3.

28.   B.L., Harleian MS 163, f. 163.

29.   C.M. Hibbard, *Charles I and the popish plot* (University of North Carolina, 1983).

30.   J.T. Gilbert (ed.), *A contemporary history of affairs in Ireland from A.D. 1641-1652...*, Irish Archaeological Society (3 vols, Dublin, 1879), i, 450, 453.

31.   R. Nugent to M. Vitelleschi, 12 Nov. 1640, Irish Jesuit Archives, Dublin, MS A, no. 71.

32.   J. Barnewall to Hugo Burgo, 18 Dec. 1640, in B. Jennings (ed.), *Louvain papers 1606-1827* (Dublin, 1968), 132.

33.   Honeyman to —, 3 Mar. 1641, Nat. Lib. Scot., Adv. MS 29.2.9, ff. 151-v.

34.   The Scottish commissioners' 'desires concerning unity in religion ... as a special mean for conserving peace in his majesty's dominions', 10 Mar. 1641, Nat. Lib. Scot., Adv. MS 33.4.6, ff.142-3.

35.   Notestein, *The journal of Sir Simonds D'Ewes*, 442.

36.   Maguire's relation, in M. Hickson (ed.), *Ireland in the seventeenth century or the massacres of 1641-2, their causes and results* (2 vols, London, 1884), ii, 344.

37.   O'Neill to Wadding, 8 July 1641, in C.P. Meehan, *The fate and fortune of Hugh O'Neill, earl of Tyrone, and Rory O'Donnell, earl of Tyrconnell* (Dublin, 1868), 545-7.

38.   *Commons' jn. Ire.*, i, 276-7.

39.   Clarke, *Old English*, 138.

40.   Ibid., 150; *Cal .S.P. Ire., 1633-47*, 339.

41.   E. Hyde, earl of Clarendon, *The history of the rebellion and civil wars in England*, W.D. Macray (ed.), (6 vols, Oxford, 1888), i, 411n.; Temple to Leicester, 22 July 1641, H.M.C., *De L'Isle and Dudley MSS*, vi, 405; same to same, 29 July, ibid, 406; same to same, 5 Aug. 1641, ibid., 407-8; same to same, 11 Aug. 1641, ibid., 410; Kent Archives Office, Maidstone, De L'Isle MSS, pt 2, V1475, Z1/9. I am grateful to Viscount De L'Isle, V.C., K.G., for permitting me to consult his family's muniments, and to Conrad Russell for directing me to this source.

42.   Russell, *The fall of the British monarchies*, 316-7, 328, 367, 369.

43. *Cal. S.P. Ire., 1633-47*, 321; O'Farralls of Longford to Dillon, 10 Nov. 1641, in Gilbert, *Contemp. hist., 1641-52*, i, 368.
44. Creichton's deposition, ibid., i, 527. We need not take seriously the claim that there was no plot to take Dublin Castle. This was first advanced in 1823 (M. Carey, *Vindiciae Hibernicae* (Philadelphia, 1823), 313-45) and has recently been revived (B. Fitzpatrick, *Seventeenth-century Ireland: the war of religions* (Totowa, New Jersey, 1989), 133-67). The claim is based on the undoubtedly inconsistent evidence supplied by the person who revealed the plot, Owen Connolly. However, there is a variety of independent evidence, apart from Connolly's statement, substantiating the existence of the plot, and this has either been ignored or unsatisfactorily explained by those who argue that the lords justice invented the plot. (See also Clarke, *Old English*, 161n).

Chapter 6   Destabilizing Ulster, 1641–2

1. Trinity College Dublin [hereafter T.C.D.], Ms 832, fol. 95.
2. T.C.D., Ms 840, fol. 1.
3. T.C.D., Ms 835, fol. 26.
4. *The last news from Ireland being a relation of the hostile and bloody proceedings of the rebellious papists there present* (London, 1641), sig A2v; *Bloody news from Norwich* (London, 1641), sig A3v; *Still worse news from Ireland* (London, 1641), 4, 6-8; *Inquisitionum in officio rotulorum cancellariae Hiberniae asservatarum repertorium*, ii, (Dublin, 1829), Monaghan, Charles II no.7; T.C.D. Ms 809, f. 297.
5. P.R.O., SP 63/260/30; Paul Walsh, *Irish chiefs and leaders* (Dublin, 1960), 166-9.
6. T.C.D., Ms 837, fols. 3-7, 12.
7. H.M.C., *Report on the manuscripts of the earl of Egmont*, i, (London, 1905), 146.
8. Bodl., Carte Ms 2, fol. 203.
9. T.C.D., Ms 838, fol. 155; Ms 834, fol. 35.
10. T.C.D., Ms 838, fol. 181; Raymond Gillespie, *Colonial Ulster* (Cork, 1985), 155.
11. T.C.D., Ms 837, fols. 89, 90; Ms 838, fol. 237.
12. Raymond Gillespie, 'The end of an era: Ulster and the outbreak of the 1641 rebellion', in Ciaran Brady, Raymond Gillespie (eds.), *Natives and newcomers: essays on the making of Irish colonial society, 1534-1641* (Dublin, 1986), 193-6, 201-2.
13. T.C.D., Ms 836, fol. 172.
14. J.T. Gilbert (ed.), *Ir. confed.*, i, (Dublin, 1882), 2.
15. T.C.D., Ms 836, fols. 44, 57v.
16. Raymond Gillespie, *Conspiracy: Ulster plots and plotters in 1615* (Belfast, 1988).

17. Gillespie, *Conspiracy*, 56; Sheffield City Library, Wentworth Woodhouse Mss, Strafford Letter Book 1, fol. 36.
18. E.M. Jope, 'Moyry, Charlemont, Castleraw and Richill: fortification to architecture in the north of Ireland, 1500-1700', *Ulster Journal of Archaeology*, 3rd ser. xxiii (1960), 97-123.
19. B.L., Egerton Ms 80, fol. 60v.
20. Gillespie, 'The end of an era', 204-7.
21. Bodl., Carte Ms 1, fol. 379.
22. P.R.O., SP 63/258/55.
23. Michael Perceval-Maxwell, 'Strafford, the Ulster Scots, and the covenanters', *I.H.S.*, xviii no. 72 (Sept. 1973), 524-51.
24. T.C.D., Ms 832, fol. 3v; Ms 835, fols. 2, 29v.
25. T.C.D., Ms 838, fols. 117v, 237.
26. T.C.D., Ms 837, fol. 144.
27. T.C.D., Ms 839, fols. 58, 112.
28. T.C.D., Ms 835, fol. 48v.
29. T.C.D., Ms 838, fol. 41, 79v.
30. T.C.D., Ms 836, fol. 76; Ms 835, fol.39.
31. T.C.D.. Ms 837, fols. 119, 124, 130, 131.
32. Gillespie, 'The end of an era', 210-12.
33. T.C.D., Ms 832, fol 55v; Ms 834, fols. 63, 84v; Ms 837, fol. 17; Ms 836, fol.31; Gillespie, 'The end of an era', 193.
34. T.C.D., Ms 833, fols. 51, 60, 65, 69; Ms 839, fol.125v; Ms 835, fols. 5, 8v; Ms 831, fol. 2, Ms 836, fols. 32, 78; Ms 834, fols. 90, 91, 182.
35. Robert Dunlop, 'The forged commission of 1641', *E.H.R.* ii (1887), 527-33.
36. T.C.D., Ms 839, fol. 45v; Ms 835, fols. 8, 35; Ms 830, fol. 174.
37. T.C.D., Ms 832, fols. 46v, 63v, 66v, 99; Ms 834, fol.77; Ms 839, fols. 3v, 127.
38. Gillespie, 'The end of an era', 203-4, 208.
39. T.C.D., Ms 809, fol.6.
40. T.C.D., Ms 836, fols. 72, 57v; Ms 839, fol. 6v; Ms 835, fol.13; Ms 834, fols. 55, 57v, 81; Ms 832, fol. 112v.
41. Gilbert (ed.), *Ir. confed.*, i, 17, 45-6.
42. Gillespie, 'The end of an era', 210; H.M.C., *Report on the manuscripts of the duke of Ormond*, new series, ii (London, 1895), 245; Breandán Ó Buachalla, 'An mheisiasacht agus an aisling', in P. de Brún, S. Ó Coileáin, P. Ó Riain (eds.), *Folia Gadelica* (Cork, 1983), 77-8.
43. Keith Thomas, *Religion and the decline of magic* (London, 1971), 490.
44. T.C.D., Ms 831, fol. 6v.
45. T.C.D., Ms 835, fols. 14, 15, 30, 35; Ms 836, ff 49, 63, 64v.
46. T.C.D., Ms 831, fol. 11.
47. James Hogan (ed.), *Letters and papers relating to the Irish rebellion, 1642-6* (Dublin, 1936), 6.

48.   T.C.D., Ms 832, fol. 56v; Ms 834, fol. 91.

49.   Nicholas Bernard, *The whole proceedings of the siege of Drogheda* (London, 1642), 68.

50.   Bernard, *Siege of Drogheda*, 84-7, 53.

51.   T.C.D., Ms 836, fols. 40v, 62.

52.   T.C.D., Ms 836, fol. 165; Ms 832, fols. 143v, 166; Ms 839, fol. 118.

53.   T.C.D., Ms 836, fols. 40v, 46, 49; Ms 834, fol. 64v; Ms 833, fols. 108, 154v.

54.   T.C.D., Ms 838, fols. 73v, 79.

55.   T.C.D., Ms 835, fols. 20v; Ms 832, fols. 84v, 105, 120.

56.   T.C.D., Ms 836, fols. 2, 38v, 39, 59.

57.   T.C.D., Ms 832, fol. 81.

58.   Robert Cole, *The last true intelligence from Ireland* (London, 1642), 2.

59.   *A relation from Belfast* (London, 1642), 5-6.

60.   *The latest and true news from Ireland* (London, 1642), 2; *News from Ireland concerning the warlike affairs in the province of Leinster* (London, 1642), 2.

61.   T.C.D., Ms 836, fols. 97, 98; Ms 809, fol. 9. The episode of the beam of light recorded by Maxwell clearly made an impact on contemporaries as it was compared to other supernatural manifestations in 1689, Andrew Hamilton, *A true relation of the actions of the Enniskillen men* (London, 1690), 35-6.

62.   T.C.D., Ms 836, fols. 89, 92, 94, 103, 112; Ms 809, fols. 10-10v.

63.   T.C.D., Ms 837, fol. 11; Ms 832, fols. 79v, 142.

64.   *Memoirs of his own life and times by Sir James Turner* (Edinburgh, 1829), 22.

65.   T.C.D., Ms 837, fol. 4; Ms 835, fol. 29.

66.   John Temple, *A history of the general rebellion in Ireland* (Cork, 1766), 97-8.

67.   James Ussher, archbishop of Armagh, *Vox Hiberniae or rather the cries from Ireland* (London, 1642).

68.   Bernard, *Siege of Drogheda*, 4.

69.   *Good and true news from Ireland being a copy of a letter sent by Mr Roger Puttock...to a brother of his* (London, 1642), sig A2-sig A2v.

70.   J.T. Gilbert (ed.), *A contemporary history of the affairs of Ireland*, i, (Dublin, 1879), 7.

71.   Gilbert (ed.), *Ir. confed.*, vol. i, 1.

Chapter 7   Violence in County Armagh, 1641

1.   T.C.D. MSS 809-839. See A.Clarke, 'The 1641 depositions', in P. Fox (ed.), *Treasures of the Library: Trinity College Dublin* (Dublin, 1986), 111–22

2.   This article is based on my moderatorship thesis, Dublin University, 1974.

3.   For more detailed accounts of the plantation of county Armagh see *N.H.I.* iii, chapter vii, and P. Robinson, *The Plantation of Ulster* (Dublin, 1984).

4.   H. Jones, 'A remonstrance of divers remarkable passages concerning the church and kingdome of Ireland', in T. Thorpe (ed.), *Original Tracts, illustrative of Irish history*, i, (1641-2), 13-16.

5.   Letters and Despatches T.C.D. MS. 844, fol. 136-137.

6.   For clarity the term '1641 Depositions' refers to the volume of Depositions as a whole; evidence given to the 1641–2 commission is referred to as a '1642 deposition' and the witness is called 'the deponent'; and evidence given to the 1652 commission is called a '1652 examination' and the witness an 'examinant'.

7.   W. Clark, 2, 7 Jan. 1641–2; W.Clark, 177, 28 Feb. 1652–3. [For the sake of brevity, when quoting evidence in the Armagh volume of the 1641 Depositions,T.C.D. MS 836, I have given the name of the deponent or examinant, the folio number of the Armagh volume and the date of the deposition or examination. As the depositions are dated according to the old calendar I have added the modern date to each reference. In some instances depositions or examinations from other volumes have been quoted. In these cases the name of the county volume has been added to the reference. Where there are direct quotations from the depositions the original spelling has been retained and the scribal contractions have been silently extended].

8.   J. Warren, 59, 21 Feb. 1652–3; N.Richardson, 67, 20 April 1642; T. Taylor, 179, 24 Feb. 1652–3; R.Newberry, 60, 27 June 1642.

9.   W. Clark, 2, 7 Jan. 1641–2.

10.   W. Clark, 177, 28 Feb. 1652–3.

11.   R. Newberry, 60, 27 Feb. 1642–3.

12.   J. Warren, 139, 21 Feb. 1652–3.

13.   J. Beere, 161, 26 Feb. 1652–3; W.Skelton, 222, 6 June 1653; J. Wisdome, 15, 8 Feb. 1641–2.

14.   T.Hayward, 147, 16 Feb. 1652–3.

15.   See 10.

16.   E. Fullerton, 50, 16 Sept. 1642; E. Price, 101, 26 June 1643.

17.   P. Taylor, 7, 8 Feb. 1641–2; C. Stanhawe, 75, 23 July 1642; R. Newberry, 61, 27 June 1642.

18.   V. Blacker, 242, undated.

19.   T. McCann, 240, 5 May 1653.

20.   R. Maxwell, Dublin, 9, 22 Aug. 1642; W. Duffeild, 49, 9 Aug. 1642.

21.   K. Cook, 92, 24 Feb. 1643–4; A. Stratford, 115, 9 March 1643–4.

22.   H. Jones, 'Remonstrance...' in T. Thorpe, *Original Tracts*, ii, 1-10.

23.   E. Hogan (ed.), *History of the War of Ireland by a British officer* (1873), 8.

24.   A. Smith & M.Clark, 73, 16 March 1642–3.

25.   J. Constable, 87, 6 June 1643.
26.   See 24.
27.   J. Grace, 52, 3 Sept. 1642.
28.   See 25.
29.   R. Maxwell, Dublin, 10, 22 Aug. 1642.
30.   E. Rolleston, 68, 21 Aug. 1642.
31.   F. Sacheverell, 107, 21 July 1643.
32.   E. Matchett, 59, 3 Sept. 1642.
33.   A. Hutchenson, 248, 19 April 1653.
34.   W. Bently, 149, 24 Feb. 1652–3; T.Dixon, 119, 26 Feb. 1652–3.
35.   T. Chambers, 37, undated.
36.   T. Chambers, 42, 2 June 1642.
37.   W. Bently, 149, 24 Feb. 1652–3.
38.   M. Brabazon, 153, 24 Feb. 1652–3.
39.   J. Henderson, 208, undated; J.Beere, Antrim, 98, 4 June 1653.
40.   T. Dixon, 119, 26 Feb. 1652–3.
41   W. Brownlow, 202, 26 Feb. 1652–3; N.Simpson, Monaghan, 182, 6
       April 1643.
42.   J. Kerdiff, Tyrone, 13, 28 Feb. 1641–2.
43.   J. Beere, Antrim, 98, 4 June 1653.
44.   N. Simpson, Monaghan, 182, 6 April 1643.
45.   W. Bently, 149, 24 Feb. 1652–3; J.Wisdome, 15, 8 Feb. 1641–2.
46.   J. Gowrly, 57, 8 Nov. 1642.
47.   W. Bently, 149, 24 Feb. 1652–3; J. Beere, 161, 26 Feb. 1652–3;
       G. Graves, 151, 23 Feb. 1652–3; M. Brabazon, 153, 24 Feb. 1652–3.
48.   J. Henderson, 250, 2 May 1653.
49.   W. Sym, 229, 19 May 1653.
50.   Proceedings of the High Court of Justice 1652–4, T.C.D. MS 866,
       fol.135.
51.   W. Skelton, 171, 26 Feb. 1652–3.
52.   J. Constable, 88, 6 June 1643.
53.   M. Harrison, 136, 11 Feb. 1652–3.
54.   J. Travers, 157, 26 Feb. 1652–3.
55.   P. Dory, 164, 21 Feb. 1652–3.
56.   A. Gill, 209, undated; W. Brownlow, 202, 26 Feb. 1652–3.
57.   W. Codd, 268, 3 June 1653; O. McKeene, 252, 5 May 1653.
58.   W.McGinn, 245, 3 May 1653.
59.   E. Fullerton, 51, 16 Sept. 1642; E. Saltenstall, 72, 1 June 1642; M.
       Harrison, 136, 11 Feb. 1652–3; A. Stratford, 115, 9 March 1643–4.
60.   J. Richardson, 234, 5 March 1641–2; M. Harrison, 136, 11 Feb.
       1652–3.
61.   E. Fullerton, 50, 16 Sept. 1642; A. Gregg, 95, 21 July 1643.
62.   R. Holland, Monaghan, 63, 4 March 1641–2; J. Constable, 88, 6 June
       1643; J. Wisdome, 15, 8 Feb. 1641–2; W. Skelton, 172, 26 Feb.
       1652–3.

63. T. Chambers, 43, 2 June 1642.
64. M. Harrison, 129, 11 Feb. 1652–3.
65. J. Parry, 62, 31 May 1642; T. Chambers, 38, undated.
66. W. Skelton, 172, 26 Feb. 1652–3.
67. H. Stewart, Down, 82, 3 March 1653–4; W. Clark, Antrim, 174, 28 Feb. 1653–4.
68. H. Simms, '1641 Depositions for County Armagh', (moderatorship thesis, Dublin University, 1974), 48–52.
69. E. Greene, 94, 24 Nov. 1643.
70. R. Maxwell, Dublin, 10, 22 Aug.1642.
71. Books of Survey and Distribution, P.R.O.N.I., Armagh, fol.53.
72. G. Hill, *An historical account of the Plantation in Ulster 1608-20* (Belfast, 1877), 125.
73. A. Clarke,'The genesis of the Ulster rising of 1641', in P. Roebuck (ed.), *Plantation to partition: essays in Ulster history in honour of J.L. McCracken* (Belfast, 1981), 32–33.
74. P. O'Quin, 238, 5 May 1653.
75. R. Warren, 9, 7 Jan. 1641–2; B. Drewrie, 46, 30 June 1642; C. Stanhawe, 75, 23 July 1642.
76. R.J. Hunter, 'The Ulster Plantation in the counties of Armagh and Cavan 1608-1641', (M.Litt. thesis, Dublin University,1968).
77. E. Saltenstall, 69, 1 June 1642; N. Richardson, 67, 20 April 1642; R. Warren, 9, 7 Jan. 1641–2.
78. See 36.
79. B. Drewrie, 46, 30 June 1642; R. Newberry, 60, 27 June 1642.
80. See 66.
81. See 27.
82. M. Phillis, 66, 15 March 1642–3.
83. G. Littlefeild, 55, 1 June 1642; J. Constable, 89, 6 June 1643.
84. See 9.
85. See 46
86. C. Stanhawe, 76, 23 July 1642; G. Pemerton, 8, 2 March 1641–2.
87. A. Workeman, 204, 28 Feb. 1652–3.
88. T. Jukes, 16, undated.
89. W. Sym, 226, 19 May 1653; R. Miles, 214, 3 May 1653; S. Hasleton, 215, 3 May 1653.
90. W. Brownlow, 202, 26 Feb.1652–3; F. Sacheverell, 107, 21 July 1643.
91. P. Taylor, 7, 8 Feb. 1641–2; T.Chambers, 38, undated.
92. P.F. Moran, 'The Irish massacre of 1641', *I.E.R.*, 2nd ser., x ([1873]), 89.
93. M. Hickson,'Depositions relating to the Irish massacres of 1641', *E.H.R.*, ii (1887), 137.
94. N. Canny, *Kingdom and colony: Ireland in the Atlantic world, 1560-1800* (Baltimore, 1988), 96.
95. P. Robinson, *The Plantation of Ulster* (Dublin 1984), 105-107, 212-3.

Chapter 8   The 1641 Rebellion and anti-popery in Ireland

1. C.Z. Weiner, 'The beleaguered Isle. A study of Elizabethan and early Jacobean anti-Catholicism', *Past and Present* 51 (1971), 27-62; Robin Clifton, 'The popular fear of catholics during the English revolution', ibid., 52 (1971), 23-55; Robin Clifton, 'Fear of popery', in Conrad Russell (ed.), *The origins of the English civil war* (London, 1973), 144-67; R.J. Bauckham, *Tudor Apocalypse* (Abingdon, 1978); M. Finlayson, *Historians, Puritanism and the English Revolution* (Toronto, 1983). Peter Lake, 'Anti-popery: the structure of a prejudice', in Richard Cust and Ann Hughes (eds), *Conflict in early Stuart England* (London, 1989), 72-106.

2. T.C. Barnard, 'Crises of identity among Irish protestants, 1641-1685', *Past and Present* 127 (1990), 51-6.

3. Henry Jones, Randall Adams, William Aldrich, Henry Brereton, William Hitchcock, Roger Puttock, John Sterne and John Watson, *A remonstrance of divers remarkable passages concerning the Church and Kingdome of Ireland* (London, 1642).

4. Henry Jones, Randall Adams, Henry Brereton, and Edward Piggott, untitled 'Discourse' (catalogued as 'A treatise giving a representation of the grand rebellion in Ireland'), B.L., Harleian MS. 5999.

5. The last and best of the traditional treatments were, respectively, the contributions of G.V. Jourdan in W.A. Philips (ed.), *History of the Church of Ireland* (3 vols, Oxford, 1933-4) and R.D. Edwards, *Church and state in Tudor Ireland* (Dublin, 1935).

6. B. Bradshaw, 'Sword, word and strategy in the Reformation in Ireland', *Historical Journal* 21 (1978), 475-502; Nicholas Canny, 'Why the reformation failed in Ireland: *une question mal posée*', *Journal of Ecclesiastical History* 30 (1979), 423-50; Karl Bottigheimer, 'The failure of the reformation in Ireland: *une question bien posée*', ibid., 36 (1985), 196-207; Steven G. Ellis, 'Economic problems of the church: why the reformation failed in Ireland', ibid., 41 (1990), 239-65.

7. D.B. Quinn and K.W. Nicholls, 'Ireland in 1534', in *N.H.I.* iii, 1-38.

8. S.G. Ellis, *Tudor Ireland: crown, community and the conflict of cultures, 1470-1603* (London, 1985) is an able introduction. D.B. Quinn, *The Elizabethans and the Irish* (Ithaca, 1966), 7-13.

9. Nicholas Canny, *The Elizabethan conquest of Ireland: a pattern established, 1565-76* (Hassocks, 1976), chapter 6, 'Elizabethan attitudes towards the Irish', 117-36; John Bossy, 'The counter-reformation and the people of catholic Ireland', in T.W. Williams (ed.), *Historical studies: viii* (Dublin, 1971), 155-70.

10. See Note 6.

11. Nicholas Canny, *The formation of the Old English élite in Ireland* (Dublin, 1975); 'Dominant minorities: English settlers in Ireland

and Virginia, 1550-1650', in A.C. Hepburn (ed.), *Minorities in history: Historical Studies xii* (London, 1978), 50-69; C.F. Brady, 'Conservative subversives: the community of the pale and the Dublin administration, 1556-86', in P.J. Corish (ed.), *Radicals, rebels and establishments: Historical Studies xv* (Belfast, 1985), 11-32; Aidan Clarke, 'The English', in P.J. Loughrey (ed.), *The people of Ireland* (Belfast, 1988), 112-24.

12. John J. Silke, *Kinsale: the Spanish intervention in Ireland at the end of the Elizabethan wars* (Liverpool, 1970), 65-70.

13. *N.H.I.* iii, 187-91; John McCavitt, 'The lord deputyship of Sir Arthur Chichester in Ireland, 1605-16' (PhD dissertation, Queen's University, Belfast, 1988), chapter 7, 215-62.

14. McCavitt, 'Sir Arthur Chichester in Ireland', loc. cit.; *N.H.I.* iii, 191-2.

15. Privy Council of England to Lord Deputy Chichester, 24 January 1606, P.R.O., State Papers, Domestic, 31/8/199, 62-5.

16. J.J. Silke, 'Primate Lombard and James I', *Irish Theological Quarterly*, 22 (1955), 131-3.

17. *Cal. S.P. Ir., 1625-32*, 297-8, 304; P.R.O., S.P. Ire., 63/246/7.

18. On the Church of Ireland, see Alan Ford, *The protestant reformation in Ireland, 1590-1641* (Frankfurt, 1985); Aidan Clarke, 'Varieties of uniformity : the first century of the Church of Ireland', in W.J. Shiels and Diana Wood (eds), *The churches, Ireland and the Irish: studies in church history 25* (Oxford, 1989), 105-22.

19. *Articles of religion agreed upon by the archbishops and bishops, and the rest of the clergie of Ireland, in the convocation holden at Dublin in the year of our lord God 1615: for the avoidance of diversities of opinions: and the establishment of consent touching true religion* (Dublin, 1615); Ford, *Protestant reformation*, 194-201.

20. Ford, *Protestant reformation*, 202-28.

21. Irish Articles of 1615, No 68.

22. Luke 14/23.

23. Aidan Clarke, *The Old English in Ireland, 1625-42* (London, 1966), 28-43; a recusancy fine was the penalty imposed in the act of uniformity (1560) for each failure to attend services of the established church.

24. C.R. Elrington, *The life of the Most Reverend James Ussher* (Dublin and London, 1848), 73-5. Some fifty years later Henry Jones, then bishop of Meath, cited the declaration as support for his increasingly unfashionable view that the pope was Antichrist: *A sermon of Antichrist, preached at Christ-Church, Dublin, Novemb. 12.* (Dublin, 1677).

25. Ford, *Protestant reformation*, 262-7; Clarke, *Old English*, 38-40.

26. Elrington, *Life of Ussher*, 76; Bodl., Carte MSS, i. 85.

27. T.C.D., MS 1188.

28. 1 Samuel 15/24. The commandment, which concerned the Amalekites, had required Saul to 'utterly destroy all that they have, and spare them not'.
29. Elrington, *Life of Ussher*, 79-86.
30. Aidan Clarke, *The Graces, 1625-41* (Dundalk, 1968).
31. Nicholas Tyack, 'Puritanism, Arminianism and Counter-Revolution', in Conrad Russell (ed.), *The origins of the English civil war* (London, 1973), 119-143.
32. Ford, *Protestant reformation*, 269-70.
33. Henry Leslie, *A treatise of authority of the church* (Dublin, 1637), The epistle Dedicatory.
34. Most dramatically, perhaps, in Sir John Clotworthy's speeches to the English House of Commons: W. Notestein (ed.), *Journal of Sir Simonds D'Ewes* (New Haven, 1923), 13-4.
35. Aidan Clarke, 'Ireland and the general crisis', *Past and Present* 48 (1970), 85-6.
36. T.W. Moody, *The Londonderry plantation, 1609-41* (Belfast, 1939), 329.
37. B. Mac Cuarta (ed.), 'Mathew De Renzy's letters on Irish affairs, 1613-1620', *Anal. Hib.* 34 (Dublin, 1987), 112.
38. 'we continuing amongst them in all love and amity without distrust', as a group of protestant petitioners asserted in 1644, *H.M.C., Ormonde MSS, new series* (London, 1903), ii, 342.
39. Sir John Temple, *The Irish rebellion* (London, 1678), 27.
40. Randall Adams (1626), Henry Jones (1624) and John Watson (1631), had been fellows of TCD; Henry Brereton (BA, 1629) and Roger Puttock (MA, 1622) were graduates. Temple had become a fellow of Trinity in 1618, during the provostship of his father.
41. Aidan Clarke, 'The 1641 depositions', in P. Fox (ed.), *Treasures of the Library: Trinity College Dublin* (Dublin, 1986), 111-22.
42. *A remonstrance of divers remarkable passages concerning the church and kingdome of Ireland* (London, 1642). W.D. Love, 'Civil War in Ireland: appearances in three centuries of historical writing', *Emory University Quarterly* 22 (1966), 57-72.
43. *A remonstrance*, 1.
44. Ibid., 3.
45. Ibid., 1.
46. Ibid., 7.
47. Ibid., 1-2.
48. Ibid., 7.
49. Ibid., 3–5.
50. Ibid., 7.
51. Adams, Brereton, Jones and Edward Piggott (BA, 1633) who had replaced the deceased Roger Puttock in the third commission in June 1642, Clarke, 'The 1641 depositions', 112.

52. Harleian MS. 5999. A sequence of 207 depositions runs from 24 March 1642 to 18 July 1643. To these was added the deposition of Sir William Stewart, taken on 12 October 1643, presumably because it contains the catholic bishop of Raphoe's alleged admission that the king's commission had been 'forged by one Plunkett'. Attention was drawn to this manuscript by Ferdinand Warner, who used it rather than the originals preserved in Trinity College Dublin, which he examined perfunctorily, to arrive at his controversial and ill-informed estimate that only 4,028 Protestants had been killed in the rebellion (*The history of the rebellion and civil-war in Ireland*, London, 1767, 294-7), Clarke, 'The 1641 depositions', 119.
53. Harleian MS. 5999, 2.
54. Ibid., 3v.
55. Ibid., 2.
56. Ibid., 21, 21v.
57. Ibid., 5v.
58. Ibid., 13.
59. Ibid., 35v.
60. 'being the most disgraceful terme wherewith (in their apprehension) they can brand a man, and importing to their sense, men of the most base contemptible and sordid condition', ibid., 21.
61. 'that is, men that lived industriously by husbandry', ibid., 21.
62. Ibid., 24.
63. Ibid., 30.
64. Ibid., 3v.
65. Ibid., 21v.
66. Ibid., 30.
67. Ibid., 9v.
68. Ibid., 2.
69. *A remonstrance*, 2.
70. Harleian MS. 5999, 9-9v.
71. Ibid., 24–24v.
72. Ibid., 17.
73. Ibid., 36.
74. Ibid., 14v.
75. Ibid., 12, 29; Juan Mariana SJ (1536-1623/4) had justified tyrannicide in *De Rege et Regis Institutione* (1559).
76. Ibid., 3v.
77. Ibid., 4v.
78. Ibid., 5v.
79. Ibid., 8, 9.
80. Ibid, 13v-14, 23v. The Polyphemus image had been used in an early pamphlet which had argued that land 'was the only religion they thirsted after. Their debts were great, their fortunes and estates

desperate, even generally. They had no other way left to repair themselves but this. And yet our Old English gentry in the pale are so dull as to be fooled with this gross conceit, that this war is only for religion. Let them take heed, their land is the flower of the whole kingdom . . . What favour could they expect in such a case, but that which Polyphemus promised to Ulysses, That he should be the last devoured.' Thomas Emitie, *That great expedition for Ireland by way of underwriting proposed, by both Houses of Parliament, and graciously assented to by His Majesty, is here vindicated* (London, 1642).

81. Harleian MS. 5999, 23v.
82. Ibid., 16–17v.
83. Ibid., 15-15v.
84. Ibid., 12-12v.
85. Ibid., 13.
86. Ibid., 18v.
87. Ibid., 19–19v, Revelation 11/ 8, 9.
88. Ibid., 31v, 33.
89. Ibid., 12.
90. Ibid., 31v.
91. Ibid., 36.
92. R. Puttock, *Good and true news from Ireland* (London, 1642).
93. Clarke, 'The 1641 depositions', 116.
94. D. Harcourt, *A new remonstrance from Ireland* (London, [1643]).
95. Harleian MS. 5999, 34v–35v.
96. R. Puttock, *A reioynder unto W. Malone's reply to the first article* (Dublin, 1632), Dedication.
97. Harleian MS. 5999, 36.
98. Ibid., 33.
99. T.C. Barnard, 'Crises of identity', 53.
100. Harleian MS. 5999, 16v.
101. Ibid., 18, 18v.

Chapter 9   1641 and the quest for Catholic Emancipation, 1691–1829

1.   A good introduction to the revisionist efforts of Curry and O'Conor is to be found in Walter D. Love, 'Charles O'Conor of Belanagare and Thomas Leland's "philosophical" history of Ireland', *I.H.S.*, xiii (1962), 1-25; see also Joseph Liechty, 'Testing the depth of catholic/protestant conflict: the case of Thomas Leland's *History of Ireland, 1773'*, *Archiv. Hib.*, xlii (1987), 13-28. For Fr O'Leary on 1641, see *An humble remonstrance to the Scotch and English inquisitors: by way of an apostrophe* [n.d: c. 1780], in Arthur O'Leary, *Miscellaneous tracts* (Dublin, 1791), 183-98.
2.   See *N.H.I.* iii, chap. xi. See also Jacqueline Hill, 'Popery and protestantism, civil and religious liberty: the disputed lessons of

Irish history 1690-1812', *Past & Present*, no. 118 (1988), 96-129; here, 100, 117, n. 93.

3. Conor Cruise O'Brien, *The great melody: a thematic biography . . . of Edmund Burke* (London, 1992), 69.

4. Mathew Carey, *Vindiciae Hiberniciae: or, Ireland vindicated: an attempt to develop and expose a few of the multifarious errors and falsehoods respecting Ireland, in the histories of May, Temple . . . and others: particularly in the legendary tales of the conspiracy and pretended massacre of 1641* (Philadelphia, 1819). Carey was said to have decided to compile this work having read William Godwin's novel *Mandeville*, 3 vols., (Edinburgh, 1817), whose hero had been scarred for life by memories of his parents' murder at the hands of Ulster Catholics in 1641 (see *DNB*).

5. *The earl of Castlehaven's review; or his memoirs of his engagement and carriage in the Irish wars* ([London], 1680, 1684). No new edition appeared until that brought out by Charles O'Conor in 1753.

6. See Maureen Wall, *Catholic Ireland in the eighteenth century: collected essays*, Gerard O'Brien (ed.), (Dublin, 1989), chap. 1.

7. 'An act for keeping and celebrating the twenty-third of October, as an anniversary thanksgiving in this kingdom', 14 & 15 Chas II, c. 23; *The book of common prayer...according to the use of the Church of Ireland* (Dublin, 1745).

8. T.C. Barnard, 'The uses of 23 October 1641 and Irish protestant celebrations', *E.H.R.*, cvi (1991), 889-920, especially 891-5; Nathanael Foy, *A sermon preached in Christ's-Church, Dublin; on the 23d of October, 1698. Being the anniversary thanksgiving for putting an end to the Irish rebellion, which broke out on that day, 1641* (Dublin, 1698), 19.

9. Barnard, 'The uses of 23 October 1641', 889, 897-8.

10. For instance, in Thomas Bartlett's recent welcome study, *The fall and rise of the Irish nation: the catholic question 1690-1830* (Dublin, 1992), only about one-eighth of the book is devoted to the period 1690-1750.

11. Patrick Fagan, *The second city: portrait of Dublin 1700-1760* (Dublin, 1986), 134, 136. See also the same author's *Dublin's turbulent priest: Cornelius Nary (1658-1738)* (Dublin, 1991).

12. Fagan, *Dublin's turbulent priest*, chap. 3; *The second city*, chap. 9.

13. Wall, *Catholic Ireland*, 1-9; Bartlett, *Fall and rise of the Irish nation*, chap. 2.

14. 9 Will. III, c. 1. This act required Roman Catholic bishops, vicars general and regular clergy to leave Ireland by 1 May 1698. It was not consistently enforced (Wall, *Catholic Ireland*, 9-31).

15. John Stoye, 'Europe and the revolution of 1688', in Robert Beddard (ed.), *The revolutions of 1688* (Oxford, 1991), 191-212; here, 191-5; Jonathan Scott, 'Radicalism and restoration: the shape of the Stuart

experience', *Historical Journal* (hereafter *Hist. Jn.*), xxxi (1988), 453-67; here, 460.

16. See Mark Goldie, 'The civil religion of James Harrington', in Anthony Pagden (ed.), *The languages of political theory in early-modern Europe* (Cambridge, 1990 edn.), 197-222; here, 210-12, 221-2.

17. See e.g., Paul Monod, *Jacobitism and the English people 1688-1788* (Cambridge, 1989); also the bibliography on Jacobitism in J.C.D. Clark, *Revolution and rebellion* (Cambridge, 1986), 174-7.

18. Wall, *Catholic Ireland*, 15-16.

19. Republished 1720; also appeared as *The impartial history of Ireland* (London, 1754, 1762, 1768), (Dublin, 1787), and as *The genuine history of Ireland* (Dublin, 1799, 1837).

20. Hugh Reily, *The impartial history of Ireland* (London, 1762), 32.

21. Linda Colley, *Britons: forging the nation 1707-1837* (New Haven & London, 1992), 200-36.

22. Wall, *Catholic Ireland*, 108-9.

23. Ibid., 14-17; C.D.A. Leighton, *Catholicism in a protestant kingdom: a study of the Irish ancien régime* (Dublin, 1994), chap. 5.

24. Bartlett, *Fall and rise of the Irish nation*, 6-9, 52-3.

25. See e.g., Thomas Leland, *History of Ireland from the invasion of Henry II*, 3 vols. (London, 1773), iii, 127-8.

26. David Berman, 'David Hume on the 1641 rebellion in Ireland', *Studies*, lxv (1976), 101-12; Hill, 'Popery and protestantism', 108-12.

27. Liechty, 'Testing the depth of catholic/protestant conflict', 13-28.

28. Robert Kent Donovan, 'The military origins of the Roman Catholic relief programme of 1778', *Hist. Jn.*, xxviii (1985), 79-102.

29. Jacqueline Hill, 'Religious toleration and the relaxation of the penal laws: an imperial perspective, 1763-1780', *Archiv. Hib.*, xliv (1989), 98-109; here, 102.

30. Bartlett, *Fall and rise of the Irish nation*, 77-81, and chap. 6.

31. Hill, 'Religious toleration and the relaxation of the penal laws', 107; Bartlett, *Fall and rise of the Irish nation*, 53-4.

32. See letter signed 'Hurlo Thrumbo', *Freeman's Journal*, 19-21 Oct. 1775.

33. See e.g., reports in *Freeman's Journal*, 24-6 Oct. 1775, 23-5 Oct. 1777, 23-5 Oct. 1781; Edward Young [bishop of Dromore], *A sermon preached in Christ-Church, Dublin; on...October 23, 1763* (Dublin, 1763), 5. For a fuller discussion of the contents of the sermons, see Barnard, 'The uses of 23 October 1641'.

34. Hill, 'Popery and protestantism', 112-14, 116-20.

35. *An historical and critical review of the civil wars in Ireland* (Dublin, 1775).

36. *Faulkner's Dublin Journal* (hereafter *FDJ*), 23-6 Oct. 1784. In 1786 *FDJ*, one of the more conservative Dublin newspapers, reported the failure of 'government' to go in state to church on 23 October without any adverse comment: *FDJ*, 21-4 Oct. 1786.

37. *Dublin Chronicle*, 23 Oct. 1788; cf ibid., 21 Oct. 1790. For reports of the corporation's observance, see e.g., ibid., 25 Oct. 1792, 24 Oct. 1793.

38. Ibid., 23 October 1788.

39. Representative Church Body Library, Braemor Park, Dublin, St Werburgh's parish account book, 1781-98, P. 326/7/2 (information for 1789, 1790 and 1791 is incomplete). The year 1792 saw the first major signs of division among Protestants over the catholic question, and it was in that year that the *Dublin Evening Post* (*DEP*), a pro-catholic paper, criticised householders in the Dublin area who had lit up their houses to mark 23 October: *DEP*, 27 Oct. 1792. During these two seven-year periods the other anniversaries on which bells were rung at St Werburgh's (excluding church holidays, contemporary military victories, and birthdays, etc. of the reigning royal family) were: 1 July (battle of the Boyne): 5/14; 12 July (battle of Aughrim): 3/14; 1 August (Hanoverian accession): 1/14; 4 November (King William's birthday), 11 or 12/14; 5 November (gunpowder plot): possibly once (payment made to ringers on 6 Nov. 1788 without specifying whether for 4 or 5 November).

40. Quoted in Hill, 'Religious toleration and the relaxation of the penal laws', 103. While it is correct to suggest that by this time some members of the British government were coming to regard catholic relief as mainly a matter of expediency (Bartlett, *Fall and rise of the Irish nation*, 91), this of course left the opposition occupying the high ground of principle.

41. See his *An essay on toleration* [1781], in O'Leary, *Miscellaneous tracts*, 266. For the sake of obtaining relief in other fields, O'Leary was prepared for Catholics to be excluded from parliament, high office and from bearing arms: ibid., 266.

42. James Kelly, 'The parliamentary reform movement of the 1780s and the catholic question', *Archiv. Hib.*, xliii (1988), 95-117.

43. Bartlett, *Fall and rise of the Irish nation*, chaps 8 & 9; Jacqueline Hill, 'The meaning and significance of "Protestant ascendancy"', in *Ireland after the union* (Proceedings of the second joint meeting of the Royal Irish Academy and the British Academy, London 1986) (Oxford, 1989), 1-22.

44. Sir John and Lady Gilbert, *Calendar of ancient records of Dublin* (*CARD*), 19 vols. (Dublin, 1899-1944), xiv, 284-7; Hereward Senior, *Orangeism in Ireland and Britain, 1795-1836* (London & Toronto, 1966), 1-2, 51.

45. J.C.D. Clark, *English society 1688-1832* (Cambridge, 1985), 253-8.

46. 'It is not a fundamental part of the settlement at the revolution, that the state should be protestant *without any qualification of the term*' (emphasis in original). *A letter from the Right Hon. Edmund*

Burke ... to Sir Hercules Langrishe,..on the subject of the Roman catholics of Ireland (Dublin, 1792), 19.

47.   *CARD*, xiv, 287.

48.   Ibid., xiv, 284-6.

49.   Bartlett, *Fall and rise of the Irish nation*, chaps 8 & 9.

50.   Jacqueline Hill, 'The politics of privilege: Dublin corporation and the catholic question, 1792-1823', *Maynooth Review*, vii (1982), 17-36; Senior, *Orangeism*, 4-21.

51.   See Barnard, 'The uses of 23 October 1641', 895; Senior, *Orangeism*, 1-2; Jacqueline Hill, 'National festivals, the state and "protestant ascendancy" in Ireland, 1790-1829', *I.H.S.*, xxiv (1984), 30-51.

52.   See e.g., *FDJ*, 2-6 Nov. 1731; 1-4, 11-15 July 1732; *Freeman's Journal*, 3-6 Nov. 1764; 13-16 July 1765; *FDJ*, 10-13 July 1784.

53.   One description that captures well the flavour of the 4 November Dublin ceremonies, recorded in 1751, is found in *The autobiography and correspondence of Mary Granville, Mrs Delany*, Lady Llanover (ed.), 3 vols. (London, 1861), iii, 54. For complaints of the non-observance of the anniversary at the end of Queen Anne's reign see the letter from John Fiens in *Freeman's Journal*, 23-7 Oct. 1764. See also Hill, 'National festivals'.

54.   *Freeman's Journal*, 4-6 Nov. 1783.

55.   See *DEP*, 5 Nov. 1778; *Freeman's Journal*, 4-6 Nov. 1779; ibid., 3-6 Nov. 1781; ibid., 4-6 Nov. 1783; *FDJ*, 4-6 Nov. 1784; ibid., 3-5 Nov. 1785; ibid., 4-7 Nov. 1786; *Dublin Chronicle*, 6 Nov. 1787; ibid., 4 Nov. 1788; *DEP*, 10 Nov. 1792.

56.   Down to 1814 the Orange oath promised only conditional loyalty to the king, constitution and the succession (i.e, they must be protestant); Senior, *Orangeism*, 192, and Appendix A, 298-301.

57.   The importance of conquest myths in Irish protestant identity is discussed in Leighton, *Catholicism in a protestant kingdom*, chaps. 2, 4, 6.

58.   The rules of the Orange Society, 1798 (Senior, *Orangeism*, Appendix A, 298-301) explain that the members had associated to honour King William III, and would annually celebrate the victory over King James at the Boyne on 1 July (Old Style: taken to be 12 July, New Style).

59.   Musgrave, *Memoirs of the different rebellions in Ireland*, 2nd edn. (Dublin, 1801), 27, 207.

60.   See e.g., *Hansard 1*, iv, cols 865-9 (13 May 1805). Duigenan was one of the first Dublin Orangemen: Senior, *Orangeism*, 76.

61.   See the letter from 'C.U.T.' to the editor, *FDJ*, 21 July 1812.

62.   *Hansard 1*, iv, cols 922-3 (13 May 1805).

63.   For hostility to Duigenan in parliament see *Hansard 1*, xi, cols. 128-9 (29 April 1808). For hostility towards the Orange Order, see Senior, *Orangeism*, 206-7, 209, 214.

64. Resolutions of the Catholic Society of Dublin (12 March 1792), *Hibernian Journal*, 14 Mar. 1792.
65. G.F.A. Best, 'The protestant constitution and its supporters, 1800-1829', *Transactions of the Royal Historical Society*, 5th ser., viii (1958), 105-27.

Chapter 10   *1641: a bibliographical essay*

1. R.M. Gilbert, *The life of Sir John T. Gilbert* (London, 1905), 296.
2. R.T. Dunlop, 'The depositions relating to the Irish massacres of 1641', *E.H.R.*, ii (1887), 339.
3. W.D. Love, 'Civil war in Ireland: appearances in three centuries of historical writing', *Emory University Quarterly*, 22, (1966), 57–72; A. Clarke, 'The 1641 depositions', in P. Fox (ed.), *Treasures of the Library: Trinity College Dublin* (Dublin, 1986), 120; T.C. Barnard, 'The Protestant Interest, 1641–1660', in Jane Ohlmeyer (ed.), *Ireland from Independence to Occupation 1641–1660* (Cambridge, 1995), 218–40.
4. Henry Jones, *A remonstrance of divers remarkable passages concerning the church and kingdome of Ireland* (London, 1642).
5. John Temple, *The Irish Rebellion* (London, 1646), i, sig. [a3[vl.]
6. T.C. Barnard, 'Crises of identity among Irish Protestants, 1641–1685', *Past and Present*, 127, (1990), 39–83.
7. R. Palmer, earl of Castlemaine, *The Catholique Apology* (n.p. 1674), 52–64; H. Reilly, *Ireland's case briefly stated* (n.p., 1695), sig. [ai], 38–46.
8. J. Crespin, *Actiones et monimenta martyrum* (Geneva, 1560); J. Foxe, *Actes and Monuments* (London 1563); S. Goulart, *Histoire des martyres persecutez et mis a mort pour la vérité de L'Évangile* (Geneva, 1582).
9. E. Wetenhall, 'The Christian law and the sword', in *Hexapla Jacobeae* (Dublin, 1686), 30–6.
10. H.M.C., *Eighth Report*, appendix, part i, sect. iii (1881), 572b–576b.
11. V. Gookin, *The great case of transplantation in Ireland discussed* (London, 1655); W. Gostelo, *Charles Stuart and Oliver Cromwell united* (London, 1655). For English examples: N. Carlin, 'The Levellers and the conquest of Ireland', *Historical Journal*, xxx (1987), 269–88; C. Hill, 'Seventeenth century English radicals and Ireland', in P.J.Corish (ed.), *Radicals, rebels and establishments: Historical Studies XV* (Belfast, 1985), 33–39; C.M. Williams, 'The anatomy of a radical gentleman', in D.H. Pennington and K.V. Thomas (eds.), *Puritans and Revolutionaries* (Oxford, 1978), 126.
12. Clarke, 'The 1641 depositions', 111.
13. *An abstract of some few of the barbarous, cruell massacres and murthers, of the Protestants and English in some parts of Ireland* (London, 1652);

R.T. Dunlop, 'The depositions', *E.H.R.*, i, (1886), 743; Barnard, 'Crises of identity', 64.

14.   Walter Harris, *Fiction unmasked* (Dublin, 1752), 171.

15.   E.McC. Dix and C.W. Duggan, *Catalogue of early Dublin-printed books, 1601–1700* (Dublin, 1898–1912), 75–84, 89–113.

16.   Jane Ohlmeyer, 'Ireland independent: confederate foreign policy and international relations during the mid-seventeenth century', in Ohlmeyer (ed.), *Ireland from Independence to Occupation*, 89–111.

17.   Barnard, 'The Protestant Interest'; R.S., *A Collection of some of the Murthers and Massacres committed on the Irish in Ireland since the 23d of October 1641* (London, 1662), 8.

18.   *A catalogue of the Bradshaw collection of Irish books in the University Library, Cambridge*, 3 vols., (Cambridge, 1916), ii, 868–9, 898–900; E.R.McC. Dix, 'Printing in the city of Kilkenny in the seventeenth century', *R.I.A. Proc.*, xxxii, C, (1914), 125–37.

19.   Castlemaine, *The Catholique Apology*, 58; R.S., *A Collection*, 7,9–10; [P. Walsh], *The Irish Colours folded* (London 1662), 3.

20.   R.S., *A Collection*, 6, 16–17,19,25.

21.   *A Continuation of the brief narrative, and the sufferings of the Irish under Cromwell* (n.p., 1660).

22.   T.C. Barnard, 'The uses of the 23 October 1641 and Irish Protestant celebrations', *E.H.R.*, cvi, (1991), 892.

23.   Barnard, 'Crises of identity', 54–5; R. Steele (ed.), *Bibliotheca Lindesiana, a catalogue of Tudor and Stuart proclamations*, 2 vols., (Oxford, 1910), ii, no. 707 (Ireland). About 1750, Walter Harris claimed that it had taken him twenty years to find the pamphlet: Pearse Street Public Library, Dublin, Gilbert Ms. 101, p. 109.

24.   Barnard, 'The uses of 23 October 1641', 892–3.

25.   T. Bartlett, *The fall and rise of the Irish nation* (Dublin, 1992), 7. I am also fortunate to have heard a conference paper at York in April 1990 given by Dr. Anne Laurence of the Open University on 'Images of 1641'.

26.   B.L., Stowe Ms. 206, fos. 240, 312; Bodl., Add. Ms. C.34, fol. 224; Barnard, 'Crises of identity', 55; *Letters written by his excellency Arthur Capel earl of Essex, Lord Lieutenant of Ireland, in the year 1675* (Dublin, 1770), 2.

27.   Introduction by Francis Maseres to J. Temple, *The Irish Rebellion* (London, 1812).

28.   *Catalogue of books printed for, and sold by, Peter Wilson, in Dame-Street, Dublin* ([Dublin], 1760), 3,11.

29.   *An abstract of some few of those barbarous, cruell massacres and murthers, of the Protestants, and English* (London [1660?]); *A collection of certain horrid murthers in several counties of Ireland. Committed since the 23. of Octob. 1641* (London, 1689). Efforts were made in 1689 to add fresh atrocities to the earlier ones, as, for example, in *A full and true*

account of the damages and murders done and committed on the estates and lives of the Protestants by the Irish rebels in Ireland (London, 1689). At later moments of crisis, we find: [T. Carte], *The Irish Massacre set in a clear light* (London, [1714]); *A brief account from the most authentic Protestant writers of the causes, motives and mischiefs, of the Irish Rebellion, on the 23d day of October 1641* (London, 1747).

30.   As in the Dublin 1724 edition. Cf. Barnard, 'The uses of the 23 October 1641', 890–3.

31.   D. Dickson, *New foundations: Ireland 1660–1800* (Dublin, 1987), 134–5.

32.   J. Hennig, 'The Anglican church in Ireland: prayers against the Irish "rebels"', *I.E.R.*, lxiv (1944), 247–9.

33.   Royal Irish Academy, Ms.I. iv. 1, annotations at pp 360–1. For the owner's interest in heraldry, J. Gibbons, *Introductio ad Latinum Blasonium. An essay to a more correct blason* (London, 1682), of which there is a presentation copy in the library of Trinity College Dublin. For the more conventional marginalia in which the fatalities are totted up, see the copy of the 1679 *Collection of certain horrid murders*, in the Bodleian Library, Oxford, pressmark, Wood 506.

34.   Bowood House, Wiltshire, Petty Mss. 4/40. This collection has recently been bought by the British Library.

35.   John Brett, *A friendly call to the people of the Roman Catholick religion in Ireland. A sermon preached at the parish-church of St. Bridget's, Dublin, on Sunday, the 23d of October 1757* (Dublin, 1757). Cf. Maureen Wall, *Catholic Ireland in the eighteenth century* (Dublin, 1989), 98.

36.   Henry Maule, *God's Goodness visible in our deliverance from popery*, 5th edition (London, 1735), 85–119. More generally on Maule's activities: T.C. Barnard, 'Protestants and the Irish language, c. 1675–1725', *Journal of Ecclesiastical History*, 44, (1993); K. Milne, 'Irish Charter Schools', *The Irish Journal of Education*, 8, (1974), 5,10,13.

37.   The official preachers were Anthony Dopping and George Sandford: *Journals of the House of Commons in the kingdom of Ireland*, 28 vols., (Dublin, 1753–91), iv, part i, 364; *Journals of the House of Lords of the kingdom of Ireland*, 8 vols., (Dublin, 1779–1800), iii, 503.

38.   'Description of Mayo', p.8; 'Description of Cavan', p.8, in Armagh Public Library, Lodge Mss., G.II.23.

39.   Robert French to William Smythe, London, 24 October 1713, in National Library of Ireland, P.C. 447/3; Barnard, 'The uses of 23 October, 1641', 889–920.

40.   R.S., *A collection of some of the murthers*, 7.

41.   Charles O'Conor in J. Curry, *An historical and critical review of the civil wars of Ireland*, 2 vols., (London, 1789), i, p.viii; J. Curry, *Historical Memoirs of the Irish Rebellion in the year 1641* (London, 1765), pp. xiv–xvi.

42.   Walter Harris, *Fiction Unmasked* (Dublin, 1752); W.D. Love, 'Charles O'Conor of Belanagare and Thomas Leland's "philosophical" history of Ireland', *I.H.S.*, xii (1962), 25. Harris alleged, for example, that the 1662 *Collection* was so rare on account of the fact that 'the priests of the Romish religion and other papists destroying all they could lay their hands on, because they knew it could not stand the test of examination'. In actuality, as we have seen, the Irish government had suppressed the tract. Pearse St. Public Library, Dublin, Gilbert Ms. 101, 109–10.

43.   Ferdinando Warner, *The history of the rebellion and civil war in Ireland* (London, 1767), 294–7. Also, T.C.D., Love Mss., Ms. 7231/ 2–5; D. Berman, 'David Hume on the 1641 rebellion in Ireland', *Studies*, lxv (1976), 101–10.

44.   Richard Musgrave, *Memoirs of the different rebellions in Ireland* (Dublin, 1801), appendix xii, separate pagination, 162–3. A copy of the 1724 edition of Temple, bound with William King's *State of the Protestants*, now in Archbishop Robinson's Public Library in Armagh, bears on the flyleaf an acrostic on the word *Eliphismatis*: 'Every Loyal Irish Protestant Heretic I shall Murder And This I Swear', to which is added, 'the pious creed of the Irish papists in the year 1794 and put in practice in 1798'.

45.   Edinburgh, 1817.

46.   Philadelphia, 1819, reprinted in 1823 and 1837.

47.   J.P. Prendergast to P.H. Bagenal, 18 February 1862, King's Inns, Dublin, Prendergast Mss.; T.C.D., Lecky Mss., Ms. 1827/254, 333; 1828/379, 400, 427, 480, 490; T.C. Barnard, 'Irish images of Cromwell', in R.C. Richardson (ed.), *Images of Cromwell: essays by and for Roger Howell, jr.*, (Manchester, 1993), 193–7.

48.   Dunlop, 'The depositions', *E.H.R.* ii, 339.

49.   M. Hickson, *Ireland in the seventeenth century: or the Irish massacres of 1641–2* (London, 1884).

50.   Froude, 'Preface', in Hickson, *Ireland in the seventeenth century*, pp.v–x; Hickson, 'The depositions', *E.H.R.* ii, 133.

51.   Gilbert, *Life of Gilbert*, 153–204; D. Knowles, *Great historical enterprises* (London, 1963), 101–34; Ambrose Macaulay, *Dr. Russell of Maynooth* (London, 1983) 255–7.

53.   Royal Irish Academy, Gilbert correspondence, Ms. 12.0.20/5, Sir T.D. Hardy to J.T. Gilbert, 3 Sep. 1870, 11 May 1871, 4 Nov. 1871;/ 6, Gilbert to Hardy, 10 Feb. 1872. As well as his widow's memoir, a more recent sketch is F.E. Dixon, 'Sir John T. Gilbert, 1829–1898', *Dublin Historical Record*, xxii, (1968), 272–4.

54.   H.M.C., *Eighth report*, appendix, part i, sect. iii, 572b–576b.

55.   Froude, 'Preface', in Hickson, *Ireland in the seventeenth century*, vii–ix; Hickson, 'The depositions', 133. So effective had been the complaints against Gilbert's supposed bias by Froude and Hickson,

that when his report was re-issued by the Historical Manuscript Commission in 1908 it was freighted with footnotes referring to Miss Hickson's alternative view.

56. 3 volumes, (London, 1872–4). On its reception, and more generally on Froude: W.H. Dunn, *J.A. Froude, a biography*, 2 vols., (Oxford, 1961–3); D. McCartney, 'J.A. Froude and Ireland: a historiographical controversy of the nineteenth century', in T.D. Williams (ed.), *Historical Studies: VIII* (Dublin, 1971), 171–90.

57. T.N. Burke, *Ireland's case stated in reply to Mr. Froude* (New York, 1873), 97, 105; cf. Barnard, 'Irish images of Cromwell', 197.

58. T.C.D., Ms. 1828/492.

59. R.T. Dunlop, 'The depositions relating to the Irish massacres of 1641', *E.H.R.*, i (1886), 741–3; ibid., ii (1887), 338–9. Also: C.H. Firth, 'Robert Dunlop', *History*, xv (1931), 310–4.

60. Dunlop, 'The depositions', 742.

61. Dunlop, 'The depositions', 741; Dunlop, *Ireland under the Commonwealth*, 2 vols., (Manchester, 1913), i, pp. vii–viii.

62. T.C.D., Mss. 1827–8/237, 255a, 472, 474, 549.

63. M. Hickson, 'The depositions', *E.H.R.* ii, 133.

64. Nicholas Canny, 'What really happened in Ireland in 1641?', in Ohlmeyer (ed.), *Ireland from Independence to Occupation*, 24–42, the substance of which has already appeared as 'In defense of the constitution? The nature of Irish revolt in the seventeenth century', in L. Bergeron and L.M. Cullen (eds.), *Culture et pratiques politiques en France et Irlande XVIe–XVIIIe siècle* (Paris, [1990]), 23–40.

65. These potential uses were first suggested by Dunlop in *Ireland under the Commonwealth*, i, p.cxviii, n.1, and later by Aidan Clarke in 'Ireland and the General Crisis', *Past & Present*, 48, (1970), 87, n.17. Among those who have heeded these suggestions: N. Canny, 'Migration and opportunity: Britain, Ireland and the new world', *Ir. Econ. & Soc. Hist.*, 12, (1985) 7–32; R. Gillespie, *Colonial Ulster* (Cork, 1985); M. MacCarthy-Morrogh, *The Munster plantation* (Oxford, 1986); B. Mac Cuarta, 'Newcomers in the Irish Midlands, 1540–1641', (unpublished MA thesis, University College, Galway, 1980); Mary O'Dowd, *Power, politics and land: early modern Sligo* (Belfast, 1991); C. Ó Murchadha, 'Land and society in seventeenth-century Clare', (unpublished PhD thesis, University College, Galway, 1982).

66. T. Fitzpatrick, 'The Ulster civil war, 1641: "the king's commission" in County Fermanagh', *Ulster Journal of Archaeology*, 2nd series, xiii (1907), 133–56; xiv. (1908), 168–75; xv. (1909), 64. His other studies were *The Bloody Bridge and other papers relating to the insurrection of 1641* (Dublin, 1903); and *Waterford during the Civil War (1641–1653)*, (Waterford, 1912).

67. His notes are now T.C.D., Mss. 7227–7241, from which I have

profited. The principal statement of his findings is in 'Civil War in Ireland', *Emory University Quarterly*, 22, (1966), 57–72.

68.   'The 1641 depositions', in Fox, *Treasures of the Library*.

69.   A. Clarke, 'The genesis of the Ulster rising of 1641', in P. Roebuck (ed.), *Plantation to partition* (Belfast, 1981), 29–45; R. Gillespie, 'The end of an era: Ulster and the outbreak of the 1641 rising', in C. Brady and R. Gillespie (eds.), *Natives and newcomers* (Dublin, 1986), 191–213; M.Perceval-Maxwell, 'The Ulster rising of 1641 and the depositions', *I.H.S.*, xxi (1978), 144–67.

70.   Clarke, 'Ireland and the General Crisis', 79–99; C. Russell, 'The British problem and the English civil war', *History*, lxxii (1987); Russell, *The fall of the British monarchies, 1637–42* (Oxford, 1991); J. Ohlmeyer, *Civil war and Restoration in the three Stuart kingdoms: the career of Randal MacDonnell, marquis of Antrim 1609–83* (Cambridge, 1993); M. Perceval-Maxwell, 'Protestant faction, the impeachment of Strafford and the origins of the Irish civil war', *Canadian Journal of History*, xvii (1982), 235–55; Perceval-Maxwell, 'Ireland and the monarchy in the early Stuart multiple kingdom', *Historical Journal*, xxxiv (1991), 279–95.

71.   As investigated, for example, in Barnard, 'Crises of identity'; 'The uses of 23 October 1641' and 'The Protestant Interest'; in as yet unpublished essays by Robert Eccleshall on 'Anglican political thought in the century after the Revolution of 1688 in Ireland'; by James Kelly on '"The glorious and immortal memory": commemoration in Ireland, 1660–1800'; and Joseph Liechty on 'Remembering 1641: The October 23 anniversary thanksgiving sermons, 1685–1770' (to all three of whom I am grateful for allowing me to read their work). See, too: J.R. Hill, 'The disputed lessons of Irish history, 1690–1812', *Past and Present*, 118, (1988), 96–129; Hill, 'National festivals, the state and "Protestant ascendancy" in Ireland, 1790–1829', *I.H.S.*, xxiv (1984–5), 30–51.

Index